2002

ETHICS AND LAW IN MODERN MEDICINE

INTERNATIONAL LIBRARY OF ETHICS, LAW, AND THE NEW MEDICINE

Editors

DAVID C. THOMASMA, *Loyola University, Chicago, U.S.A.*
DAVID N. WEISSTUB, *Université de Montréal, Canada*
THOMASINE KIMBROUGH KUSHNER, *University of California, Berkeley, U.S.A.*

Editorial Board

VOLUME 6

The titles published in this series are listed at the end of this volume.

ETHICS AND LAW
IN MODERN MEDICINE

Hypothetical Case Studies

by

David M. Vukadinovich
Attorney at Law, Foley & Lardner,
Los Angeles, CA, U.S.A.

and

Susan L. Krinsky
Tulane University School of Law,
New Orleans, LA, U.S.A.

KLUWER ACADEMIC PUBLISHERS
DORDRECHT / BOSTON / LONDON

A C.I.P. Catalogue record for this book is available from the Library of Congress.

ISBN 1-4020-0088-X

Published by Kluwer Academic Publishers,
P.O. Box 17, 3300 AA Dordrecht, The Netherlands.

Sold and distributed in North, Central and South America
by Kluwer Academic Publishers,
101 Philip Drive, Norwell, MA 02061, U.S.A.

In all other countries, sold and distributed
by Kluwer Academic Publishers,
P.O. Box 322, 3300 AH Dordrecht, The Netherlands.

Printed on acid-free paper

Printed in the Netherlands.

To my parents and grandparents.
-D.M.V

To the memory of my father, Leonard W. Krinsky.
-S.L.K

TABLE OF CONTENTS

viii

INTRODUCTION

Ethics and Law in Modern Medicine: Hypothetical Case Studies is divided into eleven chapters, each of which explores complex issues of bioethics, law, and social policy that arise in the delivery of health care. Each chapter sets out a detailed hypothetical case study for participants to read and discuss. While all of the topics presented are accessible and compelling enough to serve as the basis for stimulating group discussion, each chapter was written with a particular background in mind. Accordingly, each chapter includes references to the Appendices to this volume and to suggested outside readings and research. The Appendices include excerpts from relevant state and federal case law, statutes, and regulations that health care professionals, administrators, and attorneys deal with on a regular basis. The authors suggest that participants read all or a part of the suggested readings prior to embarking upon their analysis and discussion of each case study.

Ten of the chapters also include role assignments that are intended to provoke and guide discussion of the hypothetical fact pattern presented in that chapter. Often, the role assignments are characters involved in the hypothetical case study. For example, the roles of patients, hospital administrators, physicians, and attorneys are assigned to discuss the case study from the perspective of an individual involved in the events set forth in each of the hypothetical fact patterns. The role of arbitrator or judge is also assigned in several of the case studies so that at the end of the group discussion one or more participants may be called upon to make decisions that affect the other participants. The role assignments are crafted to represent a wide variety of points of view and with a variety of objectives in mind. The authors have found that use of the role assignments helps participants view difficult situations from a variety of perspectives, particularly when a participant is called upon to argue from a point of view that he or she does not personally hold. Each chapter also includes discussion questions pertaining to the issues raised in the case study.

Instructions and objectives are presented at the beginning of each chapter that briefly summarize the substance of the case study and topics that the authors believe to be most pertinent in that chapter.

CHAPTER 1

HEALTH CARE PROFESSIONALS AND HIV

The Duty to Warn

INSTRUCTIONS AND OBJECTIVES

This case study is designed to be discussed in conjunction with the "duty to warn" cases such as *Tarasof v. The Regents of the University of California* and statutory provisions that set out duties relative to confidentiality and obligations to make certain disclosures, particularly duties that arise when the conduct of a patient potentially endangers the health or life of a third person. The case study provides a fact pattern in which the urgency to warn is heightened both by the HIV-positive scenario and by the identity of the HIV-positive individual. The hypothetical poses questions of how far and to whom a duty to warn extends, and under what circumstances. Through the role assignments set out at the end of the case study, the participants explore the interests of the various parties and inevitable conflicts that arise between the duty to warn and confidentiality

THE CASE STUDY

Mr. and Dr. McCormick arrived at Mountain View Regional Hospital at 2:00 a.m. Their son Matthew was born several hours later and placed in the neonatal unit with a number of other newborns. The following day, Nurse Shanahan drew blood from Matthew McCormick and sent it to the laboratory to be tested for HIV. Later that afternoon, Nurse Shanahan realized that her order was to draw blood from Martin McComb and not from Matthew McCormick. Nurse Shanahan then took the blood ordered from Martin McComb without canceling the HIV test ordered on Matthew McCormick's blood.

A few days later, after the McCormicks had been discharged from Mountain View Regional Hospital, Nurse Shanahan received the results of the blood work performed on Matthew McCormick. Nurse Shanahan opened the envelope containing the results and was shocked to discover that Matthew McCormick was born HIV-positive. In a state of disbelief, Nurse Shanahan shared the story of her

1

mistake and the results of the test with Dr. Green, Dr. McCormick's obstetrician, and with Dr. Blue, Matthew McCormick's pediatrician. Doctors Blue and Green decided that since Dr. McCormick was a colleague of theirs at the hospital they should approach her with the test results. The doctors visited Dr. McCormick at her home and described to her how the test came to be mistakenly performed. They also revealed the results of the test. Dr. McCormick abrasively ordered the physicians out of her home and threatened them with a lawsuit if they revealed the test results to anyone, including hospital staff or Mr. McCormick. The doctors told Dr. McCormick that the result may have been a false positive and that a second test should be performed. Dr. McCormick refused further tests and any medical intervention.

After leaving the McCormick residence, the physicians discussed between themselves their concern for the welfare of Matthew and Dr. McCormick, as well as their concern for the health of Mr. McCormick. The doctors drove to Mr. McCormick's office where they informed him of the positive HIV-positive test result. Mr. McCormick did not understand how Matthew could have been infected with the virus and the doctors explained that the fact that Matthew was born HIV-positive necessarily indicated that Dr. McCormick was also HIV-positive. Mr. McCormick had never been tested for HIV and the doctors recommended that he be immediately tested.

Upon returning to the hospital, the doctors had lunch with various members of the staff and administration with whom they shared the story of Dr. McCormick. After lunch, the doctors approached the Chief of Staff. The Chief of Staff has called a meeting.

DICUSSION QUESTIONS

This meeting has been called to discuss the events outlined above. Each participant should formulate a position and supporting arguments on each of the issues presented below. The issues should be discussed with regard to any ethical or legal breaches that may have occurred.

1. What, if any, ethical breaches and/or legal liabilities arose by virtue of the conduct of Nurse Shanahan? Consider each of the following events:

(a) Drawing blood from the wrong infant for HIV testing;

(b) Failing to stop the HIV test on the McCormick blood after realizing that an error had occurred;

(c) Proceeding to examine the HIV test results knowing that consent had not been given to test Matthew McCormick for HIV; and

(d) Disclosing the positive test results and name of Matthew McCormick to Dr. Blue and Dr. Green with the knowledge that a positive test result from Matthew necessarily indicated Dr. McCormick to be HIV-positive.

Did any of Nurse Shanahan's acts violate either Matthew's or Dr. McCormick's right to medical confidentiality? If so, which acts and why? What course of action should have been taken by Nurse Shanahan after she discovered that she had made an error?

2. Do Dr. Blue and Dr. Green owe a duty of privacy and/or confidentiality to either Dr. McCormick or Matthew McCormick? What is the difference between a breach of the right to privacy and a breach of the duty of confidentiality? Did the doctors violate either of those duties by informing Mr. McCormick of the HIV-positive condition of his wife? Of his child? Consider California Health and Safety Code Section 121015 included at Appendix A. Did the doctors violate any duty by informing the Chief of Staff? Were the actions of the doctors consistent with honoring the doctor/patient relationship that exists between Dr. McCormick and her obstetrician? Between Matthew McCormick and his pediatrician?

3. When Dr. Blue and Dr. Green became aware of Matthew McCormick's HIV test results, what obligations arose and to whom? Were the doctors justified in disclosing the test results to Dr. McCormick? What arguments can be made to justify the doctors' decision to disclose the information to Mr. McCormick? To the Chief of Staff? To their colleagues with whom they had lunch?

Additional information. Dr. McCormick is on staff at Mountain View Regional Hospital as an orthopedic surgeon. As such, she performs invasive procedures on a regular basis. Dr. McCormick has informed the hospital that after a three week maternity leave she intends to return on a full-time basis to her position.

4. Should Mountain View Regional Hospital be able to require Dr. McCormick to be tested for HIV?

5. Should Mountain View Regional Hospital allow Dr. McCormick to perform invasive surgical procedures if she is not tested or if she tests positive for HIV?

6. Will Dr. McCormick have a cause of action against Mountain View Regional Hospital if the hospital informs her future patients of her HIV-positive status? Will patients of Dr. McCormick have a cause of action against the hospital if they become infected by Dr. McCormick without being informed by the hospital of Dr. McCormick's HIV status?

7. Does the hospital have an ethical obligation to inform Dr. McCormick's future patients of her HIV status? Can the argument be made that the doctrine of informed consent requires the hospital to inform patients of the possibility, no matter how slight, that they might be infected with HIV from Dr. McCormick during an invasive surgical procedure?

8. Can Mountain View Regional Hospital legally inform Dr. McCormick's past patients, upon whom she has performed invasive procedures, that she is HIV-positive? Does the hospital have an ethical obligation to do so?

Case Update. The story of what has happened has spread throughout the hospital. Three weeks have passed and Dr. McCormick has returned to work. Dr. McCormick has been ostracized for her uncooperative attitude and for refusing to be tested for

HIV. Dr. McCormick has decided to confront the situation head-on by being tested for HIV. The test results have confirmed that Dr. McCormick is HIV-positive. Dr. McCormick has revealed the results to the Chief of Staff and indicated that she intends to continue to practice as an orthopedic surgeon. She has also informed the Chief of Staff that she will take legal action if the hospital attempts to prevent her from performing surgery or if the hospital, or any of its agents, reveal her HIV-positive status to her patients.

9. Now that Dr. McCormick has been tested for HIV, does the Hospital have an obligation to keep the results of Dr. McCormick's HIV test confidential? Can Dr. McCormick ethically and/or legally demand that she be kept on staff without notifying her patients of her HIV status? What would be the effect if the Texas Health and Safety Code provision included at Appendix B is applicable?

10. Dr. McCormick has objected to any attempts made by the hospital to either inform former patients of her seropositive status or any general statements advising past patients to be tested for HIV. Does the hospital have an ethical or legal responsibility to:

(a) Advise former patients of Dr. McCormick to be tested for HIV?

(b) Maintain the confidentiality of Dr. McCormick's HIV status?

Is the hospital's responsibility to former surgical patients strengthened if hospital records indicate the occurrence of an event, such as Dr. McCormick being cut during surgery, that may have increased the chance of exposure of the patient to HIV?

11. Based on the issues and concerns raised by the McCormick case, what elements should be included in a newly formulated hospital policy on HIV-positive physician and confidentiality?

SUGGESTED RESEARCH

Statutory Law

Appendix A: California Health and Safety Code Section 121015.
Appendix B: Texas Health and Safety Code Section 85.204.

Case Law

Appendix C: *Tarasoff v. Regents of University of California*, 551 P.2d 334 (1976).

Texts

Annas, George J. *Standard of Care: The Law of American Bioethics.* New York City, NY: Oxford University Press, 1993, 119-31.
Munson, Ronald. *Intervention and Reflection: Basic Issues in Medical Ethics.* 4th

ed. Belmont, CA Wadsworth, 1992, 205-57.

Pence, Gregory E. *Classic Cases in Medical Ethics.* 2d ed. New York City, NY: McGraw-Hill, 1995, 413-42.

Veatch, Robert M. *Medical Ethics.* 2nd ed. Sudbury, MA: Jones and Bartlett, 1997, 395-413.

ROLE ASSIGNMENTS FOR 20 PARTICIPANTS

1. Dr. McCormick
2. Mr. McCormick
3. Mr./Ms. Bates, Esq., Attorney Representing Matthew McCormick
4. Dr. Green, Pediatrician
5. Dr. Blue, Obstetrician
6. Nurse Shanahan
7. Dr. Kramer, Chief of Staff
8. Mr./Ms. Hershey, Former Patient of Dr. McCormick, HIV-positive
9. Mr./Ms. Sandeman, Former Patient of Dr. McCormick, HIV-positive
10. Mr./Ms. Pine, Former Patient of Dr. McCormick, HIV-positive
11. Mr./Ms. Devon, Former Patient of Dr. McCormick, HIV Test Not Conclusive
12. Mr./Ms. Sharp, Esq., An Attorney Representing the Interests of Prospective Patients
13. Mr./Ms. Black, Esq., An Attorney Representing Dr. McCormick
14. Mr./Ms. Spencer, Hospital CEO
15. Mr./Ms. Greenwood, Surgical Assistant
16. Dr. Boyle, Colleague of Dr. McCormick
17. Dr. Ramsey, Director of Surgery
18. Dr. Charles, Ph.D., Bioethicist
19. Mr./Ms. Thomas, Hospital Administrator
20. Mr./Ms. Chung, Health Care Educator

Role Assignment Number 1

Assume the role of Dr. McCormick. Your primary interests are:

1. To return to work.

2. To protect what privacy you still have by preventing the release of your own test results or the results of Mr. McCormick's or Matthew's tests.

In making your arguments consider the following points:

1. No conclusive studies show a risk of infection from physician to patient.

2. Use of universal precautions prevents the spread of HIV.

3. The hospital does not conduct mandatory testing of all surgeons and there are certainly other physicians on staff who are HIV-positive.

4. Setting the precedent of releasing the results of your HIV test will discourage

physicians from being tested for HIV

Role Assignment Number 2

Assume the role of Mr. McCormick. No one else knows yet but you have been tested and you are HIV-negative.
Your primary interests are:
    1. Not contracting HIV.
    2. Seeking the best medical care for Matthew and for your wife.
    3. Quietly and quickly resolving this matter so your life can return to normal.
    4. Ensuring that your wife never again performs surgery or in any other way exposes anyone to HIV.
Think about the analogy between sharing a needle or having sexual relations with an HIV-positive person and being operated on by an HIV-positive surgeon. How do these two occurrences compare with one another? You have been extremely lucky in not becoming infected. You can only wonder how many more times you could have risked exposure without being infected and, likewise, how many more times your wife can operate without infecting someone else--if she hasn't already done so. The risk of infection, though slight, is present every time your wife operates on someone. This risk must be eliminated to prevent harm to your wife's patients.

Role Assignment Number 3

Assume the role of Mr./Ms. Bates, Esq., an attorney present to represent the interests of Matthew McCormick. You believe Matthew's primary interests are the following:
    1. Procuring the best medical treatment possible, even if Dr. McCormick is not cooperative.
    2. Ensuring that Mr. McCormick is fully informed of the risk that Dr. McCormick has exposed him to so that he can make educated health care decisions for himself and for Matthew.

Role Assignment Number 4

Assume the role of Dr. Green, Matthew's pediatrician. Consider the following:
    1. Argue that you and Dr. Blue did the right thing by confronting Dr. McCormick and informing her husband that Dr. McCormick is HIV-positive. Argue that you may have directly prevented harm to a third party likely to contract HIV (if indeed Mr. McCormick is HIV-negative). Argue that your actions are also justified by the fact that if not for your confronting Dr. McCormick, Matthew McCormick would be in danger of not being treated for his condition. Furthermore, argue that your actions did not violate doctor/patient privilege because, as Matthew's pediatrician you owe a duty to Matthew to ensure that he gets the best treatment possible. This duty includes

the duty of advising Matthew's guardians of his medical condition. Argue that you owe no duty of confidentiality to Dr. McCormick because she is not your patient.

2. Consider the argument that a duty flows from a physician to any third party who is in imminent danger. Mr. McCormick was in imminent danger of contracting HIV by having sexual relations with his wife. In making your arguments, consider the ethical principle of nonmaleficence, the decision of the California Supreme Court in *Tarasoff v. Regents of the University of California*, and California Health and Safety Code Section 121015. Argue that your actions were in compliance both with your ethical obligation and your legal duty.

3. Argue that all past patients of Dr. McCormick who may have been exposed to HIV should be tracked and notified of the potential risk of infection. As a colleague of Dr. McCormick's, you feel a responsibility to third parties who may have been exposed.

Role Assignment Number 5

Assume the role of Dr. Blue, Dr. McCormick's obstetrician.

Argue that your actions were justified. You revealed to Dr. McCormick knowledge that you had regarding her medical condition. Argue that your duty would have been breached if you did not disclose this information to Dr. McCormick because that would have allowed harm to occur that could be prevented. The fact that the test was mistakenly performed is trivial; nothing can be done about it now other than creating a new policy for similar situations in the future. In any case, you were not a party to the mistake and once you had knowledge of Dr. McCormick's HIV-positive serostatus, you had a duty to use that knowledge for the benefit of your patient. Furthermore, you believe that mandatory testing of all pregnant women would advance the health of both the woman and the child.

Also, argue that you breached no duty by informing Mr. McCormick of Dr. McCormick's status because he is a third party in immediate threat of harm. Once you discovered that Dr. McCormick was not going to be cooperative, you had a duty to prevent future harm to third parties. Also, argue that your discussion about Dr. McCormick over lunch with your colleagues was justified because you were seeking their professional advice regarding the situation. You understand that confidentiality is important but at times doctors must discuss important issues in order to make proper decisions.

Role Assignment Number 6

Assume the role of Nurse Shanahan. In making arguments to justify your actions, consider the following:

1. Argue that mistakes happen and, in the end, it is a good thing this one did or else the health of both Dr. and Matthew McCormick would be compromised. Your

actions may have even saved Mr. McCormick.

2. As to whether or not you should have looked at the results, of course you should have. The harm, if any, was done when the blood was drawn and not when the test results were viewed. Besides, the only people you informed were the doctors. Argue that adherence to the principle of nonmaleficence required you to reveal the results because nondisclosure would have resulted in harm.

Role Assignment Number 7

Assume the role of Dr. Kramer, Chief of Staff at Mountain View Regional Hospital. Consider the following:

1. Your primary interest is providing the best medical care possible to Mountain View's patients.

2. Argue that such a minimal risk of infection exists from Dr. McCormick to a patient that she should be allowed to continue to operate without disclosing her HIV-positive status. Keep in mind that no case has been documented in which a surgeon has transmitted HIV to a patient. In weighing all the factors, argue that more harm would be done by preventing Dr. McCormick from operating than from assuming the minimal risk of infecting patients. You also believe that if it is disclosed that Dr. McCormick is HIV-positive, it will create very bad publicity and unnecessary panic. In your opinion, the risk of infection is not medically significant and it should be dealt with by continuing to use universal precautions.

3. You are also concerned with the precedent that this case may have if Dr. McCormick is prevented from keeping her position. Will this lead to mandatory testing of all health care workers? How many of the best physicians and surgeons will be lost if they are found to be HIV-positive? Will physicians leave your hospital if they feel their privacy is at risk? All of these factors must be considered in deciding how to deal with Dr. McCormick.

4. As to the doctors discussing and disclosing the status of Matthew and Dr. McCormick, you feel sanctions should be imposed and that a policy should be put in place allowing for the termination of any employee who discusses the HIV status of a colleague. If your staff wishes to be tested for HIV, you advise them to go elsewhere and have it done anonymously. Furthermore, argue that Nurse Shanahan should have stopped the testing as soon as she realized her mistake and that it was not justified for her to look at the results with knowledge that consent was not given. The bottom line is that people on your staff will be infected with HIV. In your opinion, the best policy is "Don't Ask, Don't Tell."

Role Assignment Number 8

Assume the role of Mr./Ms. Hershey, a former patient of Dr. McCormick who has since tested HIV-positive.

Several years ago, Dr. McCormick performed an invasive procedure on you. Last month you tested HIV-positive during a routine physical. You are married, monogamous, and have never used intravenous drugs. While participating in the group discussion, consider the following:

1. Argue that Dr. McCormick should never again perform invasive procedures. You know that she exposed you to the virus. Even though the risk of being exposed during surgery is minuscule, it still exists and it is 100 percent preventable simply by prohibiting Dr. McCormick from performing invasive procedures in the future. The economic harm that Dr. McCormick may incur from losing her career cannot be used to justify failing to prevent the spread of a terminal disease. Doctors have an ethical obligation to do no harm. That obligation is breached when a physician knowingly engages in behavior that may potentially spread HIV.

2. Argue that Dr. McCormick should be required to inform all of her former patients of her HIV-positive serostatus. People have a right to know that they may have been exposed to HIV by Dr. McCormick. By requiring Dr. McCormick to inform her former patients, those former patients who test positive will be able to get immediate treatment to prolong their lives and they will be able to alter their behavior to prevent infecting others.

3. In the event that the hospital and Dr. McCormick refuse to disclose her status, consider the option of selling your story to a tabloid. If you do this, you will be able to make money to help pay your medical bills and you will be able to expose Dr. McCormick's status so that prospective patients will at least be able to make an informed decision as to whether or not they want her to operate on them.

Role Assignment Number 9

Assume the role of Mr./Ms. Sandeman, a former patient of Dr. McCormick who has since tested HIV-positive.

Several years ago Dr. McCormick operated on you. Your life has been a turbulent one and you realize and openly acknowledge that you may have contracted HIV from a source other than Dr. McCormick. The thought has even crossed your mind that you may have passed the virus to Dr. McCormick during your operation.

Your reasons for participating in today's discussion are:

1. To protect Dr. McCormick. She saved your life and you feel indebted to her for that. Argue that every individual has the right to privacy and that requiring Dr. McCormick to reveal her serostatus will violate her right to privacy. Discrimination against HIV-positive persons is wide-spread and if Dr. McCormick reveals her HIV status she will be discriminated against and lose her career.

2. To advance voluntary testing of all surgical candidates. You know that if you had been tested before your surgery, your life would probably be better today and Dr. McCormick might not be HIV-positive. Argue that all patients undergoing invasive surgical procedures should be tested for HIV so that health care workers can take proper precautions to avoid potential infection.

Role Assignment Number 10

Assume the role of Mr./Ms. Pine, a former patient of Dr. McCormick who has since tested HIV-negative.

About a year ago Dr. McCormick performed a highly invasive procedure on you. Today, you are healthy and HIV-negative. You believe it would be terrible to lose such a talented surgeon as Dr. McCormick just because she is HIV-positive. Further, argue that requiring surgeons to reveal their HIV statuses will cause panic and prejudice that are not justified by the minimal risk to the patient. Therefore, you respect Dr. McCormick's right to privacy and you are attending this meeting to voice your opinion in opposition to firing Dr. McCormick or requiring her to reveal her HIV status to anyone.

Role Assignment Number 11

Assume the role of Mr./Ms. Devon, a former patient of Dr. McCormick whose HIV tests are not conclusive.

You were the last patient that Dr. McCormick operated on (about six weeks ago) and a sufficient amount of time has not elapsed since possible exposure to ensure the accuracy of the HIV test. However, you have been tested and the results came back negative. You will be tested again in about a month. You respect Dr. McCormick's right to privacy but believe that she has an obligation, as your physician, to reveal to you her HIV status.

You believe that Dr. McCormick knew at the time that she operated on you that she was HIV-positive and you intend to bring a cause of action for damages resulting from the emotional distress, sleeplessness, and anxiety that have been caused by knowing that you may have been exposed to HIV by Dr. McCormick. Due to this distress, you have missed several days of work and lost wages. You plan to sue Dr. McCormick and Mountain View Regional Hospital.

Argue that all health care professionals who conduct invasive procedures should be tested and those test results should be made available to prospective patients. Consider the argument that in order for a patient to give truly informed consent to a procedure she must have knowledge of all potential risks. Since infection from an HIV-positive surgeon is a potential, albeit slight, risk the patient should have the right to know of that risk when deciding whether to have any particular surgeon perform a procedure. Had you known that Dr. McCormick was HIV-positive, you would have never consented to her performing your operation.

Role Assignment Number 12

Assume the role of Mr./Ms. Sharp, Esq., an attorney who is present to represent the interests of prospective patients of Dr. McCormick.

Your primary goal is to preserve the autonomy of all prospective patients of Dr. McCormick. Respect for autonomy includes giving patients all necessary information to allow them to make informed decisions regarding health care. Dr. McCormick and Mountain View Regional Hospital have knowledge that Dr. McCormick is HIV-positive and that she may infect patients during an invasive procedure. Patients should be informed that the risk of infection from such an occurrence is minimal but that it does exist every time an HIV-positive surgeon performs an invasive procedure. Argue that without full disclosure it is not possible for a prospective patient to make a fully informed decision about receiving care from Dr. McCormick or any other HIV-positive surgeon.

Role Assignment Number 13

Assume the role of Mr./Ms. Black, Esq., an attorney representing Dr. McCormick.

You are currently suing Mountain View Regional Hospital for testing the blood of Matthew McCormick without consent, for allowing Dr. McCormick's condition to become common knowledge throughout the hospital, and for any action decided upon today that will discriminate against Dr. McCormick on the basis of her HIV status. Argue in favor of the following:

1. Ensuring that Dr. McCormick is allowed to return to work with the full privileges and responsibilities that she enjoyed prior to this incident.

2. Protecting the privacy of Dr. McCormick's condition, both with regard to prospective and past patients.

Role Assignment Number 14

Assume the role of Mr./Ms. Spencer, CEO of Mountain View Regional Hospital.

As CEO of Mountain View Regional Hospital you are concerned with maintaining the reputation of the hospital and protecting the hospital's economic interests. Argue in favor of the following points:

1. Argue that Dr. McCormick should never again be permitted to perform invasive procedures. Maintain the position that any known risk of HIV infection must be prevented. The liability associated with infection, no matter how slim the risk, is too great to accept. If Dr. McCormick is allowed to operate, and an incident causing infection of the patient were to occur, the hospital could face incredible liability.

2. Argue that the hospital's economic interests must be protected by sealing Dr. McCormick's medical record and not notifying any of her former patients of her condition. This position makes sense because even if former patients of Dr.

McCormick are HIV-positive it will not be possible for them to prove that they were infected by Dr. McCormick. Furthermore, notification may cause more harm than good because it could cause hysteria in the general public if the media were to publicize the incident. Notification would set a dangerous precedent and there is no clear legal or ethical duty requiring the hospital to notify anyone of Dr. McCormick's HIV-positive status.

3. In lieu of Dr. McCormick practicing as a surgeon you are prepared to offer her an administrative position or a position doing research. If this not acceptable, you are prepared to offer two years' salary to Dr. McCormick if she agrees to sign a confidentiality agreement stating that she will never discuss her HIV status or any of the events leading up to her resignation.

4. Propose that a policy be instituted in the future whereby all staff members will be prohibited from discussing the HIV status of other hospital employees. Also, propose a policy prohibiting staff members from being tested for HIV or receiving HIV treatment at Mountain View Regional Hospital. The purpose behind this policy would be to separate the professional and personal lives of your employees. This will also limit hospital liability by eliminating the hospital's knowledge of employee serostatus.

Role Assignment Number 15

Assume the role of Mr./Ms. Greenwood, Director of Surgical Assistants.

You represent the interests of all of the surgical assistants at the hospital. You have personally assisted Dr. McCormick on numerous procedures and you have seen her get stuck with needles and be cut on several occasions. These injuries often occurred when Dr. McCormick's hands were in the body cavity of a patient. You know that the possibility of infection exists, both from doctor to patient and patient to doctor. You recall one specific occasion when Dr. McCormick was operating and an assisting physician cut her with a scalpel. Dr. McCormick's hand began to bleed while it was inside the body of the patient. That patient is present at today's meeting and has tested HIV-positive. No one else knows what you saw that day and the patient does not know how he/she was infected. Do you have an ethical obligation to disclose what you saw?

Role Assignment Number 16

Assume the role of Dr. Boyle, an Orthopedic Surgeon and Colleague of Dr. McCormick.

As a fellow surgeon of Dr. McCormick you are interested in protecting her and your fellow physicians. Argue that any risk that does exist of physician-patient infection is minimal and that if anyone is at risk it is the surgeons. Adamantly oppose any policy requiring physicians to be tested for HIV or requiring physicians to disclose their HIV statuses after they have been tested. Maintain the position that, so long as universal precautions are followed, the risk to patients is not significant enough to justify ruining someone's career that they have worked years to achieve. Consider the following points:

1. If Dr. McCormick is required to reveal her status to past patients, this will establish grounds for the involuntary testing of all physicians and health care workers and subsequent release of their test results.

2. If involuntary testing is implemented, many talented surgeons will be discriminated against.

3. If talented surgeons like Dr. McCormick are prevented from performing surgery because they are HIV-positive, this will do more harm than good because potential patients of Dr. McCormick will be forced to see less experienced and less talented surgeons. This will inevitably result in a lower quality of care than if the better, though HIV-positive, surgeons were allowed to operate.

4. If health care workers are required to divulge their HIV status they will simply not be tested. This will compromise their own health and put their sexual partners and possible future children at risk.

Role Assignment Number 17

Assume the role of Dr. Ramsey, Director of Surgery at Mountain View Regional Hospital. As director of surgery you feel that all surgeons have a right to privacy and that the law and hospital policy should protect this right. If patients know that a surgeon is HIV-positive they will not go to him or her and it is possible that they will delay surgery and suffer damage to their health. Also, argue that an individual needing surgery will be unable to make an informed decision as to whether to see an HIV-positive surgeon. This is because the patient will make a decision based on fear without understanding the minuscule likelihood of an event occurring which might cause the surgeon to bleed inside the body cavity of the patient and, even if such an event were to occur, the fact that enough virus would not likely enter the body of the patient to infect him or her. This is an area where physicians must paternalistically make decisions for patients because patients will not be able to make reasonable decisions for themselves.

Role Assignment Number 18

Assume the role of Dr. Charles, Ph.D., a Bioethicist on staff at Mountain View Regional Hospital. Consider the following:

1. Because consent had not been given for the HIV test on Matthew McCormick's blood, it was unethical to allow the test to proceed and it was unethical for Nurse Shanahan to look at the results or for the doctors to pursue the matter. Confidentiality has clearly been violated and Dr. McCormick must be compensated

for damages resulting from that breach.

2. Now that knowledge that Dr. McCormick is HIV-positive is widespread, it cannot be ignored. Dr. McCormick has an ethical obligation to inform her past and potential patients of her serostatus. A patient may consent to surgery by Dr. McCormick only if that patient's consent is truly informed. Therefore, Dr. McCormick should be permitted to continue on staff so long as she informs all potential patients of her HIV-positive status.

3. If it is discovered that Dr. McCormick performed surgery on patients knowing that she was HIV-positive, but without informing her patients of the risk which they were undertaking, then Dr. McCormick should be held liable to those patients who are HIV-positive, provided that it can be shown that Dr. McCormick was the source of their HIV infection. If this is shown, then Dr. McCormick should be held liable for such patients' medical bills and incidental damages.

Role Assignment Number 19

Assume the role of Mr./Ms. Thomas, an administrator at Mountain View Regional Hospital concerned with the formulation of HIV/AIDS policy.

You are most concerned with maintaining the integrity of the physician/patient relationship. Because you believe that the physician/patient relationship has been breached by the doctors discussing Dr. McCormick's serostatus over lunch, you believe that Dr. Blue and Dr. Green should be punished and that Dr. McCormick deserves to be compensated. You do not, however, believe that the doctors or Nurse Shanahan breached their duties with their other actions. Argue that both doctors had a physician/patient relationship with both Dr. and Matthew McCormick which required them to reveal the test results. Further, upon discovering that Dr. McCormick was not going to be cooperative, you believe that the doctors had an ethical obligation to inform Mr. McCormick of Matthew's HIV status in order to ensure that he gets proper treatment. You also believe that the doctors were justified in disclosing the test results to Mr. McCormick because he was a third party in imminent danger of infection (if he has not already been infected).

Role Assignment Number 20

Assume the role of Mr./Ms. Chung, a Health Care Educator employed by Mountain View Regional Hospital. When teaching people about HIV you always stress that any risk is too great to accept. Argue that this applies to the case at hand. Just as condoms are not 100 percent effective in preventing risk, neither are universal precautions. There is a risk that a surgeon with HIV may be cut or pricked during surgery causing him or her to bleed. If the physician's blood mixes with the blood of the patient, infection may occur either from the physician to the patient or from the patient to the physician. You encourage everyone with whom you speak to be tested for HIV. Doctors should be examples and should all be tested. Because there is a risk that an HIV-positive surgeon will infect a patient, he or she should not perform invasive procedures.

CHAPTER 2

EMERGENCY CARE AND HIV

Treatment Policy and Practice

INSTRUCTIONS AND OBJECTIVES

This chapter sets forth hypothetical events occurring one night in the emergency department of City Hospital. The central issues presented in this chapter are treatment of HIV-positive persons, confidentiality rights verses the duty to warn, and the ability of health care professionals to withhold or administer care based on a potential threat to their own health. Discussion of the case study should focus on whether the procedures followed and the acts undertaken were appropriate and, if not, what steps can be taken to improve hospital protocol. In addressing each of the issues presented, participants should consider the ethical principles of autonomy, beneficence, nonmaleficence, and justice. Participants should also consider the needs and desires of individuals, both receiving and administering health care, verses an overarching public policy perspective.

THE CASE STUDY

The following is a record of a few hours of activity in the emergency department at City Hospital. The record is being presented for review by the professional staff and administration of City Hospital in order to resolve ethical and legal issues. These issues have arisen in the context of City Hospital's policies and procedures for treating HIV-positive persons who present at the hospital's emergency department.

12:00 a.m. A transient, "Mr. Doe," is brought into the emergency department by police. Mr. Doe is unconscious with a blood alcohol level of .20. He was found floating unconscious in a park pond and is soaking wet. Emergency department staff take Mr. Doe into an examining room to remove his wet clothing, dry him off, and allow him to sleep off his stupor. While removing Mr. Doe's jacket, Nurse Jackson reaches into a deep pocket. When she removes her hand, a hypodermic needle is sticking through her latex glove and into her palm. Blood is visible on the syringe and it appears to have been used for injection of intravenous drugs. Upon inspection, Nurse Jackson finds needle marks on the inside of both of Mr. Doe's arms.

12:15 a.m. Jack Smith, a local man known to be suffering from full-blown AIDS, is brought into the emergency department by ambulance. He has been hit by a drunk driver. His condition is critical and he needs immediate surgery to stop profuse internal bleeding. Mr. Smith is covered with blood. The surgeon on call is Dr. Reed. Dr. Reed knows Mr. Smith and has knowledge that Mr. Smith has been suffering from AIDS for well over two years. In Dr. Reed's opinion, Mr. Smith does not have long to live, even with surgery, as he will soon die from AIDS. Dr. Reed evaluates the situation and decides that to perform the highly invasive surgery required to save Mr. Smith's life would create such a risk of HIV infection to herself and other staff that the dangers of performing the procedure outweigh any benefit that Mr. Smith might gain from the surgery. Confronted by the chief of the emergency department, Dr. Reed refuses to perform the surgery. A second surgeon is called in. It will take about 45 minutes for the second surgeon to arrive.

12:22 a.m. Afraid that she might have been exposed to HIV, Nurse Jackson draws blood from the still unconscious Mr. Doe. Nurse Jackson sends the blood to the laboratory to be tested for HIV. Nurse Jackson includes only an identification number on the blood sample and does not label the specimen as belonging to Mr. Doe.

12:27 a.m. Ms. Snow arrives in the emergency department after being shot in the chest with a cross-bow. Dr. Reed quickly leaves Mr. Smith and the confrontation with the emergency department chief to attend to Ms. Snow. Upset by the Smith situation, Dr. Reed forgets to put her face mask and eye shield back into place. Upon gently pulling upon one of the arrows, blood sprays from Ms. Snow's chest, covering Dr. Reed's face and entering her mouth, nose, and eyes.

12:43 a.m. Jack Smith dies. The second surgeon has not yet arrived.

1:07 a.m. Upset by the death of Mr. Smith, Dr. Hancock, a resident, confronts Dr. Reed. In the course of their shouting match, Dr. Hancock reveals that he is HIV-positive.

1:22 a.m. A local prostitute arrives at the emergency department after having been badly beaten. She is crying and incoherent. Dr. Hancock attends to cleaning her up. During their exchange, the prostitute reveals that the man who beat her is Mr. Garcia, manager of the convenience store located across the street from the emergency department. The prostitute mutters that Mr. Garcia may have beaten her but that she got the best of him because she has AIDS and now "so will he."

DISCUSSION QUESTIONS

The Case of Mr. Doe

1. Was Nurse Jackson justified in drawing blood from Mr. Doe without his consent for purposes of an HIV test? Should the circumstances under which Nurse Jackson drew the blood be considered in evaluating her actions? Was Nurse Jackson justified in her actions if she does not tell anyone the results of the HIV test?

2. How does the California statute included at Appendix A affect your analysis of the issues surrounding Nurse Jackson's interaction with Mr. Doe?

3. Did Nurse Jackson violate Mr. Doe's right to privacy or his right to confidentiality or both? What is the difference between the right to privacy and the right to confidentiality? How is each of those rights violated?

4. If Nurse Jackson was not justified in drawing the blood, what course of action should she have taken?

5. Does Nurse Jackson have an obligation to inform Mr. Doe that she drew his blood for purposes of performing an HIV test? Does Nurse Jackson have an obligation to disclose the results of the HIV test to Mr. Doe?

6. Who, or what entity, should pay for the HIV test performed on Mr. Doe's blood?

7. If the test result comes back positive, does Nurse Jackson have a legal duty to disclose the results to friends of Mr. Doe who Nurse Jackson knows share needles with him? Does she have an ethical obligation to do so? What is the effect of California Health and Safety Code Section 121010 included at Appendix A?

8. Suppose that Nurse Jackson did not draw blood from Mr. Doe while he was unconscious but instead waited until he regained consciousness to obtain his informed consent to draw blood for the test. If Mr. Doe refuses to consent to the test, does Nurse Jackson have any grounds upon which compel Mr. Doe to give blood? Does Mr. Doe have an obligation to give the blood? If so, what is the nature of that obligation—legal or ethical?

9. Assume that Nurse Jackson did not draw blood and that Mr. Doe refused to consent to the HIV test. If Nurse Jackson finds blood on the inside of Mr. Doe's shirt sleeve, can Nurse Jackson ethically send such a specimen to the laboratory for testing without Mr. Doe's knowledge or consent? Why or why not? If Nurse Jackson decides to do that, would it violate Mr. Doe's right to privacy or confidentiality? Would it violate Mr. Doe's right to privacy or confidentiality if he abandoned his old shirt from which the blood sample was taken?

The Case of Mr. Smith and Dr. Reed

1. Was Dr. Reed justified in refusing to operate on Mr. Smith? Why or why not?

2. Was Dr. Reed justified if she knew that only either Mr. Smith or Ms. Snow could be saved, therefore, she chose to save the patient whom she judged to have the greater chance of achieving a better quality and longer life?

3. Can the fact that a person has AIDS be used to deny him scarce medical resources based on the premise that even if he is saved at that moment, he will not be

able to achieve the same quality or quantity of life as would be achieved if the resources were utilized by an otherwise healthy individual?

The Case of Ms. Snow and Dr. Reed

1. Can Dr. Reed compel Ms. Snow to be tested for HIV? Is there any difference between the Reed-Snow interaction and the Jackson-Doe interaction?

2. In order to justify requiring Ms. Snow to be tested for HIV, can it convincingly be argued that if Ms. Snow did infect Dr. Reed, then Dr. Reed, as an emergency department physician, would be putting other patients at risk of infection?

3. Should Dr. Reed be disciplined for not wearing her face mask?

4. Did Dr. Reed assume the risk of HIV infection by not following universal precautions and wearing her face mask?

The Case of Dr. Hancock

1. Should Dr. Hancock be dropped from the residency program because he is HIV-positive? Can it be argued that it constitutes bad public policy to train HIV-positive persons to be physicians? What if Dr. Hancock is a surgical resident who plans on spending his career performing invasive, exposure-prone procedures?

2. Should Dr. Hancock be able to sue City Hospital on the basis of discrimination if he is fired or sanctioned for being HIV-positive?

3. What other options does City Hospital have to deal with Dr. Hancock?

The Case of The Prostitute and Mr. Garcia

1. Does Dr. Hancock have any obligation to offer HIV testing or counseling to the prostitute? Should he be required to inquire how she knows that she is HIV-positive? Does he have an obligation to investigate further as to how the prostitute contracted HIV or whom she may have infected?

2. Does Dr. Hancock have an ethical obligation or a legal duty to keep information given to him by the prostitute confidential?

3. Does Dr. Hancock owe any duty to Mr. Garcia? If Dr. Hancock has a physician/patient relationship with the prostitute that requires him to keep the prostitute's medical information confidential, are there any grounds upon which Dr. Hancock may have an obligation to Mr. Garcia that trumps his duty of confidentiality to the prostitute? What is the effect of California Health and Safety Code Section 121015 included at Appendix A? Of the *Tarasoff* case included at Appendix C?

4. Assume that over the past few years, Mr. Garcia has been treated by Dr. Hancock for various ailments. Although the treatment has all been within the emergency department setting, Mr. Garcia has not seen any other physician and he considers Dr. Hancock to be his primary care physician. Does Mr. Garcia have a physician/patient relationship with Dr. Hancock? If so, does that relationship impose any additional duties on Dr. Hancock? If so, how should Dr. Hancock's duty to the

prostitute be balanced against Dr. Hancock's duty to Mr. Garcia?

5. What course of action should Dr. Hancock take according to California Health and Safety Code Section 120975 included at Appendix A? Does the statute apply given the fact that the prostitute self-disclosed her HIV status and did not receive an HIV test?

6. If several days pass and Dr. Hancock sees the prostitute "negotiating" with Mr. Garcia, does Dr. Hancock have any obligation to intervene, either for the sake of the health of the prostitute (to prevent her from being beaten) or for the sake of the health of Mr. Garcia (to prevent him from being exposed to HIV)?

7. Suppose that at the time that the prostitute disclosed her HIV status to Dr. Hancock, Dr. Hancock informed her that he could not keep her statements confidential. Would that change the course of action that Dr. Hancock should take? If so, why?

SUGGESTED RESEARCH

Statutes

Appendix A: California Health and Safety Code Sections 120975 through 121020.

Case Law

Appendix C: *Tarasoff v. Regents of the University of California*, 551 P.2d 334 (Cal. 1976).

Texts

Annas, George J. *Standard of Care: The Law of American Bioethics*. New York City, NY: Oxford University Press, 1993, 119-31.

Munson, Ronald. *Intervention and Reflection: Basic Issues in Medical Ethics*. 4th ed. Belmont, CA: Wadsworth, 1992, 205-57.

Pence, Gregory E. *Classic Cases in Medical Ethics*. 2nd ed. New York City, NY: McGraw-Hill, 1995, 413-42.

Veatch, Robert M. *Medical Ethics*. 2nd ed. Sudbury, MA: Jones and Bartlett, 1997, 395-413.

ROLE ASSIGNMENTS FOR 12 PARTICIPANTS

1. Nurse Jackson
2. Mr. Doe
3. Dr. Reed
4. Dr. Hancock
5. Attorney representing the survivors of Mr. Smith
6. Mr. Garcia
7. The HIV-positive prostitute

8. Ms. Snow
9. A Representative of the Residency Program Sponsoring Dr. Hancock
10. The Chief of Staff of City Hospital
11. Mr./Ms. Hemingway, a patients' rights advocate
12. Hospital Administrator with authority to render decisions (This role assignment may be assigned to multiple participants.)

Role Assignment Number 1

Assume the role of Nurse Jackson. No one but you knows yet, but Mr. Doe tested positive for HIV. You have since tested negative but must be tested again in a few months to confirm that result. Argue to justify taking blood from Mr. Doe to perform the HIV test. Consider the following:

1. You were exposed to HIV during the course of caring for Mr. Doe.
2. You only tested Mr. Doe for your own personal purpose of knowing whether you were exposed to HIV.
3. You were exposed to HIV as a direct result of Mr. Doe's illegal activity (i.e., his drug use).
4. If you did not test Mr. Doe, you would have to wait about six months to determine whether you were infected with HIV by Mr. Doe.
5. As a health care worker, it is possible that you may endanger third parties by accidentally exposing them to blood-borne diseases which you carry. By testing Mr. Doe, you may have protected the health of countless emergency department patients.

Role Assignment Number 2

Assume the role of Mr. Doe. Consider the following arguments:

1. Nurse Jackson invaded your privacy by drawing your blood for HIV testing without your consent. If Nurse Jackson wanted to know your HIV status she should have waited until you regained consciousness and then sought your informed consent to draw your blood for testing.
2. Nurse Jackson violated your autonomy rights by having your blood tested for HIV without revealing the results of the test to you.
3. If Nurse Jackson reveals the results of the HIV test to anyone, including the other people present at this meeting, she will be violating your right to medical confidentiality. If she does that, you intend to seek retribution through legal action.
4. By taking your blood without obtaining your informed consent, Nurse Jackson committed a battery upon your person.

Role Assignment Number 3

Assume the role of Dr. Reed. While participating in today's discussion, consider the following:

1. Argue that your decision not to treat Mr. Smith was justified because you could only treat either Ms. Snow or Mr. Smith. Given their conditions, one of them would die. Your decision to treat Ms. Snow was justified because Ms. Snow will

have a longer life and a better quality of life than Mr. Smith would have had if he had been saved. As a physician, you are called upon to allocate scarce resources and you have an ethical obligation to allocate those resources in the manner which produces the greatest amount of good for the greatest number of people. That is exactly what you did.

2. Argue that Ms. Snow should be required to be tested for HIV because she may have exposed you to the virus. If she is HIV-positive, you have the right to know so that you can take appropriate steps to promote your own well-being and prevent possible spread of the virus to your patients.

3. Argue that Dr. Hancock should be dismissed from the residency program because it is likely that he may expose patients to HIV in the emergency department. Emergency department work is fast-paced and often highly invasive. As such, it is reasonably foreseeable that an emergency department physician might get cut and expose a patient or another health care worker to any blood-borne disease that he or she carries, including HIV. Argue that HIV-positive physicians who insist on treating patients violate their duty of nonmaleficence to those patients because those physicians may potentially harm the patients by exposing them to HIV.

Role Assignment Number 4

Assume the role of Dr. Hancock. While participating in today's discussion, consider the following:

1. Argue that if you are forced to resign or are fired, that would constitute discrimination against you based on your HIV-positive serostatus. Consider the fact that there has never been a documented case of a health care worker infecting a patient with HIV. Because the risk of transmission is minimal, so long as universal precautions are followed, HIV-positive health care workers do not present a realistic threat to patients. Because there is no articulable risk, there are no grounds for terminating your employment.

2. Argue that firing HIV-positive health care workers constitutes bad public policy because such a policy would encourage health care workers to avoid being tested for HIV and it would force them to conceal their serostatus. That would be detrimental to the health of HIV-positive health care workers because they would not seek the care that is necessary to preserve their own health out of fear of losing their jobs.

3. Argue that Dr. Reed should be fired for not treating Mr. Smith and that the District Attorney should consider prosecuting her for manslaughter. Mr. Smith could have been saved if Dr. Reed had fulfilled her legal obligation and delivered care to him. It is not the place of emergency department physicians to play God by deciding who should be treated and who should be left to die. The fact that Mr. Smith was known to be HIV-positive did not give Dr. Reed warrant to refuse to treat him.

4. Argue that Ms. Snow should be allowed to refuse to consent to being tested for HIV. Every individual has the right to autonomy in making health care decisions. If Ms. Snow wishes to refuse to be tested then her wishes must be respected. Besides, had Dr. Reed followed universal precautions by wearing her face mask she would not have been exposed to Ms. Snow's blood. Dr. Reed should bear the consequences

of her own negligence.

Role Assignment Number 5

Assume the role of an attorney representing the survivors of Mr. Smith. While participating in today's discussion, consider the following:

1. Argue that Dr. Reed should be prosecuted for manslaughter. Dr. Reed caused the death of Mr. Smith by failing to act, as legally required, to save Mr. Smith's life. Additionally, argue that Dr. Reed should be terminated and have her license to practice medicine revoked. If those punishments are not pursued then it sends the message to physicians that they can play God and decide who lives and who dies. Furthermore, if Dr. Reed is not punished, it sets the precedent that HIV-positive persons are not entitled to the care which other persons are afforded.

2. Argue that Dr. Hancock must not be fired or forced to resign. HIV-positive health care professionals present only a minimal risk of infection to their patients. The risk of an HIV-positive patient infecting a health care worker is substantially greater than that of a health care worker infecting a patient, yet no one would ever suggest that HIV-positive persons should elect not to seek health care in order to protect health care professionals. Why then should HIV-positive health care professionals be denied the right to pursue their careers? So long as universal precautions are followed, both patients and health care workers will be protected.

Role Assignment Number 6

Assume the role of Mr. Garcia. While participating in today's discussion, consider the following:

1. Argue that Dr. Hancock has an obligation to disclose to you any medical information about the prostitute that may be relevant to your health. Formulate your argument based on the requirements of the California statutes included at Appendix A and the *Tarasoff* decision included at Appendix C. Also base your arguments on the fact that Dr. Hancock is your physician, therefore, he owes a duty to you to help protect your health.

2. Argue that the prostitute has no right to confidentiality because she has indicated that she will use HIV as a weapon. Argue that because Dr. Hancock has knowledge that the prostitute will act in a particular way with the intent to do harm to you, Dr. Hancock has a duty to prevent the harmful act by notifying you of the potential danger.

Role Assignment Number 7

Assume the role of the HIV-positive prostitute. While participating in today's discussion, consider the following:

1. Argue that you have a right to medical confidentiality. You disclosed your HIV status to Dr. Hancock during the course of receiving treatment. Because you gave Dr. Hancock that information while receiving treatment from him, Dr. Hancock

is obligated to keep the information confidential. Furthermore, Dr. Hancock has no definite knowledge that you and Mr. Garcia engage in unsafe conduct or that Mr. Garcia is at risk of exposure.

2. Argue that even if Dr. Hancock is Mr. Garcia's physician, the relationship that the two of them have cannot trump your own relationship with Dr. Hancock. When a person discloses information to a physician, she does so with the understanding that it will be kept confidential. If that basic assumption is broken, then public confidence in the health care establishment will be undermined and people will be hesitant to disclose sensitive information to health care professionals. That would impede the ability of physicians to adequately care for their patients.

3. Argue that Mr. Garcia is at risk because of his own acts. Mr. Garcia is free to refrain from sexual activity with prostitutes, and he is free to use a condom. Mr. Garcia knows that his acts carry risk and he has freely chosen to take that risk. You cannot be held responsible for Mr. Garcia's lack of discretion.

4. Argue that by informing Mr. Garcia of your HIV status, Dr. Hancock would be putting you at risk of being beaten by Mr. Garcia.

Role Assignment Number 8

Assume the role of Ms. Snow. While participating in today's discussion, consider the following:

1. Argue that your right to privacy will be violated if you are required to be tested for HIV without your consent. Argue that an unconsented test would also violate your right to autonomy in making health care decisions and your right to refuse unwanted health care. Also argue that requiring an unconsented HIV test would constitute a battery and establish a public policy that would allow individual rights to be trumped. Such a policy would undermine patient confidence in the medical establishment.

2. Argue that Mr. Doe has the right to refuse to be tested for HIV. Just because he was unconscious when he presented at the emergency department does not mean that he does not have a privacy interest or a right to autonomy.

3. Argue that in both your case and the case of Mr. Doe, the health care professionals were potentially exposed to HIV due to their own negligence. In your case, Dr. Reed was in violation of hospital policy when she failed to replace her face mask in accordance with universal precautions. In the case of Mr. Doe, Nurse Jackson was simply acting incompetently by sticking her hand into Mr. Doe's pocket without first looking into the pocket to see if there was any danger. Neither you nor Mr. Doe should have your rights compromised on account of someone else's negligence.

Role Assignment Number 9

Assume the role of a representative of the residency program sponsoring Dr. Hancock. While participating in today's discussion, consider the following:

1. Argue that Dr. Hancock must be dismissed from the medical residency program. HIV is potentially spread through a physician being cut during an invasive

procedure. Though the risk of infection is small, the risk is present whenever an HIV-positive physician treats an HIV-negative patient. Being HIV-positive is a medical condition and not a social status. The duty of nonmaleficence requires that doctors do no harm. Allowing patients to potentially be exposed to HIV is to cause them harm. An HIV-positive physician is, therefore, ethically required to refrain from performing invasive procedures, and a medical school is ethically required to prevent an HIV-positive resident from potentially harming patients. Plenty of other opportunities exist for Dr. Hancock to pursue a lucrative career in which he will not be a threat to patients.

2. Argue that Mr. Doe and Ms. Snow should both be required to be tested for HIV. Nurse Jackson and Dr. Reed were potentially exposed to HIV while saving the lives of Mr. Doe and Ms. Snow. Health care professionals must have some rights to help protect and promote their own welfare. The invasion of the privacy rights of Mr. Doe and Ms. Snow would be minimal as only Nurse Jackson and Dr. Reed would know the results of the tests. Informing any third party of the HIV test result would constitute a violation of confidentiality and would be subject to sanctions.

Role Assignment Number 10

Assume the role of the Chief of Staff of City Hospital. While participating in today's discussion, consider the following:

1. Argue that Nurse Jackson was justified in her actions. Mr. Doe was engaged in illegal activity. Mr. Doe should not enjoy a privacy right in using illegal drugs that overrides Nurse Jackson's interest in knowing whether she was exposed to HIV. Favoring the rights of criminals over the rights of health care professionals constitutes bad public policy.

2. Argue that Dr. Reed was justified in refusing to treat Mr. Smith. Emergency department physicians and health care professionals are called upon to make tough choices everyday that affect who lives and who dies. Dr. Reed weighed the risks and benefits and decided that to treat Mr. Smith would cause a significant risk of infection to herself and the emergency department staff. Dr. Reed's choice was also justified by the fact that she could only save either Ms. Snow or Mr. Smith. The fact that Ms. Snow will have a longer and better quality of life than Mr. Smith could have had is a legitimate factor to be considered in deciding how to allocate limited resources.

3. Argue that Ms. Snow should be required to be tested for HIV. Health care professionals must have the ability to protect and promote their own health when they are potentially exposed to HIV or other diseases. Ms. Snow should be tested for HIV and the results should be revealed to Dr. Reed. Dr. Reed, however, should be required to keep the results of the test confidential.

4. Argue that Dr. Hancock should be terminated. HIV is potentially spread through a physician being cut during an invasive procedure. Though the risk of infecting a patient is small, it does exist. It does not constitute sound economic policy for the hospital to assume liability for employing an HIV-positive resident. Furthermore, the limited resources that the hospital has available to train physicians should not be spent on training HIV-positive persons.

5. Argue that Mr. Garcia should be informed that the prostitute is HIV-positive. It is common knowledge that Mr. Garcia utilizes the services of the prostitute and, thus, that he is at risk of contracting HIV from her. The duty of nonmaleficence can be understood to require health care professionals to prevent harm to anyone known to be at risk. Mr. Garcia should be informed that the prostitute is HIV-positive in order to protect his health.

Role Assignment Number 11

Assume the role of Mr./Ms. Hemingway, a patients' rights advocate. In arguing in support of patient autonomy and informed consent, consider the following:

1. Every individual has the right to privacy. A person's HIV serostatus is protected by that right and no one can compel another person to disclose his or her serostatus. Therefore, Mr. Doe and Ms. Snow have the right to refuse being tested for HIV.

2. A right to medical confidentiality exists which protects communications between doctors and patients. Anything that is said during the course of treatment is protected. The communication that occurred between the prostitute and Dr. Hancock is confidential, and Dr. Hancock cannot disclose that information to a third party without the consent of the prostitute.

3. Informed consent means that patients understand all risks associated with treatment before they undergo a procedure. Part of the risk associated with any procedure is the risk of being infected with HIV from an HIV-positive physician. In order for a patient to give truly informed consent, he must understand that there is a risk of contracting HIV from his physician. Therefore, Dr. Hancock should be allowed to stay in the residency program but he should be required to inform his patients that he is HIV-positive before performing any invasive procedure. Patients should then be given the opportunity to refuse to be cared for by Dr. Hancock if they do not wish to assume that risk.

4. All patients have the right to emergency medical care regardless of whether they are HIV-positive. Dr. Reed should be dismissed because she refused to care for Mr. Smith. By choosing to enter medicine, physicians assume the risk of being exposed to infectious diseases. Universal precautions should be followed to protect physicians. If doctors such as Dr. Reed do not wish to assume the risk of being exposed to HIV then they should not enter the medical profession. It is unacceptable for an emergency department physician to arbitrarily decide who she will or will not treat.

Role Assignment Number 12

Assume the role of a hospital administrator with authority to render a decision in each of the cases presented today. While participating in today's discussion, listen to all arguments presented and ask questions which you deem relevant. At the end of today's meeting, you will be called upon to render the following decisions:

1. Whether to sanction Nurse Jackson;
2. Whether to sanction Dr. Reed; and

3. Whether to fire or limit the privileges of Dr. Hancock.

CHAPTER 3

A REVOLUTIONARY POLICY?

Mandatory Disclosure of HIV Serostatus

INSTRUCTIONS AND OBJECTIVES

This chapter makes a "modest proposal" in an attempt to force participants to look at the stigma of HIV-positive status in a different light. The hypothetical leads participants to think about whether there might be a way to eliminate the social and medical stigma of HIV, whether availability of information might be a way to eliminate that stigma, and what the other effects of the availability of information might be. While the proposal appears benign on its face, further examination may uncover legal, ethical, and other problems, which participants are asked to identify and evaluate.

THE CASE STUDY

Welcome to the Horizons Health Maintenance Organization Annual Policy Analysis Conference. The topic today is mandatory HIV/AIDS testing and disclosure. You have been invited to attend this meeting because of your expertise in HIV/AIDS policy and management. You and your colleagues will be reviewing an innovative and highly controversial policy that has been proposed by the California branch of our organization. In evaluating the proposed policy, please take into account the policy's effect on health care workers, patients, the HMO, our community, and society as a whole. Remember to address issues of cost/benefit, confidentiality, privacy, informed consent, and the ethical principles of autonomy, nonmaleficence, beneficence and justice. A copy of the proposed policy with community comments follows below:

Openness and Candor in HIV/AIDS Disclosure
A Proposed Policy

Statement of Purpose. The purpose of this proposed policy is to eliminate the social stigma and phobia that surrounds HIV/AIDS in the context of health services. The goal is to educate both health care workers and patients as to the minimal risks associated with HIV infection during the rendering of medical services and thereby eliminate discrimination against HIV-positive health care workers and patients. This policy asserts that through wide disclosure of HIV serostatus, both by health care workers and patients, health care delivery may be improved, legal claims may be reduced, and the spread of HIV may be contained, all while eliminating the social stigma associated with being HIV-positive.

Article I. Mandatory Testing of Health Care Workers.

(a) Effective immediately, all health care workers employed by Horizons HMO shall be required to be tested for HIV.

(b) The results of all HIV tests conducted on Horizons employees shall be kept in the Medical Records Office and shall be open to inspection by any and all Horizons health care workers and enrollees.

(c) All employees shall be tested for HIV every three months.

(d) Any Horizons health care worker who refuses HIV testing shall be granted severance and referred elsewhere for employment.

Article II. Statement of Non-Discrimination Based On HIV Serostatus.

(a) The position of employment of health care workers undergoing HIV testing shall not be altered based on the results of an HIV test.

(i) This section applies to personnel conducting exposure-prone invasive procedures, as well as to all other health care workers employed by Horizons.

(ii) Should an employee responsible for conducting exposure-prone invasive procedures test positive for HIV, his or her employment shall not be altered and he or she shall be permitted to continue performing exposure-prone invasive procedures.

(iii) Should an employee who tests positive for HIV wish to begin conducting exposure-prone invasive procedures which he or she has not previously performed, that individual's HIV status shall not be considered in evaluating his or her qualifications to be trained to conduct such procedures.

(b) Should an employee test negative for HIV, the negative test results shall not be used to his or her advantage or disadvantage in any case.

(i) HIV-negative employees shall in no way be favored over HIV-positive employees.

Article III. Mandatory Testing of Health Care Recipients.

(a) All persons receiving health services as enrollees of Horizons HMO shall be required to be tested for HIV, except as exempted by Article IX of this text.

(b) The results of all HIV tests conducted on Horizons patients shall be kept in the Medical Records Office and shall be open to inspection by all Horizons health care workers.

(c) The results of HIV test results of Horizons enrollees shall not be open to inspection by other Horizons enrollees nor to inspection by any third parties, including but not limited to insurance providers or employers.

(d) All Horizons enrollees shall be tested for HIV every three months or as close thereto as is practicable.

(e) All Horizons enrollees undergoing exposure-prone invasive procedures must have a current HIV serostatus test result on file with the Horizons Medical Records Office.

Article IV. Statement of Non-Discrimination Against Patients Based on HIV Serostatus.

(a) No patient shall be discriminated against by any health care worker based on the patient's HIV serostatus.

(b) A patient's HIV serostatus shall not be grounds for a health care worker to refuse to provide care to that patient.

(i) This provision applies both in the case of an HIV-positive patient receiving care from an HIV-negative health care worker and in the case of an HIV-negative patient receiving care from an HIV-positive health care worker.

Article V. Use of Universal Precautions.

(a) Universal precautions shall be followed at all times regardless of the HIV serostatus of the patient, health care worker(s), or blood product(s) involved.

(b) Health care workers not following universal precautions shall be subject to sanctions in accord with Horizons policy.

Article VI. Purpose of Recording HIV Serostatus.

(a) Records of HIV serostatus shall be maintained so that all parties may be fully informed.

(b) HIV serostatus information shall be referred to in case of breach of universal precautions so that the person affected may know if a risk of potential infection has occurred.

(c) HIV serostatus shall be maintained as common knowledge to combat the secrecy which has surrounded that information in past years and which has given rise to unfounded fears of infection and unjustified discrimination.

Article VII. Duty of Confidentiality.

(a) Horizon records indicating the serostatus of enrollees and health care workers shall be treated as confidential and privileged information. Although the number of persons privileged to access that information is large, that does not relinquish those persons' responsibility to maintain a duty of confidentiality with regard to that information.

(b) Persons with access to the HIV serostatus records are prohibited from discussing the contents of those records with anyone not privileged to access the records.

(c) Enrollees are prohibited from disclosing the serostatus of Horizons health care workers to any other Horizons enrollees or third parties.

Article VIII. Enrollee Consent to Disclosure and Non-Discrimination.

(a) All enrollees of Horizons HMO must agree to and sign the following statement upon enrollment with Horizons:

I, _____, understand that, as an enrollee of the Horizons Health Maintenance Organization, I am required to undergo routine testing for HIV. I understand that the results of those tests indicating my HIV serostatus (i.e., whether I have HIV) shall be made available for inspection by all health care workers employed by Horizons. I understand that after I have been tested for HIV, the results of HIV tests conducted on all Horizons employed health care workers shall be made available to me for my review.

I hereby consent to receive treatment by health care workers who are assigned to my case based on my needs regardless of the HIV serostatus of those health care workers. I understand that this means that I may be treated by health care workers who are HIV-positive. I relinquish any right or privilege to refuse health care services based on the HIV serostatus (positive or negative) of the health care worker(s) assigned to me.

I understand that information on the serostatus of health care workers is provided for my own personal knowledge and that such information is not provided by other health maintenance organizations. I further understand that all information regarding the serostatus of Horizons employees is confidential. I will not disclose or discuss any information regarding the serostatus of any Horizons employee with any other Horizons enrollee or third party.

I agree to the above statement and all other provisions of the Horizons "Policy of Openness and Candor in HIV/AIDS Disclosure."

_____

Signature   Date

Article IX. Exception For Enrollees Refusing to Submit to HIV Testing.

(a) Compliance with this article exempts enrollees refusing to undergo HIV testing from Articles III and VII above.

(b) If an enrollee or prospective enrollee objects to being tested for HIV, he or she may enroll with Horizons HMO but he or she shall not be granted access to the files containing information on the HIV serostatus of Horizons health care workers.

(c) In the case that such an exempted patient becomes aware of the HIV serostatus of any Horizons health care worker, he or she may not use that knowledge to discriminate against that health care worker and he or she is bound to keep that information confidential.

Article X. Informed Consent and Disclosure.

(a) By enrolling in the Horizons HMO, all enrollees give informed consent to be cared for by HIV-positive health care workers.

   (i) Article X section (a) applies to all procedures including invasive surgical procedures.

(b) By enrolling with Horizons HMO, all enrollees consent to disclosure of their HIV serostatus to health care personnel employed by Horizons.

   (i) Disclosure of patient serostatus does not extend beyond health care workers employed by Horizons.

(c) By accepting employment with Horizons, all health care workers consent to disclosure of their HIV serostatus to all enrollees of the Horizons HMO and to all other health care workers employed by Horizons.

COMMUNITY COMMENTS

After drafting the Openness and Candor in HIV/AIDS Disclosure Policy, the public relations committee in California conducted a notice and comment period during which the policy was released and comments were received. The following is a summary of comments received during a thirty day period. The comments are listed following the name of the individual or organization submitting them. Please take account of the comments in evaluating the policy.

AIDS Action Committee. The AIDS Action Committee applauds the mandatory disclosure policy as a bold move towards eliminating the social stigma of being HIV-positive. The Committee, however, cautions Horizons regarding the confidentiality of the records, both of patients and the health care workers. Horizons members may not fully understand with whom they may discuss the HIV status of physicians. For example, a Horizons member who has submitted to the policy may not understand that he or she is not permitted to discuss the HIV status of a Horizons physician with another Horizons member who has not consented to HIV disclosure. The Committee also warns that adequate treatment and counseling must be provided to all persons testing positive for HIV and that HIV/AIDS education should be made available to all Horizons HMO enrollees and employees.

The United Coalition of HIV-Positive Health Care Workers. The Coalition objects to the disclosure policy as a breach of the fundamental rights of privacy and confidentiality. It is inevitable that the HIV status of health care workers will be disclosed to other health care providers. This will make it impossible for those HIV-positive health care workers to find work with any organization other than Horizons.

National Organization of Hospital Administrators. The Organization opposes implementation of the policy based on the fact that it is simply not a sound economic decision. The cost of testing all patients and health care workers will be astronomical. That allocation of resources is not warranted considering the minimal risk that exists for the spread of infection during medical procedures. The policy is also not sound as it requires the testing of all persons regardless of whether they perform or undergo exposure-prone invasive procedures. If a health care professional poses no risk of infection to patients then why should he or she be tested? In this case, the price of knowledge is greater than the cost of ignorance.

Commission of Health Care Managers. The Commission asserts that the policy will be ineffective. The main problem is that it allows HIV-positive surgeons to continue to conduct exposure-prone invasive procedures. If the goal is to reduce the spread of HIV, then HIV-positive surgeons should not be permitted to perform exposure-prone invasive procedures. Furthermore, the liability involved may be increased with this policy. If informed consent is found not to exist based on the patient agreement then the HMO may be liable for knowingly allowing HIV-positive health care workers to conduct exposure-prone procedures. Horizons may then be responsible for putting those patients at risk of potential infection. Alternatively, if a health care worker is required to perform an invasive procedure on an HIV-positive patient and that health care worker becomes infected as a result, then he may have a cause of action against the HMO. The fact that people may not always make the correct decision in matters concerning HIV/AIDS does not mean that their ability to make those decisions should be taken away from them. Education, and not compulsion, will eliminate discrimination.

Dr. Alice McCormick, M.D. (HIV-positive Orthopedic Surgeon). I applaud the policy. This acceptance of the existence of HIV-positive health care workers and physicians is greatly needed. This policy will allow HIV-positive health care workers to receive the medical care we need and deserve without forfeiting our careers and incomes. HIV-positive health care workers should not be discriminated against because of their HIV status because HIV status does not affect a physician's ability to do his or her job.

Dr. Reed, M.D. (HIV-negative Emergency Department Physician). I agree that all patients and physicians should be tested, but I disagree with requiring anyone to do anything with which they are not comfortable. If a physician does not want to treat someone who is HIV-positive then he should not be forced to put his life on the line to save that person. Physicians who are HIV-positive should acknowledge that they can no longer safely do their jobs and resign from the practice of medicine. HIV is a medical condition and not a social status. If a physician is HIV-positive, he has an ethical obligation to recognize the risk of infection that his medical condition poses to his patients and recognize that his medical condition compromises his ability to safely care for his patients. Though the risk of infecting a patient is small, a risk does exist and it is not the place of the physician to decide whether the patient should assume that risk. At the very least, HIV-positive physicians should inform their patients of their HIV-positive serostatus so that each patient can make a truly informed decision which considers all risks presented by the procedure and the physician. The best idea would be for HIV-positive doctors to treat only HIV-positive patients--that way no one can get hurt.

Dr. Danielle Ross, Ph.D. (Bioethicist). This policy may appear to mock the principle of autonomy that underlies bioethics but in reality the policy embraces autonomy. The policy allows individuals to adopt and adapt to a system that chooses to tear down the walls of secrecy and myth that society has erected around HIV-positive persons. If people don't like the policy then they can go elsewhere for care. The policy gives people knowledge, and knowledge can never be bad.

Freddie Law, Esq. I wholeheartedly embrace this policy. The first time a patient tells someone that one of the Horizons physicians has AIDS, and sooner or later that will happen, I'll sue and I'll win. After that, when someone gets HIV from one of the health care workers, I'll sue and I'll win. Most definitely adopt the policy--it will keep plaintiff's attorneys like me in business.

Dr. Elroy Smith, M.D. (Chief of Staff, General Hospital). The policy looks good because it requires people to do what they should do without being required--that is, get tested. The problem is that because of people like Mr. Law, the policy will never work. A patient may come to Horizons today and think that the policy is good because the possibility of actually being treated, let alone being operated on, by an HIV-positive health care worker seems remote. When the time does come for the patient to undergo an invasive procedure, however, the patient will find every reason why the HIV-positive health care worker should not perform the procedure. In the end, we cannot mandate social justice and nondiscrimination by trumping the rights of the individuals. People must have the autonomy to make their own decisions even if those decisions are often ignorant.

Ms. Jaimie Stone. As a current enrollee of Horizons and a married mother of three, I agree that all physicians should be required to inform their patients if they are HIV-positive prior to performing any kind of invasive procedure that might create a risk of exposure no matter how small the risk. As a married woman, however, I see no reason why I should be tested for HIV. It is obvious that I don't have AIDS and I will never agree to be tested.

Mr. John Simpson. As an HIV-positive member of Horizons, I would vote for this policy. I got HIV from a blood transfusion, and I think that people need to be made aware of the risks associated with receiving medical treatment. People should know whether their doctor is HIV-positive so that they can make truly informed decisions. This policy will promote that end.

DISCUSSION QUESTIONS

1. Does the Openness and Candor Policy promote or violate the principle of autonomy? Does the policy enhance or detract from the concept of informed consent?

2. What effect does the policy have on the ethical obligations of beneficence and nonmaleficence?

3. How is the bioethical principle of justice affected by the Openness and Candor Policy?

4. If a Horizons enrollee were to consent to the policy, test negative for HIV, and later require an invasive procedure to be performed by an HIV-positive surgeon, should Horizons be able to require that the enrollee receive care from the HIV-positive surgeon even if the patient objects? What, if anything, would be Horizons' recourse against the enrollee for refusing treatment by the HIV-positive surgeon? Could Horizons ethically refuse to provide care to that enrollee?

5. Does the policy violate the autonomy of physicians to choose their patients? Should a physician be allowed to refuse to care for HIV-positive persons because of

the patient's HIV serostatus?

6. Has HIV/AIDS been treated as a disease or a social status? How should it be treated? How, if at all, have HIV-positive persons been discriminated against? Has such discrimination been justified? Would implementation of the Openness and Candor Policy have an effect on the way in which HIV/AIDS is viewed by society? Would the effect of the policy be positive or negative from a public policy perspective?

7. Does the knowledge gained from the policy justify the economic cost of universal testing? What factors should be considered in determining the true economic cost of the policy? Consider the following: the cost of testing on regular intervals; the money saved from early intervention and treatment of persons who test positive; the costs incurred from infections that occur from allowing known HIV-positive health care workers to continue performing invasive procedures; the money saved from infections which are prevented because individuals discover that they are HIV-positive; the cost of lawsuits stemming from implementation of the policy; and other costs incurred and saved.

8. Currently, under California statutory law, HIV test results are given heightened confidentiality protections above and beyond the protections that are given to other medical information. A copy of the California statute is included at Appendix A. How does the Openness and Candor in HIV/AIDS Disclosure Policy compare and contrast with the current California law?

9. Should HIV-positive health care workers be required to inform patients of their status before conducting invasive procedures? Should HIV-positive patients be required to inform their physicians of their HIV serostatus before undergoing invasive procedures?

10. If implemented, would the policy achieve its stated purpose of eliminating the social stigma and phobia that surround HIV/AIDS in the context of health services?

11. Does the policy promote HIV/AIDS education? If so, how? If not, why not?

12. Will implementation of the policy help to eliminate discrimination against HIV-positive persons?

13. Will legal claims likely be reduced or increased due to implementation of the policy?

14. Will the spread of HIV likely be reduced or increased due to implementation of the policy?

15. What would be the likely consequences of attempting to implement the policy on a society-wide basis as opposed to only applying it to enrollees of Horizons HMO?

SUGGESTED RESEARCH

Statutory Law.

Appendix A: California Health & Safety Code Sections 120975-121020.

Texts.

Munson, Ronald. *Intervention and Reflection: Basic Issues in Medical Ethics.* 4th
   ed. Belmont, CA: Wadsworth, 1992, 205-57.
Pence, Gregory E. Classic *Cases in Medical Ethics.* 2nd ed. New York City, NY:
   McGraw-Hill, 1995, 413-42.
Veatch, Robert M. *Medical Ethics.* 2nd ed. Sudbury, MA: Jones and Bartlett, 1997,
   75-101.

CHAPTER 4

MINORS AND HEALTH CARE

The Limits of Consent and Confidentiality

INSTRUCTIONS AND OBJECTIVES

Chapter 4 uses a narrative of recent occurrences at the hypothetical Wayward Clinic to focus on the rights of minors to consent to and receive health care. Participants explore issues surrounding the confidentiality protections that apply to minors and the related conflicts that arise in the context of minors' rights versus their parents' rights. In addition, some scenarios offer the opportunity to balance confidentiality protections against the duty to warn where both the patient and the endangered third party are minors.

THE CASE STUDY

The Wayward Clinic is located in the heart of the city of Metropolis in the state of Columbia. Wayward Clinic provides primary health care and general counseling services to a large number of street kids who are generally runaways between the ages of ten and 17. Wayward Clinic also provides free HIV testing and sponsors a drug and alcohol abuse counseling program.

Over the past several months, several teenagers have been frequenting the clinic on a regular basis. It appears that they are coming to the clinic mostly because they have nowhere else to go and no one else with whom to talk. Some of the staff of the clinic have befriended the teenagers.

Billy is 15 years old and was kicked out of his house about six months ago. He has been living on the streets and "crashing at friends' houses." Billy has confided in Rick, a licensed counselor at the clinic, that he has been sexually active with numerous partners and that he does not use condoms. Billy likes to brag about his sexual exploits and has told Rick many stories about his girlfriend, Rhonda. Billy says he is tired of Rhonda, though, and that he is trying to get together with Lisa, a high school girl who volunteers time working at the clinic. Rick has noticed "track marks" on Billy's arms but Billy denies that he uses intravenous drugs. Rick convinces Billy to be tested for HIV, and the test comes back positive.

Another teen who frequents the clinic with Billy is his friend Jason. Jason initially came to the clinic for emergency medical treatment when he was beaten up after a drug deal went bad. Jason is known to have engaged in many high-risk behaviors, including intravenous drug use, but he refuses to be tested for HIV. Jason has seen the clinic physician, Dr. Schwartz, on a regular basis over the past few months, and he has been treated for chlamydia. Often, when Jason visits the clinic, he is visibly under the influence of drugs or alcohol. Jason is 13 years old. After several counseling sessions, Rick has convinced Jason to enroll in a drug and alcohol abuse counseling program sponsored by the Wayward Clinic. The program is federally funded and is offered to teenagers who have addiction problems.

Another teen who has been coming into the clinic is Connie. Dr. Schwartz has known that Connie is HIV-positive for over a year. Connie is sexually active and frequently engages in prostitution. Connie visits the Wayward clinic for free condoms. Connie says that she only uses condoms so she won't get pregnant but that if someone gets AIDS from her it is his own fault for having sex with her. Connie frequently and openly talks about being HIV-positive. Dr. Schwartz believes that both Jason and Billy know that Connie is HIV-positive. Connie is 11 years old.

One other teen, Vera, has been visiting the clinic to obtain prenatal care. Vera is 15 years old and four months pregnant.

DISCUSSION QUESTIONS

1. Billy, Jason, and Connie are all minors. To what, if any, medical treatment can any of the them consent under the statute included at Appendix D?

2. Dr. Schwartz wants to know whether he can inform Billy's and Connie's parents that they are HIV-positive. Dr. Schwartz hopes that by doing so, Billy and Connie may get proper medical attention and also stop engaging in behaviors that put others at risk. Does Dr. Schwartz owe a duty of confidentiality to Billy and Connie? If so, is that duty violated by Dr. Schwartz informing each of their parents of their HIV statuses? Consider application of the California statutes included at Appendices A and D.

3. Can Dr. Schwartz legally justify notifying Billy's and Connie's parents of Billy's and Connie's HIV statuses based on the theory that the parents can consent to medical treatment for Billy and Connie? Consider the effect of applying the statute included at Appendix D.

4. Can Rick contact Jason's parents to inform them that Jason has been using illegal drugs. Can Rick contact Jason's parents to inform them that Jason is participating in the drug and alcohol addiction program? Consider application of the federal regulations included at Appendix E. Assume that Rick is a licensed psychotherapist. Does your analysis change if Rick learns that Jason's father is an alcoholic and that Jason's relationship with his mother is estranged?

5. Assume that seven months pass and that Jason has not visited the clinic. Can

Rick now approach Jason's parents without breaching his obligation of confidentiality? What if two years pass? At what point in time, if any, will Rick's duty of confidentiality to Jason expire?

6. One night, Jason comes into the clinic extremely high. Jason asks Dr. Schwartz to test him for HIV. Dr. Schwartz hesitates because of Jason's stupor but he then agrees. Dr. Schwartz prepares to draw Jason's blood but before he can do so Jason loses consciousness. Does Dr. Schwartz have Jason's informed consent to test him for HIV? Should Dr. Schwartz continue with the test?

7. One evening, Billy comes into the clinic in need of immediate medical attention. His nose is broken and profusely bleeding and his left arm is broken. Billy tells Dr. Schwartz that he tried to go home but that when he got there his father lost his temper and beat him. If the statute included at Appendix F is applicable, does Dr. Schwartz have an obligation to report the beating as child abuse? Does such a report breach Dr. Schwartz's duty of confidentiality to Billy?

8. Does the fact that Connie is open with her friends about being HIV-positive change the duty that the clinic staff owes to Connie? Should a different obligation be imposed upon Dr. Schwartz, who found out that Connie is HIV-positive by giving her an HIV test, than is imposed upon the clinic receptionist, who overheard Connie telling her friends that she is HIV-positive?

9. Connie is killed in a car accident. Connie's father had heard that his daughter frequently visited the clinic. Connie's father comes to the clinic in an attempt to discover what was happening in his daughter's life before she was killed. Can Dr. Schwartz inform Connie's father that Connie was HIV-positive? Can Dr. Schwartz inform Connie's father that she was working as a prostitute? Can Dr. Schwartz release Connie's medical record to her father? What is the effect of the statute included at Appendix A?

10. Billy's girlfriend, Rhonda, comes by the clinic one day looking for Billy. She tells Rick that she is really in love with Billy. Should Rick tell Rhonda that Billy is HIV-positive? That he has chlamydia? Should disclosure of the fact that Billy is HIV-positive be treated differently than disclosure of the fact that he has chlamydia? If so, why? What is the effect of the California statute included at Appendix A?

11. A few days after Rhonda's visit to the clinic, Billy breaks up with her and asks Lisa (the high school girl who volunteers at the clinic) out on a date. Lisa is clean-cut and at first she hesitates but then she decides that she is attracted to Billy's reckless lifestyle. Should Rick intervene in any way?

12. Can Rick reveal that Billy is HIV-positive if Lisa confides in Rick that she plans on having sex with Billy? Consider application of the California statute included at Appendix A.

13. Lisa does not ordinarily have access to patient records but Rick does. Rick decides to leave Billy's chart out where Lisa can easily review it. Lisa does look at the chart and she discovers that Billy is HIV-positive. Has Rick violated any legal or ethical duty owed to Billy? If so, what duty has he violated?

14. Dr. Schwartz decided to draw blood from Jason on the night when Jason passed out at the clinic. The HIV test results come back positive. What is the proper ethical and legal course of action for Dr. Schwartz to take? What if Billy does not remember consenting to or being tested?

15. One day when Billy and Lisa are talking at the clinic, Billy tells Lisa that he has been making money by donating blood. Each time he donates blood he is paid ten dollars. Rick overhears Billy telling this to Lisa. Does Rick have a duty to inform the blood bank that Billy is HIV-positive? Does Lisa? Consider application of the statute included at Appendix A.

16. Can Vera legally consent to prenatal care? Assume that several months pass and Vera gives birth to a daughter. One day, Vera and her daughter visit the clinic. Vera asks Dr. Schwartz to treat her daughter for a runny nose. Vera also asks Dr. Schwartz to prescribe birth control pills to her and to examine a large mole on her back. Under the statute included at Appendix D, can Vera legally consent to:

    a. Treatment of her daughter?

    b. A prescription for birth control pills?

    c. Examination and/or removal of the mole on her back?

SUGGESTED RESEARCH

Statutes

Appendix A: California Health and Safety Code Sections 120975 *et seq.*
Appendix D: California Family Code Sections 6500 *et seq.*
Appendix E: Title 42, Code of Federal Regulations, Part 2
Appendix F: California Penal Code Sections 11164 *et seq.*

Case Law

Appendix C: *Tarasoff v. Regents of the University of California* 551 P.2d 334 (1976).

Texts

Beauchamp, Tom L. and Childress, James F. *Principles of Biomedical Ethics.* 4th ed. New York, N.Y.: Oxford University Press, 1994, 418-29.

ROLE ASSIGNMENTS FOR 10 PARTICIPANTS

1. Rick (clinic counselor)
2. Dr. Schwartz (clinic physician)

3. Billy
4. Jason
5. Vera
6. Connie's mother or father
7. Representative of Connie's interests
8. Rhonda (Billy's girlfriend)
9. Lisa (clinic volunteer)
10. Clinic Director

Role Assignment Number 1

Assume the role of Rick, the clinic counselor. Your primary concern is to ensure that all of the patients at the clinic receive the best medical attention possible. Based on the statutes and case law included in the Appendices, formulate arguments in support of each of the following premises:

1. That, whenever possible, parents of minors should be informed and involved in treatment decisions regarding their minor children.

2. That parents should be entitled to have access to the health records of their minor children.

3. That health professionals should intervene to prevent harm to innocent third parties.

Role Assignment Number 2

Assume the role of Dr. Schwartz, the clinic physician. Based on the statutes and case law included in the Appendices, formulate arguments that will justify each of your actions in the case study. Additionally, formulate arguments in support of each of the following acts:

1. Informing Billy's and Connie's parents that they are each HIV-positive.

2. Informing Rhonda and Lisa that Billy is HIV-positive.

3. Requiring Vera's mother to consent to treatment of Vera for which Vera is not specifically authorized to consent to on her own behalf.

Role Assignment Number 3

Assume the role of Billy. Based on the statutes and case law included in the Appendices, formulate arguments that will protect your rights to privacy and confidentiality and your right to consent to medical treatment without parental intervention. Specifically, formulate arguments in support of each of the following:

1. Preventing Dr. Schwartz from notifying your parents that you are HIV-positive.

2. Preventing Dr. Schwartz and Rick from notifying Lisa and Rhonda that you are HIV-positive.

3. A determination that you are a mature minor under the statute included at Appendix D and, therefore, that you are entitled to consent to medical treatment on your own behalf.

Role Assignment Number 4

Assume the role of Jason. Based on the statutes and case law included in the Appendices, formulate arguments in support of the following:

1. That Dr. Schwartz never obtained your informed consent and, therefore, that he violated your autonomy rights and committed a battery when he tested you for HIV.

2. That Rick is prohibited by the Federal statute included at Appendix E from informing your parents that you use drugs and from making any disclosures of information that you tell him while participating in counseling.

3. That, under the applicable statutes, you should be entitled to consent to medical treatment and counseling services without the intervention of your parents.

Role Assignment Number 5

Assume the role of Vera. Argue that, based on the statutes included in the Appendices, you are legally authorized to consent to prenatal care for yourself and to medical treatment on behalf of your daughter. Additionally, formulate arguments to support the fact that after the birth of your daughter you should be legally entitled to consent to medical care for yourself, even if the statute does not specifically authorize you to consent. Argue that it makes no sense that you should be legally authorized to consent to treatment for your daughter but not be permitted to consent to treatment for yourself.

Role Assignment Number 6

Assume the role of Connie's mother or father. Based on the case law and statutes included in the Appendices, formulate arguments in favor of Dr. Schwartz and Rick disclosing to you information about Connie's lifestyle before she died and providing you with a copy of Connie's medical record. Consider the different duties that apply to Dr. Schwartz and Rick and the information that each of them can divulge to you without breaching their duties.

Role Assignment Number 7

Assume the role of a representative of Connie's interests. Formulate arguments to protect Connie's interests in privacy and confidentiality. In so doing, consider the nature and duration of the doctor-patient relationship. Also formulate arguments as to why a duty of confidentiality should apply to both Dr. Schwartz and Rick.

Role Assignment Number 8

Assume the role of Rhonda (Billy's girlfriend). Formulate arguments in support of Dr. Schwartz and Rick disclosing to you the fact that Billy is HIV-positive and the fact that he has chlamydia. Assume that both Dr. Schwartz and Rick know that you and Billy have been sexually active. Based on the case law and statutes included in the Appendices, argue that Dr. Schwartz and Rick each owe a duty to you as a third party in imminent danger of harm that outweighs their duties of confidentiality to Billy.

Role Assignment Number 9

Assume the role of Lisa (the clinic volunteer). Based on the case law and statutes included in the Appendices, formulate arguments to justify Rick's decision to leave Billy's chart out for you to review and to warn you of Billy's HIV-positive status. Argue that the duty owed to a third party in imminent danger of HIV infection outweighs the duty of confidentiality which health care professionals owe to patients.

Role Assignment Number 10

Assume the role of the Director of the Wayward Clinic. You are most concerned with minimizing liability. Argue that confidentiality and privacy must be preserved no matter what the circumstances. Argue that laws requiring doctors to divulge patient confidences to protect third parties place doctors in a conflict of interests between the good of their patients, which requires honoring confidences, and the good of third parties, which requires breaching those confidences. Maintain the position that because doctors have a relationship with their patients, it is that duty which must be honored and not the duty which is owed to third parties.

CHAPTER 5

THE RIGHTS TO REFUSE AND DEMAND
MEDICAL TREATMENT

The Bounds of Autonomy and Futility

INSTRUCTIONS AND OBJECTIVES

The five different scenarios presented in this chapter each raise issues on the periphery of decisions about death. Some individuals whose imminent death may be inevitable want to devote resources to preventing it; others whose death can be prevented wish to refuse the use of interventions that will delay it. Definitions of life and death are implicated, as are issues of quality of life, and using resources with little prospect of gain. Participants are asked to analyze the scenarios in the context of the ethical principles of autonomy, beneficence, nonmaleficence, and justice. At the same time, participants will need to consider the hypothetical cases in the context of cost-benefit analysis and in the context of the competing interests that may be present. The scenarios raise difficult emotional issues, but require decisionmakers to consider all of the options.

THE CASE STUDY

Five cases will be presented at today's meeting. Each of the five cases concerns an individual who is currently a patient at St. Jude's Hospital in Big Valley, California. Parties present at today's meeting include the patients and their representatives, family members of the patients, the patients' physicians, and members of the Hospital administration and ethics advisory committee. Also present are five individuals who have authority to render a treatment decision in each of the five cases. Descriptions of the five cases follow with discussion questions.

The Victim Case

Vinnie and Velma Victim were on their honeymoon skiing at Wonderland. Vinnie, feeling invincible, ignored the double black diamond warning sign and sped off the side of Hemlock Ridge Run. Upon hitting the expert run, Vinnie lost control of his skis and tumbled 200 feet down the side of the mountain. Vinnie hit the bottom of the slope with tremendous force. Velma called the ski patrol, and two paramedics soon arrived at Vinnie's body. The paramedics detected no pulse and immediately transported Vinnie to St. Jude's Hospital via helicopter. In the emergency department at St. Jude's, cardiopulmonary resuscitation was administered and Vinnie's heart was restarted. Vinnie remains at St. Jude's in a permanent vegetative state.

Six months have passed since Vinnie's accident. Vinnie remains in the intensive care unit of St. Jude's, where he has been intubated and placed on a respirator. Dr. Gregory, a neurosurgeon, has determined that during his fall, Vinnie struck his forehead on a boulder, cracking his skull open and dislodging a large portion of his forebrain. Because Vinnie's forebrain is absent from his cranium, the damage is irreversible. Dr. Gregory has determined that Vinnie has no chance of regaining consciousness. It has not been determined whether Vinnie could breath on his own if the respirator is removed.

Two days ago, a tumor was discovered in Vinnie's bladder. It has not been determined whether the tumor is malignant, but it is evident that the tumor is putting pressure on Vinnie's urinary tract. If not removed, the tumor may completely block Vinnie's urinary tract resulting in death.

The Mosby Case

Mrs. Mosby is 72 years old. She lives with her son and his family on their ranch in Willow's End, California. Last week, Mrs. Mosby was diagnosed as having advanced cancer in her one kidney (the other was removed twenty years ago after a severe infection). It has been determined that the cancer has spread beyond the kidney but it is not certain to what extent. Doctors have informed Mrs. Mosby that her condition is terminal. Mrs. Mosby and her son Jack appear before the committee today to request that a kidney be transplanted from Jack into Mrs. Mosby. It is known that Jack is a suitable donor because tests were conducted many years ago when it was thought that Mrs. Mosby would need a transplant. Mrs. Mosby is positively determined that she will live to be at least 100 years old. She accepts the fact that after she receives the transplant she will have to undergo chemotherapy to combat the cancer. Mrs. Mosby's physicians have determined that Mrs. Mosby may have a minimally longer life if the transplant is performed but that the cancer has most likely spread to a point that she will not live more than a year even with a successful transplant.

Mrs. Mosby is independently wealthy and pays cash for all of her medical care. She has made it clear that she will leave a generous gift to St. Jude's from her estate if the hospital accedes to her wishes and performs the transplant.

The Brewer Case

Bobby Brewer has been ill with various ailments his entire life. His latest battle has been the worst. Bobby has been receiving radiation therapy for Hodgkin's disease (a malignant disorder of lymphoid tissue) for over a year. Bobby had his 18th birthday last week. The day after his birthday, physicians took biopsies of Bobby's lymph tissue and discovered that the malignancy had spread more extensively than originally thought. Because of the advanced stage of the cancer, physicians have recommended that more aggressive chemotherapy and anti-cancer treatments be immediately started. Bobby has been informed of the degree to which the cancer has spread, as well as of his chances of survival both with and without the more aggressive treatments. Bobby has been told that chances of curing the disease are much greater if he consents to chemotherapy and anticancer drugs. In fact, about 70 percent of patients in Bobby's condition who undergo such treatments survive for at least five years. It is estimated that Bobby would only need to undergo the treatments for several months. Doctors have informed Bobby that without the more aggressive treatments he will have a life expectancy of only six to eight months. Despite the relatively good odds that Bobby could regain a normal healthy life, he refuses to consent to the chemotherapy and anticancer drugs.

The side effects of the more intense treatments include: nausea, vomiting, and diarrhea severe enough to require hospitalization; hair loss; anemia; increased susceptibility to infection; and abnormal bleeding.

The Braun Case

Just over two years ago, Pam Braun was brought to St. Jude's emergency department after being hit by a drunk driver. Paddles were used to restart Pam's heart and it was considered a miracle that she was "brought back to life." During the accident, however, Pam's fifth vertebrae was severely damaged, and Pam is now a quadriplegic. Though Pam's mental capacity is intact, she wishes that it were not. Pam considers her daily life to be miserable as she cannot feed herself or engage in any of the sports or outdoor activities that she used to find rewarding. Pam will never be able to return to her career as a white water rafting guide. Pam says that her life has been reduced to watching television and staring at the walls. Pam feels that her life is simply not worth living.

Currently, Pam is a patient at St. Jude's because two weeks ago she began to starve herself in order to "end her meaningless suffering." Pam's brother brought her to the hospital against her expressed wishes and the attending physician placed Pam on intravenous nutrition and hydration without asking for Pam's consent. Pam comes before the committee today to demand that she be allowed to use a highly controversial device developed by a physician in the Netherlands. The device is an oral syringe specially designed to be filled with a lethal dose of a pancuronium bromide solution and inserted into an individual's mouth. The individual may then maneuver the syringe with his or her tongue to inject the solution and cause death.

Regardless of the hospital's decision regarding use of the oral syringe, Pam demands that all medical devices currently attached to her body, specifically the intravenous feeding tube, be removed. Pam also demands that the regular injections of antibiotics that she has been receiving be stopped.

The Miller Case

Judy Miller is a 32 year old follower of the Jehovah's Witness faith. Judy is the mother of three children between the ages of two and seven years of age and is currently pregnant with her fourth child. Due to extensive complications, Dr. Roth, Judy's obstetrician, has recommended that a cesarean section procedure be performed. Dr. Roth has also notified Judy that because of her specific condition, there is a 75 percent chance that she will require a blood transfusion as a result of the cesarean. Judy has agreed to undergo the cesarean section but she refuses to consent to a blood transfusion. Judy has further stated that she would not find it justifiable for a transfusion to be performed based on a physician deeming it necessary as an emergency. Judy also objects to a transfusion being performed pursuant to a court order.

Judy's refusal to consent to the transfusion stems from the Jehovah's Witness belief that consumption of blood products prevents eternal life. Judy will not consent to the cesarean procedure unless the hospital guarantees that a transfusion will not be performed under any circumstances. Judy has stated that if the hospital will not accede to her wishes, she will give birth at her home with only the assistance of a midwife. Dr. Roth has concluded that if natural childbirth is attempted, the lives of both Judy and her yet to be born child will be endangered. Judy and her husband have been separated for over a month, and the whereabouts of the husband are not known.

DISCUSSION QUESTIONS

The Victim Case

1. Is Vinnie alive? Consider the cardiopulmonary and higher brain definitions of death. What would be the result of applying each of those definitions to Vinnie? Which is more appropriate to apply?

2. Should the respirator be removed? If the respirator is removed and respiratory distress results, should CPR be administered?

3. Should nutrition and hydration be terminated?

4. Should surgery be performed to remove the tumor? Would performing surgery be futile given Vinnie's condition?

5. If it is discovered that Vinnie does have cancer, would chemotherapy and anticancer drugs be futile treatment? Consider that the anticancer treatments could extend Vinnie's quantity of life by combating the cancer but that they could not

improve his quality of life.

6. How does each of the following courses of treatment differ from the others:

a. Doing nothing and allowing Vinnie to die of complications caused by the bladder tumor;

b. Disconnecting the respirator and allowing Vinnie to die from respiratory distress;

c. Disconnecting nutrition and hydration and allowing Vinnie to starve to death; and

d. Removing the tumor and maintaining support, but allowing Vinnie to die of cancer.

7. If it is determined that measures should not be taken to extend Vinnie's life, is there an ethical obligation to ensure that Vinnie's death is not prolonged? If so, how should that be achieved?

The Mosby Case

1. Is performance of the kidney transplant futile? Would it be futile if it extended Mrs. Mosby's life by two years? By one year? By six months? By three months?

2. Should the transplant be performed?

3. Does Mrs. Mosby have a right to demand that the transplant be performed even if her doctors deem it to be futile? Can the hospital ethically perform the transplant if it is deemed to be medically futile?

4. Must a minimum benefit to Mrs. Mosby be guaranteed in order for the hospital to ethically and/or medically justify removal of the kidney from Jack? If so, how should such a threshold be determined?

5. Even if the transplant is medically futile and/or ethically suspect, can the promise of a monetary gift from Mrs. Mosby justify its performance?

6. Does refusing to perform the transplant deny Mrs. Mosby her autonomy right? Does refusal to perform the transplant violate the principle of beneficence or the principle of nonmaleficence?

7. Can Jack be said to have freely given informed consent to donate his kidney? Is it the role of the hospital to take account of such considerations?

8. If it is agreed that the transplant will be performed, and it is later discovered that Jack is not a suitable donor, should Mrs. Mosby be placed on an organ recipient waiting list to receive a donor kidney? If so, should the fact that Mrs. Mosby pays cash be considered in determining her priority over others?

9. If Mrs. Mosby is denied Jack's kidney and she is denied a place on an organ recipient waiting list, should Mrs. Mosby be allowed to pay an unrelated third party to donate his or her kidney? What public policy concerns would be implicated by allowing that course of action?

The Brewer Case

1. Is the aggressive anticancer treatment futile? Would the treatment be futile if

Bobby had only a 50 percent chance of living five years? A 20 percent chance? A ten percent chance? A two percent chance?

2. Can the hospital ethically allow a patient, who can almost certainly be cured, to refuse to consent to treatment?

3. Does justification exist for the hospital to deliver treatment to Bobby without obtaining his consent? Should a guardian be appointed to make health care decisions for Bobby even though he is a legal adult?

4. If Bobby is not given treatment and dies, can his death be said to be the result of the failure to treat?

5. Can Bobby's refusal of medical treatment be distinguished from Pam's refusal in the Braun case? If so, how?

6. To what extent should a patient's motive for refusing care be considered in honoring his or her refusal? For example, Pam is refusing care because she wants to die (Braun Case), Judy is refusing care because of her religious convictions (Miller Case), and Bobby is refusing care because he wants to live a "normal" life for a few months. Should those different motivations be considered in a subjective evaluation as to whether or not to honor each patient's wishes or should an objective standard be utilized that treats all patients the same without regard to personal motivation?

The Braun Case

1. Does the hospital violate any ethical obligation that it owes to Pam by refusing to allow her to use the oral syringe? Does the hospital violate any ethical principle by supplying Pam with the syringe (possibly nonmaleficence)?

2. How, if at all, does each of the following acts by the hospital differ from the others:

a. Stopping the antibiotic injections and allowing Pam to die from a kidney infection;

b. Disconnecting Pam from the intravenous nutrition and hydration and allowing her to starve to death;

c. Giving Pam an oral syringe and pancuronium bromide separately and not placing the syringe in her mouth;

d. Giving Pam an oral syringe filled with pancuronium bromide and inserting it into her mouth; and

e. Inserting a needle into Pam's arm and administering a lethal dose of medication.

3. Can death be definitively determined to be a harm to the patient? Can death ever be justified as a means of stopping pain? What if drugs are available to treat the pain?

4. Can a patient rationally choose to die, or does an individual's desire to die necessarily indicate that he or she is not of sound mind? What facts, if any, affect your response to that question? Consider factors such as the patient's age, prognosis, and diagnosis.

The Miller Case

1. To whom does the hospital owe a duty? To Judy? To her unborn child? To Judy's children? To Judy's husband? What duty, if any, is owed to each? How should each of those duties be balanced against the others?

2. Should the effect on Judy's children of her refusal to consent to the transfusion be considered by the hospital in determining whether to honor Judy's wishes?

3. If the hospital agrees not to give Judy a transfusion and, during the course of the cesarean a transfusion is needed, what would be the ethical course of action? Should the hospital abide by the agreement even if it means that Judy will die? Should a transfusion be performed without Judy's consent? If failure to give the transfusion would endanger the life of Judy's unborn child, should the course of action be altered?

4. One doctor has suggested that the hospital proceed with treating Judy and, if necessary, give Judy a transfusion without informing her. Would that course of action be acceptable? Would that course of action result in harm to Judy? If so, what would the harm be?

SUGGESTED RESEARCH

Case Law

Appendix G: *Cruzan v. Director, Missouri Department of Health*, 110 S.Ct. 2841 (1990).
Appendix H: *Bouvia v. Superior Court*, 179 Cal.App. 3d 1127, 225 Cal.Rptr. 297 (Cal. Ct. App. 1986).
Appendix P: Vacco v. Quill, United States Supreme Court (June 26, 1997)

Texts

Annas, George J. *Standard of Care: The Law of American Bioethics.* New York City, N.Y.: Oxford University Press, 1993, 85-115 & 240-45.
Beauchamp, Tom L. and Childress, James F. *Principles of Biomedical Ethics.* 4th ed. New York City, N.Y.: Oxford University Press, 1994, 120-81, 189-258 & 271-318.
Engelhardt, H. Tristam, Jr. *The Foundations of Bioethics.* 2nd ed. New York City, N.Y.: Oxford University Press, 1996, 239-50 & 288-57.
Furrow, Barry R., Johnson, Sandra H., Jost, Timothy S. and Schwartz, Robert L. *Health Law Cases, Materials and Problems.* 3rd ed. St. Paul, Minn., 1997, 1031-1201.
Munson, Ronald. *Intervention and Reflection: Basic Issues in Medical Ethics.* 5th ed. Belmont, CA: Wadsworth, 1992, 189-242.

Pence, Gregory E. *Classic Cases in Medical Ethics.* 2nd ed. New York City, NY: McGraw-Hill, 1995, 34-89.

Veatch, Robert M. *Medical Ethics.* 2d ed. Sudbury, MA: Jones and Bartlett, 1997, 363-94.

ROLE ASSIGNMENTS FOR 20 PARTICIPANTS

1. Velma Victim (Vinnie's wife)
2. Mr./Mrs. Victim (Vinnie's parent)
3. Dr. Gregory
4. Mrs. Mosby
5. Mrs. Mosby's physician
6. Bobby Brewer
7. Mr./Mrs. Brewer (Bobby's parent)
8. Bobby Brewer's Oncologist
9. Pam Braun
10. Eric Braun, Pam's Brother
11. Representative of The Managed Death Coalition
12. Member of St. Jude's Ethics Advisory Board
13. Judy Miller
14. St. Jude's Chief Financial Officer
15. St. Jude's Hospital Administrator
16. Hospital Administrator with Responsibility to Determine a Course of Action in the Victim Case
17. Hospital Administrator with Responsibility to Determine a Course of Action in the Mosby Case
18. Hospital Administrator with Responsibility to Determine a Course of Action in the Brewer Case
19. Hospital Administrator with Responsibility to Determine a Course of Action in the Braun Case
20. Hospital Administrator with Responsibility to Determine a Course of Action in the Miller Case

Role Assignment Number 1

Assume the role of Velma Victim, Vinnie's wife. Though you were deeply in love with Vinnie, you have accepted the fact that he is dead and gone forever. Your goal today is to have Vinnie declared legally dead. Argue that the hospital should simply recognize the higher brain death definition and declare Vinnie to be dead.

If your arguments are not accepted, argue for measures to be taken that will result in Vinnie's condition complying with the cardiopulmonary definition of death. Consider each of the following means of achieving that end:

1. Administering a lethal dose of morphine;

2. Removing the respirator;

3. Terminating nutrition and hydration; and

4. Refusing consent to remove the bladder tumor.

You should also mention that Vinnie once told you that he would never want to live as a vegetable. Argue that Vinnie's wishes should be honored.

You do not want to appear heartless, but Vinnie's continued existence in this vegetative state greatly affects your life. You want Vinnie to be declared legally dead so that you can sue the ski resort for damages, collect Vinnie's life insurance, and remarry. Society cannot really expect you to remain married to a dead man--can it?

Role Assignment Number 2

Assume the role of Mr./Mrs. Victim, Vinnie's parent. Argue against Velma's efforts to declare Vinnie dead. You are present at today's meeting to see that Vinnie gets the best care available and to ensure that no one is allowed to kill your son. You believe that so long as Vinnie's heart beats, he is alive and should not be killed just because he is unconscious. Consider each of the following points:

1. Vinnie's body is warm, his heart is beating, his eyes are open, and he even moves when subjected to painful stimuli.

2. Doctor's have said that Vinnie cannot think, but how do we really know that? Can we take the chance of "flipping the switch" that sustains Vinnie's thoughts?

3. No harm is done by just leaving Vinnie alone and letting him die when the time comes. If an error is to be made, it should be on the side of life.

As to the mass in Vinnie's bladder, by all means it should be surgically removed. It is a simple operation that will save Vinnie's life. Furthermore, if Vinnie has cancer, anticancer treatments should be administered. Such treatments should not be deemed futile because the treatments would accomplish their purpose of combating Vinnie's cancer. An extension of the length of Vinnie's life is an end worth pursuing even if his quality of life cannot be improved.

Role Assignment Number 3

Assume the role of Dr. Gregory, Vinnie's physician. In your opinion, Vinnie has permanently and irreversibly lost his capacity for all higher brain functions. Because Vinnie's brain is literally absent from his head there is no hope of repair or rehabilitation. Because Vinnie's condition cannot be improved, recommend that the respirator be removed. Vinnie's brain stem was only slightly damaged and you predict that Vinnie will continue to breath without the respirator. If that occurs, argue for discontinuation of nutrition and hydration. Argue that any treatment, including nutrition and hydration, is futile and unethical because it confers no benefit to Vinnie. As to the bladder tumor, it should be left alone. In sum, Vinnie cannot be said to be alive in any significant way because the signs of life that are evident in his body do not manifest personhood.

Role Assignment Number 4

Assume the role of Mrs. Mosby. You are independently wealthy and you are used to getting what you want. You have the resources to pay the expenses of the transplant and you know from previous tests that Jack is a perfect organ donor match. You refuse to acknowledge the argument that the surgery would be futile just because you have cancer. You are determined to live, and you have the money to pay for the best available treatment. You do not understand how anyone can tell you what you can and cannot do with your own money and your own body. Even the skeptical doctors acknowledge that by receiving the transplant you will most likely live longer than if you do not receive the transplant. Any extension of your life, no matter how slight, proves that the operation is not futile. Besides, no one is being hurt by the transplant and people will even benefit because of the gift that you will leave if your demands are met. The only action that is futile is to do nothing.

Role Assignment Number 5

Assume the role of Mrs. Mosby's physician. You have been treating Mrs. Mosby for nearly 40 years. You know Mrs. Mosby to be a very controlling individual who has achieved a great deal in her life. In your medical opinion, you do not think that the transplant will be of any benefit to Mrs. Mosby and, in fact, the trauma of the surgery may shorten her life. Not only would the operation be futile, in that it would provide no medical benefit to Mrs. Mosby, but the procedure would create a risk to Jack. Someday, Jack may be in a situation where he needs both of his kidneys. The kidney is clearly more valuable to Jack than it would be to Mrs. Mosby.

Furthermore, the only reason the surgery is even being considered is because Mrs. Mosby is bribing the hospital by paying cash and promising to leave a substantial endowment to the hospital. A transplant would not even be considered if Mrs. Mosby were not rich. You find it offensive to the concept of medical justice that money can so blatantly be used to buy the opportunity to undergo a futile procedure. You also believe that Mrs. Mosby is manipulating Jack by threatening to revoke his inheritance if he does not donate the kidney. In your medical opinion, Mrs. Mosby will die within a year, with or without the transplant. In your personal opinion, Mrs. Mosby should take her own kidney and all of her money with her to the grave.

Role Assignment Number 6

Assume the role of Bobby Brewer. All of your memories are of being sick, going to the hospital, and being poked and prodded by doctors and nurses. There has never been a time in your life when you have been healthy or during which you have lived a normal life. You are now refusing the anticancer treatments, quite simply, because you are tired. You have lost your desire to fight for your life. Your one last wish is to live life outside the hospital and without medications, even if that means that you will soon die. Right now you feel relatively good but the anticancer medications would make you very ill.

Argue that now that you are an adult, no one can tell you how to live your life. You want to live the rest of your life outside the hospital without machines and without medications. You are here today to exercise your autonomy and declare that you want to be left alone. You consider the aggressive treatments to be harmful because they would rob you of the opportunity to live a normal life, even if only for a few months. You just do not believe that you will ever be cured.

Role Assignment Number 7
Assume the role of Mr./Mrs. Brewer, Bobby's father/mother. Bobby is your only son and you have always wanted the best for him. You respect your son's autonomy but you do not think that he can make proper decisions at this time because he has been through a great deal of trauma and is on several medications. You want to be granted a durable power of attorney to make health care decisions for your son. You believe that this will be the last battle that Bobby will have to fight and you believe that the only way to save your son's life is for you to demand treatment. Because Bobby is young, you believe that you and the hospital have a moral obligation to save his life. If the hospital allows your son to die it would be like killing him. Argue that to allow a preventable death is nothing short of murder. You realize that Bobby is an autonomous individual but, just as society does not condone suicide, the hospital should not condone a patient choosing to die. Additionally, though Bobby is autonomous, you believe that he cannot competently exercise his autonomy because of his youth, his fatigue from being ill, and depression from being in the hospital and on medications.

Role Assignment Number 8
Assume the role of Bobby Brewer's oncologist. In your medical opinion, Bobby's condition is treatable and Bobby may return to a normal healthy life with the anticancer treatments. You think that Bobby is merely depressed and that his failure to consent should be overridden by appointing his father or mother as guardian for purposes of consenting to treatment. Bobby is young and has an excellent chance of living a long life. To allow Bobby to throw his potential away is ridiculous. It also does not make sense that last week, when Bobby was 17, he had no say as to his treatment and only his parents could consent. Just because he is now a week older does not mean that he should suddenly be able to choose to die and throw away all of the treatment and effort that have already been exerted on him. Autonomy is an important principle, but sometimes it must give way to the protection of third parties who will be harmed if the patient acts irrationally. Bobby's parents are innocent third parties who will be harmed if Bobby is allowed to die. Argue that society and the hospital have a duty to protect the sanctity of life and that doctors have a duty to heal the sick whenever it is within their power to do so. A few more months of treatment is a small price for Bobby to pay in order to be cured. Bobby lacks the wisdom to know that, in the big picture, consenting to the treatment is the only rational choice.

Role Assignment Number 9

Assume the role of Pam Braun. You have one goal, and that is to end your life. You would prefer that you be allowed to use the oral syringe because you consider that to be the most humane means of achieving death. Death by the syringe will be quick, clean, and painless. The final act of causing death will be your own. Though someone must put the syringe in your mouth, the actual injection will only happen when you cause it. Our society refuses to allow animals to suffer as you are suffering. Why then should doctors require you to continue your futile existence?

In the event that you are denied the ability to humanely terminate your life with the oral syringe, you unconditionally demand that the intravenous nutrition and hydration be stopped. Doctors may be able to deny you the ability to take action with the syringe but they cannot force you to tolerate unconsented, invasive, and intrusive infringement upon your body. It is your life that is at stake and no one should be able to require you to submit to unwanted procedures. You only ask that you be recognized as an autonomous and competent individual and be allowed to rationally choose to die. In arguing for your position, consider each of the following points:

1. Actively terminating someone's life and allowing someone to starve to death have the same result and the same purpose--to cause the person to die.

2. Death by the oral syringe could be attributed only to you because the last act resulting in death would be your own.

3. No one is pressuring you to kill yourself.

4. The principle of autonomy includes the right to refuse treatment.

5. You are a competent adult.

Role Assignment Number 10

Assume the role of Eric Braun, Pam's brother. Since Pam's accident, you have been her primary care-giver. You feed and wash Pam and administer her medications. You understand that it is incredibly difficult for Pam to accept her condition, but you believe that she can find meaning in her life if she only tries. You refuse to accept murdering Pam to be an acceptable option. If the hospital allows Pam to use the oral syringe or if they remove the feeding tube, you will pursue legal action. You believe that all human life is sacred and that murder cannot be justified just because it takes place in a hospital or just because the victim is in a wheelchair. Condoning the murder of people in wheelchairs sends the message to all disabled persons that they are inherently less valuable than the rest of society. Argue that the choice to die cannot be rational and that the very fact that someone wishes to die indicates definitively that they have a psychological problem that needs treatment. Argue that a person cannot rationally or competently choose death and that guardians should be appointed for individuals who purport to do to make health care decisions on their behalf.

You are at this meeting to demand that Pam be kept on intravenous nutrition and be given adequate psychological help. You are also here to ask that you be recognized as Pam's surrogate decision maker for health care decisions until such time as she recovers psychologically (i.e., until she no longer claims that she wants to die).

Role Assignment Number 11
Assume the role of a representative of The Managed Death Coalition. You are present today to fight for Bobby Brewer's right to refuse treatment, Pam Braun's right to die, and Judy's right to refuse consent to the blood transfusion. In formulating arguments to achieve your goal, consider each of the following :
  1. Every adult of sound mind is an autonomous agent capable of directing his or her own life. As part of directing one's life, an individual has a fundamental right to make personal decisions that affect his own body. Within the realm of such decisions are the use of contraception, abortion, the right to die, and the right not to be subjected to unwanted touching. Unconsented treatment is an unwanted touching and a battery.
  2. One aim of medicine is to prevent harm. Pain and suffering are harms. If the only way to prevent pain and suffering is death, then death should be considered to be a medically acceptable option for individuals to choose. As an acceptable option, death should be made as humane and painless as possible.
  3. Disabled persons, such as Pam, should be given aid in dying out of respect for their autonomy. To deny Pam the use of the oral syringe is to treat her as less of a person than if she were able to use her limbs. That is because refusing to allow Pam to use the oral syringe denies Pam access to something (i.e., a painless death) that any other mobile person can achieve without aid. To prohibit Pam from ending her life is to make paternalistic judgments on her behalf.
  4. Bobby Brewer is a legal adult. Just because he has made a decision with which others do not agree does not mean that he is incompetent. Bobby has the unqualified right to reject unwanted treatment.
  5. Judy, like everyone else, has the unqualified right to refuse treatment even if it results in her death. Judy's decision is one of principle and conviction. Judy's decision is made more difficult by the fact that Judy has children who may suffer on account of her decision. The right to refuse health care, even if death results, however, cannot be prejudicially bestowed only upon persons without children.

Role Assignment Number 12
Assume the role of a member of the St. Jude's Ethics Advisory Committee. Argue the following:
  1. Vinnie is no longer a person because he does not manifest the attributes which are necessary for personhood. Vinnie is not self-conscious, he has no self-control, he does not meet minimal intelligence thresholds, he has no sense of time, and he has no ability to communicate or relate with others. Because Vinnie is not a person, the moral duty that is owed to persons does not apply to him.

2. Bobby is an autonomous individual. His wishes must be honored because he is not requiring any action of anyone. He is only asking to be left alone to die of natural causes.

3. Pam, like Bobby, is an autonomous individual. Her wish to use the oral syringe, however, must not be facilitated because that would require a positive action on the part of another autonomous individual which would most likely offend the moral sensibilities of that individual. Pam should be taken off food and hydration and allowed to die of starvation. Allowing Pam to starve to death is morally distinguishable from facilitating the use of the oral syringe because removing the intravenous feeding tube is only the taking away of a previously performed act. The removal of the feeding tube is not a positive action which causes death, because after the tube is removed, it is up to Pam as to whether or not she wishes to eat or to starve. Pam should also be allowed to refuse antibiotics and any other medications.

4. Argue that Judy's case is unique. If she allowed to forgo the cesarean, she will die of natural consequences. If Judy is admitted to St. Jude's for the cesarean procedure, but is then allowed to die from lack of a blood transfusion, her cause of death would be the performance of the cesarean--a positive act of another. You believe that the cesarean and the transfusion should be viewed as one act and either consented to together or rejected as one. Argue that if doctors perform an act (the cesarean) which necessitates a further act (the transfusion), but then do not perform the further act (the transfusion), the doctors may be ethically and legally responsible for the end result (Judy's death). Therefore, either treat Judy and give her all the treatment she needs, or allow her to die on her own.

5. Mrs. Mosby should be given the transplant so long as all parties consent and no one is harmed.

Role Assignment Number 13

Assume the role of Judy Miller. As a Jehovah's Witness, you are required by your faith not to consume any blood products, including the receipt of blood through a transfusion. You believe that as an adult, you have the right to refuse any unwanted medical treatment, even if such a refusal results in your own death. Formulate arguments to require the hospital to perform the cesarean section without performing a blood transfusion. Consider the following:

1. Any medical procedure that is performed without obtaining the informed consent of the patient is a battery. You have specifically stated that under no circumstances will you consent to a blood transfusion. Thus, if an unwanted transfusion is performed, you will bring a legal cause of action against both the hospital and the physician ordering the procedure.

2. You understand that without receiving a transfusion you may die. You have discussed that possibility with your children, and you accept that risk. You are willing to sign an agreement with the hospital and the physician stating that you assume the risk of undergoing the cesarean without a transfusion and that you will not bring a legal cause of action against either the physician or the hospital if an

adverse outcome results from you not receiving a transfusion.

3. In the event that the hospital will not guarantee that you will not be given a transfusion, you will give birth at your home with only the assistance of a Jehovah's Witness midwife. Certainly, it can be argued that the hospital would be putting you at risk by refusing to provide you with the cesarean section procedure.

Role Assignment Number 14
Assume the role of St. Jude's Chief Financial Officer. Your primary concern is to ensure the financial integrity of actions undertaken in each case. Formulate a response to each case that considers the economic impact on to the hospital. With regard to each case, consider the following:

1. Mrs. Mosby pays all of her bills in cash and has promised to leave a substantial endowment to the hospital if she is given the transplant. She is a consumer who can afford to pay for what she wants. Even if Mrs. Mosby gains no benefit from the transplant, the gift that she will leave to the hospital may benefit countless others. Performing the transplant is, therefore, an economically beneficial transaction.

2. Vinnie's insurance does not cover all of his expenses and his family cannot meet the deficit. The hospital loses money everyday that Vinnie's vegetative state is sustained. If Vinnie is "unplugged," his bed can be given to a paying patient. If there is no other overriding reason to provide Vinnie treatment, economics dictate that he should be taken off support.

3. Bobby Brewer has insurance that covers all of his expenses. His care will not be indefinite and he may even be cured. It is a profitable transaction for the hospital to treat Bobby.

4. If Pam Braun is allowed to use the oral syringe, the hospital will probably be sued by her brother, therefore, that is not an economically wise option. If Pam is allowed to starve to death, the hospital should get a court order for the removal of the feeding tube before it is removed in order to protect against liability. In any case, to avoid potential liability, Pam should not be permitted to die in the hospital.

5. To avoid liability to Judy or her children, and possibly even to avoid criminal liability, the hospital should execute a written agreement with Judy before providing her with any treatment.

Role Assignment Number 15
Assume the role of an administrator at St. Jude's Hospital. In responding to each case, consider the following:

1. The overriding purpose of the health care profession is to heal people. The integrity of the profession and the trust that people put into the profession depend upon the health care community fulfilling its purpose. If doctors help kill their patients, people will fear their doctors. Physicians who are feared cannot be trusted.

2. The health care profession must adhere to ethical principles without being swayed by bribery or threatened with blackmail. The transplant for Mrs. Mosby is a

futile procedure because she has cancer. Her money should not be allowed to buy a procedure that doctors determine to be medically futile. Similarly, Judy should not be permitted to threaten the hospital by stating that she will not seek medical attention if St. Jude's does not agree to abstain from administering life-saving procedures that may become necessary. Just as we do not allow patients to threaten suicide if they are not prescribed certain medications, we cannot allow Judy to threaten the hospital. If Judy wishes to seek medical attention then she must submit to the best judgment of the doctors, even if that means straying from her religion.

3. Argue that the hospital has a duty to keep Vinnie, Bobby, and Pam alive. Vinnie's life is now being sustained and there is no reason to alter his condition. Vinnie should be given all the care that is necessary to keep him alive.

4. Bobby is exercising poor judgment which should not be followed. If a court orders the hospital to stop treating Bobby, then he should be discharged. He should not be allowed to stay in the hospital and die.

5. Of the three patients, Pam is the furthest from death as she is not even sick. No justification can be made for the taking of a perfectly healthy life just because the person living it is a quadriplegic. If Pam is killed or allowed to die it sets a precedent that people who are not perfect are disposable.

6. As soon as death is deemed to be permissible under one set of circumstances, the slippery slope will be embarked upon and life will become disposable. It is not acceptable for the medical profession, whose purpose it is to save people, to aid in killing its patients.

Role Assignment Number 16

Assume the role of a hospital administrator with authority to choose a course of action in the Victim case. At the end of today's meeting, you must determine how to proceed with treatment of Vinnie Victim. Consider each of the following options:

1. Leave Vinnie intubated and connected to the respirator and allow Vinnie to die from the bladder tumor;

2. Leave Vinnie intubated and connected to the respirator and remove the bladder tumor;

3. Disconnect Vinnie from the respirator and allow him to die when and if respiratory distress occurs;

4. Disconnect Vinnie from nutrition and hydration and allow him to starve to death;

5. Administer a lethal dose of medication to stop Vinnie's heart; or

6. Formulate another option of your own design.

Role Assignment Number 17

Assume the role of a hospital administrator with authority to choose a course of action in the Mosby case. At the end of today's meeting, you must determine how to proceed with treatment of Mrs. Mosby. Consider each of the following options:

1. Allow Mrs. Mosby to receive the transplant from Jack;

2. Refuse to perform the transplant from Jack, but allow Mrs. Mosby to be placed on an organ recipient waiting list;

3. Refuse to perform the transplant from Jack, and refuse to place Mrs. Mosby on an organ recipient waiting list, but agree to perform the transplant if Mrs. Mosby can find a third party willing to donate one of his or her kidneys;

4. Refuse to take part in any course of treatment that involves Mrs. Mosby receiving a kidney transplant; or

5. Formulate another option of your own design.

Role Assignment Number 18

Assume the role of a hospital administrator with authority to choose a course of action in the Brewer case. At the end of today's meeting, you must determine how to proceed with treatment of Bobby Brewer. Consider each of the following options:

1. Allow Bobby to refuse any or all treatment;

2. Follow the wishes of Bobby's parents, and attempt to have one of them appointed as Bobby's guardian for purposes of making health care decisions;

3. Try to persuade Bobby to consent to the treatment; or

4. Formulate another option of your own design.

Role Assignment Number 19

Assume the role of a hospital administrator with authority to choose a course of action in the Braun case. At the end of today's meeting, you must determine how to proceed with treatment of Pam Braun. Consider each of the following options:

1. Place the oral syringe filled with lethal medication in Pam's mouth;

2. Provide Pam with the syringe and the lethal medication without placing them in her mouth;

3. Refuse to take part in any activity involving the oral syringe;

4. Disconnect Pam from the intravenous nutrition and antibiotics and allow her die from starvation and/or infection;

5. Attempt to have Pam's brother appointed as her guardian for purposes of making health care decisions; or

6. Formulate another option of your own design.

Role Assignment Number 20

Assume the role of a hospital administrator with authority to choose a course of action in the Miller case. At the end of today's meeting, you must determine how to proceed with treatment of Judy Miller. Consider each of the following options:

1. Agree to perform the cesarean without performing the transfusion;

2. Agree to perform the cesarean on the condition that a transfusion will be performed if it becomes necessary;

3. Agree to perform the cesarean and agree to not perform the transfusion but then perform the transfusion if it becomes necessary;

4. Agree to perform the cesarean and agree not to perform the transfusion, but then perform the transfusion if it becomes necessary without informing Ms. Miller; or

5. Formulate another option of your own design.

CHAPTER 6

RELIGIOUS FREEDOM AND
THE RIGHT TO REFUSE CARE

What Are The Limits?

INSTRUCTIONS AND OBJECTIVES

The scenarios presented in this chapter are all ones in which decisions are being made in the context of the parties' religious beliefs. Health care decisions and religious decisions are each among the most private of concerns. When they are combined, the tension between what might be the "right" decision in a strictly medical context and what might be the "right" decision in a strictly religious context comes to the fore. Participants are presented with situations in which recommended or essential medical care is being refused on the basis of religious beliefs. The situations are further complicated by a number of variations: parents making decisions for their minor children of various ages; minor children expressing their own wishes; parents making decisions for themselves that will affect others; and a variety of religions ranging from mainstream to the fringe.

Participants are invited to focus on the conflict between the individual's First Amendment right to religious freedom, on the one hand, and the state's interest in promoting life, on the other. The scenarios further provide participants with the opportunity to look beyond what the parties state, to what might underlie their stated wishes—a risky endeavor, at best. There is also the temptation, particularly in the scenarios involving less well known religions, to second-guess the parties' decisions. The slippery slope that ensues can be quite enlightening.

The five different fact patterns presented in this chapter can be used individually or as a comprehensive case study.

THE CASE STUDY

Today's meeting will focus on five recent cases involving the right of individuals to refuse medical care because of their religious convictions. These cases are currently pending at various hospitals throughout the United States. Judges are present at today's meeting who have authority to render a decision and order care, if deemed appropriate, in each case. Recommendations should be made to each of the judges so that they can render decisions at the end of today's meeting. The cases are summarized as follows:

The Morgan Case

Patients: The Morgan Family: Ann (age 40), Jason (age 17), Mark (age 14), and Natalie (age 18 months)
Location: St. Jude's Hospital, Tampa, Florida
Patients' Religious Affiliation: Jehovah's Witness

Last night, Ann Morgan was hit by a drunk driver while driving with her three children. Mrs. Morgan, her two sons, Jason and Mark, and one daughter, Natalie, were all severely injured. Mrs. Morgan and her husband had been devout members of the Jehovah's Witness Church for over twenty years. Mr. Morgan died six months ago after refusing a blood transfusion which became necessary during a coronary by-pass. Mrs. Morgan is the primary care-giver of the children and she earns an annual income of $50,000 which supports the family. The Morgans have no living relatives. The Morgan children have all been raised according to the beliefs of the Jehovah's Witness Church.

Upon being admitted to St. Jude's Hospital in Tampa, Florida, it was brought to the attention of the attending physician that all of the Morgans were wearing bracelets identifying themselves as Jehovah's Witnesses. The bracelets stated that under no circumstances were the Morgans to receive blood transfusions or infusions of any blood products. At that time, all of the Morgans except Natalie were unconscious. Dr. Reeves stabilized the Morgan children without use of blood or blood products but he ordered blood to be given to Mrs. Morgan when it became evident that she would die without the transfusion. Mrs. Morgan at no time consented to the transfusion and, because it was an emergency situation, no court order was sought.

Judge Arnold is present today to order any treatment that is deemed medically necessary and legally appropriate. Currently, all of the Morgans are conscious and in need of further medical attention. Their situations are outlined below.

Jason is in need of a blood transfusion as he lost a substantial amount of blood at the time of the accident and he has continued lose blood since being admitted to the hospital. Dr. Reeves was able to stabilize Jason but his condition has worsened, and Dr. Reeves believes that without a blood transfusion Jason will die. Jason and Mrs. Morgan are now both fully conscious, and both refuse to consent to the transfusion. Jason is four months away from his 18th birthday and claims that he should be recognized as an emancipated minor in order to refuse the transfusion.

Mark is in need of invasive exploratory surgery of the abdomen to determine the extent of the injuries he sustained from the accident. Dr. Reeves believes that it is highly probable that Mark will require a blood transfusion during the course of the surgery. Mrs. Morgan refuses to consent to the blood transfusion although she has granted consent for the exploratory procedure to be performed. Mark is fully conscious and he claims that if a blood transfusion is required he would rather die than undergo the procedure.

Natalie is in stable condition but she requires infusion of several substances which contain minor blood components. Mrs. Morgan has refused to consent to the use of any substances that contain even trace amounts of blood components.

Mrs. Morgan was badly cut in the accident and she requires extensive surgery which will most likely require a blood transfusion. Mrs. Morgan will only give consent to the surgery if it is guaranteed that another blood transfusion will not be performed. Dr. Reeves claims that the surgery cannot be performed without a transfusion.

The Donovan Case

Patient: Thomas Donovan (age 5)
Location: City Hospital, Akron, Ohio
Patients' Religious Affiliation: Christian Scientist

Thomas Donovan is five years old and developmentally challenged. Mr. and Mrs. Donovan are devout members of the Church of Christian Science. Thomas became ill four days ago at school during recess. He was sent home, and his condition has progressively worsened. Thomas currently suffers from acute abdominal pain, and his temperature has risen to 102 degrees. Thomas vomits persistently and has been unable to eat any solid food. Mr. and Mrs. Donovan have refused to seek conventional medical attention for Thomas claiming that it is prohibited by their religious beliefs. Since Thomas became ill, the Donovans have been praying with him that he will be healed, but Thomas' condition has only worsened.

In the past, the Donovans have utilized various medical services for themselves and their family members. Four years ago, the Donovans' oldest son, Ralph, broke his leg. The Donovans immediately sought medical attention and had the leg set. Mr. Donovan regularly visits the dentist and has had two root canal procedures during which he received anesthesia. During the births of their children, Mrs. Donovan received medical attention and even had a cesarean procedure for the birth of Thomas. The Donovans claim that those procedures were all within the tenets of the Christian Science belief system.

Judge Hughes is present today with the authority to order care for Thomas if determined to be legally appropriate. Judge Hughes also has the authority to find the Donovans guilty of child neglect if appropriate under the applicable Ohio law.

The Schott Case

Patient: Margie Schott (age 22)
Location: County Hospital, Los Angeles, California
Patient's Religious Affiliation: Jehovah's Witness

Yesterday evening, Margie Schott was brought to County Hospital in Los Angeles, California. Ms. Schott intentionally slashed both of her wrists with a razor blade in an apparent suicide attempt. Ms. Schott wrote the following note before inflicting the injuries:

> Dear Mom and Dad,
>
> I can no longer go on living in this world. I'm sorry. And to whoever may find me, I am a Jehovah's Witness. If you find me, do not let the doctors give me a blood transfusion. I must not be given any blood. It is against my will.
>
>   Signed, Margie Schott

Since being admitted to the hospital, Ms. Schott's mother and father have arrived. They testify to the fact that Ms. Schott was raised as a Jehovah's Witness and they attest to her continued adherence to the faith. Ms. Schott's parents have pointed out that Margie usually wore a bracelet to notify doctors not to give her any blood or blood products but that she had taken the bracelet off before inflicting the wounds.

Judge Cohen is present today to order any medical care that is found to be legally appropriate.

The Brahma Case

Patient: Conrad Brahma (age 11)
Location: General Hospital, Seattle, Washington
Patient's Religious Affiliation: Rastafarian

Daimon and Ruthie Brahma are followers of Rastafarian beliefs. They have, likewise, raised their son, Conrad, according to those beliefs. Part of living according to their tradition involves being completely vegan. The Brahmas eat no meat or any dairy products. Additionally, the Brahmas purchase no animal products, including wool or leather clothing, products that have been tested on animals, or goods which contain any animal by-products. Once a year, the Brahmas travel to Africa to rejuvenate their faith.

Last week, Conrad became ill and the Brahmas took him to Seattle General Hospital. Conrad was diagnosed as being diabetic and the attending physician asked permission of the Brahmas to give Conrad insulin. Mr. Brahma inquired whether the insulin contained animal by-products. The physician said that it may contain trace elements. Mr. and Mrs. Brahma then left the hospital, taking Conrad with them against medical advice.

The Brahmas are now seeking care for Conrad from a Rastafarian faith-healer. Seattle General Hospital is seeking a court order for Conrad to receive insulin treatment. Without the insulin treatments, physicians believe that Conrad's diabetes will continually worsen and possibly cause his eventual death.

Judge Bowen is present today with authority to order insulin treatment for Conrad if it is found to be legally warranted.

The Constanza and Phillips Cases

Patients: Rob Constanza (age 23), Suzy Phillips (age 4)
Location: University Medical Center and Charity Hospital, New Orleans, Louisiana
Patients' Religious Affiliation: Commune of the Scarab and the Hen

The Commune of the Scarab and the Hen was founded in 1992 in the French Quarter of New Orleans, Louisiana. The sect now has 38 members who live together in commune style, tending to each other's needs and sharing in all possessions and responsibilities. The Commune members abide by a set of philosophical and spiritual principles which are set forth in a book entitled *The Immortal Law*. Among the 72 principles given in The Immortal Law are the following three:

> 1. Puncture not your body. A punctured body creates a pierced
> Soul and a pierced Soul cannot float in the Heavens.
> 2. Eat not dust, nor mold, nor filth, nor chemicals made by man.
> To do so pollutes the body and, with it, the Soul.
> 3. To save the body from the afflictions that cause others to
> destroy the Soul, meditate, then chant, then pray until the pains can
> no longer stay.

The first of the principles has been interpreted by Commune members to mean that any breakage of the skin weakens the human soul, endangering the soul's ability to survive eternally. There is some controversy among Commune members as to exactly how many punctures the body and, in turn, the soul, can withstand before it loses its immortal life, but all members agree that a large incision, as might result from invasive surgery, immediately destroys the soul's ability to have eternal life. The second tenet has been interpreted by Commune members to mean that both organically manufactured and artificially synthesized medications must be avoided. The third principle has been interpreted to mean that when a person is afflicted with a condition that would cause the medical establishment to give injections, conduct surgery, or prescribe medications, a commune member must refuse such care and meditate, chant, and pray for relief and healing.

Currently, two cases involving members of the Commune are at issue at New Orleans hospitals. Rob Constanza was admitted to University Medical Center three days ago with chest pains. He has been diagnosed as suffering from a congenital heart defect which requires invasive surgery to be corrected. Mr. Constanza has refused to consent to the procedure. Mr. Constanza has a two year old daughter who lives with him in the Commune. The child's mother lives in England and has not seen the girl for over a year.

Suzy Phillips has been diagnosed as having an acute inner ear infection. Doctors at Charity Hospital have recommended antibiotics to cure the infection. Suzy's mother, Martha Phillips, has refused to consent to any antibiotic treatment. Without antibiotics, Suzy may completely lose hearing in her left ear. Suzy's life is not threatened by the ear infection even if the infection goes completely untreated.

DISCUSSION QUESTIONS

The Morgan Case

1. What factors should be considered in determining whether or not to order a blood transfusion for Ann Morgan?

2. Were Mrs. Morgan's autonomy rights violated when Dr. Reeves ordered her to undergo a blood transfusion after having read the bracelet which specifically stated blood transfusions to be unconsented? If so, was that violation justified? What, if any, factors weigh in favor of finding the transfusion to be justified?

3. Was a battery committed upon Mrs. Morgan by giving her a transfusion without her consent? Should either the physician or the hospital be held liable to Mrs. Morgan for damages if a battery was committed? What factors should be considered?

4. What would be the public policy implications of a hospital protocol stating that Dr. Reeves should not have ordered the transfusion to save the life of Mrs. Morgan?

5. What factors should be considered in determining whether Jason Morgan should be granted emancipated minor status? What are the policy implications of granting Jason that status?

6. Should Mark Morgan be granted emancipated minor status? Should he be allowed to refuse the blood transfusion? Should Mrs. Morgan be allowed to refuse the transfusion on Mark's behalf? If Mark and Mrs. Morgan were to disagree as to whether consent should be given for a transfusion, whose wishes should be honored?

7. What course of action should be taken with Natalie Morgan? Should Mrs. Morgan be permitted to refuse care on Natalie's behalf? What factors should be considered? If care is ordered for Natalie, does this violate any rights of Mrs. Morgan?

8. Should minors be granted the same health care autonomy rights that adults are given? Why or why not?

9. How much deference should be given to minors in determining what care they receive?

The Donovan Case

1. Should courts and/or hospital administrators attempt to measure the faith of individuals refusing medical treatment on account of their religious beliefs? If so, how should that be done? Should Judge Hughes attempt to reconcile the Donovans' past acts of receiving medical care with their wishes for Thomas?

2. Have the Donovans violated the Ohio statute included at Appendix I? If so, which sections? If not, why not?

3. What are the public policy implications of the Ohio statute? What public policy considerations should be weighed in evaluating the effects of the statute?

The Schott Case

1. What factors are relevant to determining whether a transfusion should be ordered for Ms. Schott? Is the cause of her injury relevant? Is evidence of her deep religious convictions relevant?

2. Is Ms. Schott's desire to refuse a blood transfusion motivated from religious convictions or from a suicidal intent? Should either motivation be considered in deciding whether to administer the transfusion? If so, which motivation should be given priority?

3. Would it be a violation of Ms. Schott's autonomy to order her to undergo a transfusion? Would ordering an involuntary transfusion violate Ms. Schott's First Amendment rights? Would it be a battery?

4. What are the public policy implications of not ordering a transfusion for Ms. Schott? What are the implications of ordering a transfusion? Which course of action establishes a more desirable public policy precedent?

The Brahma Case

1. Should care be ordered for Conrad? Why or why not?

2. Should a court consider the underlying religious belief system in determining whether to honor a refusal to consent to medical care? Should followers of more widely accepted religions be given more deference than followers of less well-known faiths?

3. How much, if any, weight should be given to the expressed desires of Conrad? Remember that he is 11 years old. What effect would the statute included at Appendix D have if it were applicable to the Brahma case?

The Constanza and Phillips Cases

1. Should the size and reputation of the Commune of the Scarab and the Hen be considered in determining whether medical care should be ordered for Mr. Constanza and Suzy Phillips? Is it likely that such factors will be taken into consideration even if not explicitly stated?

2. Should Mr. Constanza be ordered to undergo the surgery? What are the arguments for and against such an order?

3. Which, if any, of Mr. Constanza's rights would be violated if he were ordered to undergo the procedure against his will?

4. How much, if any, weight should be given to the effect that Mr. Constanza's decision will have on his daughter? If Mr. Constanza dies as a result of his refusal of care, would that constitute child abandonment? If the fact that Mr. Constanza has a child is considered as a factor by the judge, does that mean that parents have limitations placed upon how they may exercise their religious freedom that are not placed upon persons without children? What would be the effect if the case included at Appendix J were applicable to the facts presented?

5. How does Mr. Constanza's case compare with the case of Ann Morgan? How do the cases differ?

6. Should care be ordered for Suzy Phillips? Why or why not?

7. How does the case of Suzy Phillips compare with the cases of Natalie Morgan, Thomas Donovan, and Conrad Brahma? Should the fact that Suzy's condition is not life-threatening be considered?

8. What would a strict utilitarian approach dictate in each of these cases? What would a strict deontological approach dictate? Which approach has preferable results?

General Questions

1. How much weight, if any, should be given to the testimony of religious elders? Should more or less credibility be given to Mr./Ms. Snow, founder of the Commune of the Scarab and the Hen, than to leaders of the Jehovah's Witnesses or Christian Scientists?

2. Consider the following state interests:

(a) The preservation of the sanctity of life;

(b) Prevention of suicide;

(c) Preservation of the integrity of the medical profession; and

(d) Protection of innocent third parties.

How should each of those state interests be weighed against the autonomy rights of the individuals involved in each of the cases? Under what circumstances, if any, should each of the state's interests trump the expressed desires of the individual?

SUGGESTED RESEARCH

Statutes

Appendix D: California Family Code Sections 6500 et *seq.*
Appendix I: Ohio State Code Section 2151.03.

Case Law

Appendix H: *Bouvia v. Superior Court*, 179 Cal.App.3d 1127, 225 Cal.Rptr. 297 (Cal. Ct. App. 1986).
Appendix J: *In re Dubreuil*, 629 So.2d 819 (Fla. 1993).
Appendix P: Vaccco v. Quill, United States Supreme Court (June 26, 1997).

Texts

Annas, George J. *Standard of Care: The Law of American Bioethics.* New York City, NY: Oxford University Press, 1993, 85-97.
Engelhardt, H. Tristam. *The Foundations of Bioethics.* 2nd ed. New York City, NY: Oxford University Press, 1996, 288-374.

ROLE ASSIGNMENTS FOR 24 PARTICIPANTS

The Morgan Case

1. Mrs. Morgan
2. Jason Morgan
3. Mark Morgan
4. Guardian ad litem for Natalie Morgan
5. Jehovah's Witness Representative
6. Dr. Reeves
7. Judge Arnold

The Donovan Case

8. Guardian ad litem for Thomas Donovan
9. Mr./Mrs. Donovan
10. Christian Science Representative
11. Judge Hughes

The Schott Case

12. Guardian ad litem for Ms. Schott
13. Judge Cohen

The Brahma Case

14. Mr./Mrs Brahma
15. Guardian ad litem for Conrad Brahma
16. Representative of Seattle General Hospital
17. Rastafarian Faith-Healer
18. Judge Bowen

The Constanza/Phillips Case

19. Rob Constanza
20. Guardian ad litem for Suzy Phillips
21. Martha Phillips
22. Guardian ad litem for Rob Constanza's daughter
23. Mr./Ms. Snow, founder of the Commune of the Scarab and the Hen
24. Judge Davis

Role Assignment Number 1

Assume the role of Mrs. Morgan. Based on the relevant case law and readings, argue for the following:

1. Jason should be declared a mature minor and be allowed to make his own decisions regarding whether to receive a transfusion. If Jason is not granted mature minor status then no medical treatment, including a blood transfusion, should be administered without your consent.

2. Mark also should be granted mature minor status. Although he is only 14, Mark is deeply committed to the principles of the Jehovah's Witnesses. It must be remembered that Mark's father died because of his own refusal of blood products. If Mark were forced to receive blood products, he would live his whole life knowing that he failed to live up to his father's expectations. In the absence of being declared a mature minor, Mark should not be subjected to any medical care without your consent.

3. Natalie is too young to voice her own preferences but you have every intention of raising her as a Jehovah Witness. Any unconsented medical treatment would be a violation of your right to freedom of religion and you will not consent to any medical treatment that involves use of blood products.

4. You are willing to die for your beliefs and you will not consent to any further blood transfusions. You consider the blood transfusion that was performed on you to be a battery and members of your church have equated such unconsented transfusions with rape. You consider your own death to be less of an evil to your children than saving your life and forsaking your religious beliefs.

5. You will bring a cause of action for battery against the physician and the hospital if any unconsented care is administered to you or any of your children.

Role Assignment Number 2

Assume the role of Jason Morgan. Based on the relevant case law and readings, argue for the following:

1. Of primary importance to you is that you are declared a mature minor. You are only four months away from being declared a legal adult and it makes no sense for you to be denied the freedom to control you own body and future just because the auto accident fortuitously occurred now rather than four months from now. You want to be declared a mature minor so that you can refuse the blood transfusion.

2. You also believe that you should be declared a mature minor under the statute included at Appendix D because you have accepted the responsibilities of an adult since your father died. You hold a part-time job, you pay your own expenses, including car and medical insurance, and you help take care of your younger brother and sister.

3. If you are not declared a mature minor and the transfusion is ordered by the court, you would not consider it to be the burden of the court but you would take full responsibility for forsaking your religion. As a Jehovah's Witness, you believe that such an action by the court would jeopardize your eternal life.

Role Assignment Number 3

Assume the role of Mark Morgan. Argue for the following:

1. You have been raised as a Jehovah's Witness, and that is the only life that you know. You have always been told that if a person consumes blood, including through a transfusion, they will not live eternally. However, you are only 14, and you do not want to die.

2. You think you should be able to make your own decision and be declared a mature minor because you thoroughly understand your religious beliefs and you know the consequences of consuming blood. To evidence your religious convictions, you may point out that you attend church services twice a week, you volunteer after school for the Jehovah's Witnesses, and you read the Bible and other religious books nightly.

3. You also understand that your father died because of his religious beliefs, but you are not sure that you can do the same.

4. Your understanding of the Jehovah's Witness faith is that it is a sin for a Jehovah's Witness to consent to a blood transfusion. You also believe, however, that if a transfusion is ordered and you are not able to stop it, you will not be held spiritually responsible for receiving the transfusion.

Role Assignment Number 4

Assume the role of a guardian ad litem for Natalie Morgan. You are present at the meeting today to represent the best interests of Natalie Morgan. In arguing for a court order for Natalie to receive the minor blood components she needs, consider the following:

1. Most Jehovah's Witness elders do not forbid the use of minor blood components. The decision whether or not to receive such substances, such as gamma globulin, is left to "individual conscience." This means that if Natalie were an adult practicing Jehovah's Witness she would be able to consent to the treatment that she requires without being condemned by Church officials. Because Natalie would be able to consent if she were an adult, Mrs. Morgan should not be able to sacrifice her daughter over a belief that is controversial even within her own belief system.

2. Because she is a child, Natalie is not able to hold any religious beliefs of her own. Accordingly, she should not be martyred on account of her mother's beliefs.

3. The treatment should be ordered because it is clearly within Natalie's best interest to live rather than to die. She is far too young to be able to consent or refuse consent on her own behalf, therefore, the court should step in to protect Natalie's best interest.

Role Assignment Number 5

Assume the role of an Elder of the Jehovah's Witness Church. Argue for the following:

1. Mrs. Morgan should be allowed to refuse the blood transfusion for herself. It is settled law in this country that an individual has the right to refuse medical care even if such a refusal results in death. It may be argued that the state has a compelling interest in this case to order care because Mrs. Morgan is the primary care-giver of her children but you know that if Mrs. Morgan were to die, there are several Jehovah's Witness families that would adopt the Morgan children. Furthermore, Mrs. Morgan should be able to refuse the transfusion because it is not certain that she will she die if she does not receive the transfusion. Mrs. Morgan should be allowed to consult Jehovah's Witness physicians to discuss the feasibility of using blood volume expanders and administering excessive liquids before the operation to prevent the need for a transfusion during the operation.

2. Jason Morgan should be declared a mature minor and be allowed to make his own decision, whatever that might be. Jason is only four months away from his

eighteenth birthday and it simply does not make sense that Jason should be denied the right to determine his own fate based on such a legal technicality. Furthermore, you believe that Jason qualifies as a mature minor under the statute included at Appendix D. Jason is a deep believer in the Jehovah's Witness faith and his beliefs should not be compromised.

3. Mark Morgan should be allowed to assent to whatever medical treatment he prefers. This means that Mrs. Morgan should be able to decide upon a medical protocol for her son and the Judge Arnold should be able to determine a medical protocol. Both of those protocols should then be presented to Mark and he should be allowed to choose between them. Mark is an advanced 14 year old and he understands his actions and the consequences of each course of treatment. By allowing Mark to assent to treatment that has been consented to by either Mrs. Morgan or Judge Arnold, Mark will be allowed to choose between two options that are both purported to be in his best interest.

4. Mrs. Morgan should be allowed to determine what is best for Natalie. Part of religious freedom is the ability to raise one's children according the religion of one's choice. This means that parents should be able to determine what is best for their children. Jehovah's Witnesses leave the consumption of minor blood components to the conscience of the individual. In this case, the conscience to be followed is that of Mrs. Morgan.

In arguing in support of Ms. Schott's right to refuse an unwanted blood transfusion, consider the following:

1. If Ms. Schott is given a blood transfusion, it will destroy her immortal existence. Ms. Schott's parents attest to the fact that she has been a long-time member of the Jehovah's Witnesses and that she would be disgraced if her beliefs were infringed upon.

2. Ms. Schott's act of attempted suicide cannot be morally justified but neither can the act of forcing a unconsented transfusion upon a Jehovah's Witness. This is truly a case where two wrongs do not make a right.

3. An unconsented blood transfusion is an extremely serious offense when committed against a devout Jehovah's Witness, such as Ms. Schott. Many have compared the act with rape. Such an act must not be sanctioned by the state.

Role Assignment Number 6

Assume the role of Dr. Reeves. Argue for the course of action that will save the most lives. Consider the following:

1. You owe a duty of beneficence to all of your patients. That means that you must maximize utility. It is within your means to save the lives of all of the Morgans. There is no reason to allow any of them to die. The children, in particular, must be saved.

2. You recognize that Mrs. Morgan has an autonomy right that must be respected. You believe, however, that she should be required to undergo the transfusion because she owes a duty of support to her children. Besides, she has already had one

transfusion, what harm can a second transfusion do? If receiving a blood transfusion means that she will not have immortal life, then the damage has already been done and Mrs. Morgan should make the best of it by continuing to live for her children. Furthermore, under one understanding of Jehovah's Witness beliefs, if a transfusion is ordered by a court then the court, and not the individual, is be morally responsible for administration of the transfusion.

Role Assignment Number 7

Assume the role of Judge Arnold. You have authority to order treatment for any or all of the Morgans. Listen carefully to all arguments made for and against treatment and decide the following:

1. Should a blood transfusion be ordered for Mrs. Morgan? Consider the state's interests in the preservation of life, the prevention of suicide, the protection of the integrity of the medical profession, and, especially, the protection of innocent third parties.

2. What course of action should be taken with regard to Jason Morgan? Consider the following: (a) granting mature minor status to Jason Morgan; (b) ordering a blood transfusion for Jason; or (c) allowing Mrs. Morgan to make Jason's medical decisions.

3. What course of action should be taken with regard to Mark Morgan? Consider the following: (a) granting mature minor status to Mark Morgan; (b) ordering a blood transfusion for Mark; or (c) allowing Mrs. Morgan to make Mark's medical decisions.

4. What course of action should be taken with regard to Natalie Morgan? Consider the following: (a) ordering the use of blood components to save Natalie's life; or (b) allowing Mrs. Morgan to make Natalie's medical decisions.

Role Assignment Number 8

Assume the role of guardian ad litem for Thomas Donovan. You are present today to represent the best interests of Thomas Donovan. In arguing for immediate care to be administered to Thomas, consider the following:

1. Thomas is developmentally disabled and not old enough or mature enough to formulate a religious belief. Because Thomas cannot himself be said to be a Christian Scientist, he should not suffer on account of the beliefs of his parents.

2. The Donovans have previously sought medical care for their oldest son and for themselves. Their refusal to treat Thomas is nothing more than discrimination against him because he is developmentally disabled. Because of the Donovans' prior willingness to receive medical care and to consent to care for their older son, it appears that they are not entirely opposed to receiving traditional medical care. Therefore, a court should not find such an opposition to medical treatment to now

exist. Additionally, it would be unethical for a judge to interpret the Ohio statute in any way that allows the Donovans to discriminate against Thomas.

Role Assignment Number 9

Assume the role of Mr./Mrs. Donovan. In arguing in support of your right to make health care decisions for Thomas, consider the following:

1. Ohio law specifically allows parents to seek faith-healing for their children.

2. The instances of past utilization of health care by your family have all been permissible within the Christian Science belief system because they were "mechanical" in nature. Thomas' condition appears to not be mechanical, therefore, medical attention in his case would be against Christian Science beliefs. Accusations that you are discriminating against Thomas because he is developmentally disabled are preposterous. You have permitted Thomas to receive traditional medical care on numerous occasions when such care has not been contrary to your religious beliefs. In the instant case, it appears that traditional medical treatment would not be consistent with your belief system, therefore, you will not consent to such treatment. Furthermore, it is not the role of the state to determine what is morally permissible for you or your family within your religious belief system.

3. You are actively seeking a cure for Thomas by proven Christian Science methods of prayer. The First Amendment guarantees your right to freedom of religion. Your acts are a manifestation of that right.

4. In any event, you simply will not allow Thomas to be treated in any manner that is not consistent with your religious beliefs. If you must, you will hide Thomas from state officials so that he can be treated as you see fit, consistent with your religious beliefs.

Role Assignment Number 10

Assume the role of a representative of the Christian Science Church. Argue that the Donovans have a fundamental right to treat Thomas as they see fit in accordance with the teachings of the Church of Christian Science. Consider the following:

1. Under the statute included at Appendix I, the Donovans have a statutory right to seek faith-healing for their son.

2. Christian Science beliefs distinguish between mechanical and nonmechanical medical care. The instances of fixing a broken arm, having dental work, and even having a cesarean section are all mechanical in nature and, thus, are allowed by the Christian Science Church. Nonmechanical care includes chemotherapy, radiation treatment, and drug treatment. Those treatments are not permitted.

3. It would be within the tenants of the Church of Christian Science for the Donovans to have Thomas examined to determine whether his malady is mechanical. If it is discovered to be mechanical, such as a bowel obstruction, it would be permissible for the malady to be repaired. If the disorder were found to be

nonmechanical, such as cancer, the Christian Science Church would require the Donovans to refrain from nonmechanical medical treatment.

Role Assignment Number 11

Assume the role of Judge Hughes. You have authority to order medical treatment for Thomas if you find that failure to treat Thomas would be a violation of Ohio law. You should rely on the Ohio statute included at Appendix I in rendering your decision. Listen carefully to all arguments presented and then answer the following questions:

1. Should medical treatment be court ordered for Thomas?

2. If so, precisely what treatment should be ordered? For example, should only a diagnosis be required or should more intensive care be ordered even if it would be in contravention of the Donovans' beliefs?

Role Assignment Number 12

Assume the role of a guardian ad litem for Ms. Schott. You are present at today's meeting to represent the best interests of Ms. Schott. In arguing for a blood transfusion to be administered to Ms. Schott, consider the following:

1. The state has an interest in the preservation of life and the prevention of suicide. Ms. Schott has an autonomy right to determine her own health care based on religious principles but because Ms. Schott's intent, as demonstrated by her acts, is to end her life and not solely to abide by her religious convictions, the state's interests must prevail.

2. Ms. Schott attempted suicide. That is an act that is prima facie indicative of a mental disorder. The fact that Ms. Schott was not in full possession of her faculties when she wrote the note indicates that it should not be taken as a serious expression of her convictions.

3. Finally, if an error is made, it should be made on the side of life. Ms. Schott can be saved and she may someday be grateful. If Ms. Schott is allowed to die there will be no subsequent opportunity for her to change her mind.

Role Assignment Number 13

Assume the role of Judge Cohen. You have authority to order a blood transfusion to save the life of Ms. Schott. Listen carefully to all arguments made and render a decision at the end of today's meeting.

Role Assignment Number 14

Assume the role of Mr./Mrs. Brahma, Conrad's parent. In arguing against a court order requiring Conrad to receive insulin, consider the following:

1. You and your family have been completely vegan for 20 years. To your knowledge, Conrad has never eaten any meat or dairy product nor used any product that came from or was tested on an animal. Conrad has strictly enforced his own adherence to your (and his) spiritual beliefs. Conrad has been with you to Africa every year since he was born and he has a deep knowledge of Rastafarian beliefs and culture.

2. To order the insulin treatment would violate your right to freedom of religion, your right to raise your child as you see fit, and your right to autonomy in choosing medical care.

3. To order the insulin treatment also ignores the proven record of faith-healing and it imposes a value system upon you which you do not honor.

4. Requiring the insulin treatment violates the bioethical principle of nonmaleficence insofar as it does harm by violating your will and the will of your son.

5. Any treatment of Conrad that is not consistent with your belief system will be unwanted and unconsented. As such, you will consider it to be a battery upon your son.

Role Assignment Number 15

Assume the role of a guardian ad litem for Conrad Brahma. You are present to defend the best interests of Conrad. In arguing that the insulin treatment should immediately be ordered by the court, consider the following:

1. Conrad is a minor. As such, decisions must be made on his behalf which are in his best interest. It is clearly not in Conrad's best interest to become ill or die.

2. The medical profession owes duties of beneficence and nonmaleficence to Conrad. If Conrad is allowed to die when he can easily be saved with routine treatment, both of those duties will be violated.

3. The right to freedom of religion allows for freedom of beliefs but when those beliefs result in practices that adversely affect innocent individuals, the practices can and must be regulated. If an individual claimed to have religious beliefs that condoned human sacrifice, such a practice would not be protected by the First Amendment. The Brahmas are attempting to sacrifice their son for the sake of their own beliefs. That cannot be permitted.

Role Assignment Number 16

Assume the role of a representative of the Seattle General Hospital. In arguing that Conrad should be ordered to receive insulin, consider the following:

1. The insulin treatment that is required will need to be administered on a regular basis for years, most likely permanently. If Conrad truly has the belief that receiving the insulin is morally wrong, then he will have the opportunity to exercise his autonomy and cease taking the insulin when he turns 18. At that time, Conrad will have the legal capacity to refuse any and all unwanted treatment.

2. The integrity of the medical profession requires saving the lives of vulnerable individuals when those with charge of them refuse to act in their best interest.

3. The ethical principles of beneficence and nonmaleficence require Seattle General Hospital to do everything in its power to save Conrad's life. That means that the best medical procedures must be used. Faith-healing is not proven and it cannot, with any degree of certainty, claim to be capable of saving Conrad. Insulin treatment, however, can and will save Conrad.

Role Assignment Number 17

Assume the role of a Rastafarian Faith-Healer. You were trained as a Rastafarian faith-healer in Africa and you are a highly respected individual within the Rastafarian community. You have treated over 1,000 individuals and have seen prayer and meditation save countless lives. Your practices have a proven history and they represent an alternative method of healing that is widely accepted in other parts of the world. Just because people in Seattle do not subscribe to your beliefs does not mean that you are wrong. You and the Brahmas have only Conrad's best interest in mind. His best interest is clearly to live according to his beliefs. You fully believe that he can live according to his beliefs if he is allowed to be healed by faith. Furthermore, the First Amendment guarantees the Brahmas the right to be Rastafarian, and part of being Rastafarian entails being vegan and practicing faith-healing.

Role Assignment Number 18

Assume the role of Judge Bowen. You have authority to decide whether to order insulin treatment for Conrad Brahma. Listen to all arguments carefully and consider the applicable statutes before rendering your decision of whether to order treatment for Conrad.

Role Assignment Number 19

Assume the role of Rob Constanza. In arguing that you have the right to refuse the heart surgery, consider the following:

1. It is settled law in the United States that an individual may refuse medical care even if such refusal results in that individual's death. For a court to order the

invasive heart surgery would be for the court to order a battery. You have a fundamental autonomy right to refuse the invasive procedure.

2. The argument that the state has an interest in ordering you to undergo the procedure to protect your daughter must be rejected because your daughter will not be abandoned if you die. The Commune is prepared to raise your daughter, and that is precisely what you would like to have happen if you die.

3. The state also cannot argue that it has an interest in preventing suicide because you are not suicidal. Your intent is not to die. You only desire is to live according to your religion. To have the surgery would violate your religion and it would destroy your immortal existence--a price that is clearly not worth paying for a few more years on earth.

Role Assignment Number 20

Assume the role of guardian ad litem for Suzy Phillips. You are present to represent the best interests of Suzy. In arguing that Suzy must be ordered to receive antibiotics, consider the following:

1. Mrs. Phillips has the right to martyr herself for her religion but she does not have the right to sacrifice her daughter's well-being. Suzy is suffering from a common childhood malady that is easily cured. It is clearly in Suzy's best interest to receive antibiotics. No good will come from allowing Suzy to lose her hearing because her mother is a member of a cult.

2. Even if the Commune is deemed to be a credible religion, the beliefs of the Commune do not appear to assert that Suzy will suffer any great consequence from receiving antibiotics, as would occur if she were to undergo surgery. *The Immortal Law* prohibits receiving drugs, such as antibiotics, but it does not lay down the punishment that will occur if such drugs are taken. The Commune itself, therefore, does not even strictly forbid the required treatment.

3. The duties of beneficence and nonmaleficence dictate that Suzy must be given the best care to promote her interests. In this case, Suzy's hearing can and must be saved.

4. The bottom line is that even if it is desirable from a public policy point of view to allow individuals to refuse treatment on account of their religious beliefs, such tolerance should only be granted to credible religious traditions. The Commune more closely resembles a dissident cult than a religion.

Role Assignment Number 21

Assume the role of Martha Phillips. In arguing for the right to refuse antibiotic treatment for Suzy, consider the following:

1. You have a First Amendment right to freedom of religion. That freedom includes the freedom to practice as a Commune member. Practicing as a Commune member entails utilizing faith-healing rather than medical interventions.

2. The fact that the Commune is small and relatively new should not be held against it. The size or notoriety of a religion does not affect the sincerity with which its followers believe and it is not the role of any man to judge the truth of another's religion.

3. This is not a life and death situation. Suzy will only incur a chance of losing some of her hearing in one ear. That is not a large enough injury to warrant abridgment of First Amendment freedoms and autonomy rights.

Role Assignment Number 22

Assume the role of a guardian ad litem for Rob Constanza's daughter. You are present at today's meeting to protect the best interests of Mr. Constanza's daughter. In arguing that Mr. Constanza should be required to undergo the heart surgery, consider the following:

1. Mr. Constanza is the primary care-giver of his daughter. The girl's mother has played no part in caring for her and has not seen her in over a year. If Mr. Constanza dies he will be abandoning his daughter. Part of Mr. Constanza's obligation as a father is to care for his child. By choosing to die, Mr. Constanza will be breaching that obligation. Furthermore, Mr. Constanza owes a duty to the state to care for his child. If Mr. Constanza dies, it is likely that his daughter will become a ward of the state. If that occurs, the state will incur the economic burden of raising the child. The state, therefore, has an economic interest in Mr. Constanza receiving care.

2. Mr. Constanza should also be required to undergo the surgery because it is in his daughter's best interest to be raised by her natural father.

3. Mr. Constanza does have an autonomy right to determine his own health care, but that right was abridged when he became a father. The duty that he owes to his child and to the state to care for his child now takes precedence over his right to refuse health care.

Role Assignment Number 23

Assume the role of Mr./Ms. Snow, the founder of the Commune of the Scarab and the Hen and the author of *The Immortal Law*. Argue that Mrs. Phillips should be allowed to refuse consent on behalf of her daughter and that Mr. Constanza should be allowed to refuse consent to the surgery. Rely on the following in making your arguments:

1. You are the final authority as to what is permitted and what is forbidden to members of the Commune. As author of *The Immortal Law*, you have final say with regard to its interpretation.

2. If Mr. Constanza undergoes the heart surgery, his soul will be destroyed and he will be condemned to nonexistence for all of eternity. An order for Mr. Constanza to undergo the procedure would be the equivalent of a spiritual death sentence.

3. Mrs. Phillips must be allowed to refuse consent to the antibiotics for her daughter. Antibiotics, like all chemicals, pollute the human soul and weaken its ability to live for all of eternity. Mrs. Phillips and Suzy must be allowed to exercise their religious freedom and refuse the treatment. The damage to Suzy's soul from receiving the treatment will be much worse than the damage to her body from not receiving it. Furthermore, the Commune will chant and pray to heal her.

Role Assignment Number 24

Assume the role of Judge Davis. You have the authority to order care for Mr. Constanza and for Suzy Phillips. Before rendering your decisions, listen to all arguments carefully and ask any questions you deem relevant.

CASE UPDATES

Since the commencement of this meeting the following developments have occurred:

The Morgan Case

Mrs. Morgan's condition remains unchanged. Jason Morgan consented to and received a blood transfusion without informing Mrs. Morgan. Jason died an hour ago. It has been concluded that he would not have died if he had been given a blood transfusion sooner. Mark Morgan consented to and received a blood transfusion without informing Mrs. Morgan. Natalie Morgan died at about the same time as Jason. Natalie's death could have been prevented with the infusion of various minor blood components.

The Donovan Case

The Donovans agreed to allow a Christian Scientist physician to examine Thomas. The physician has diagnosed Thomas as suffering from a rare viral infection. Without treatment, the infection can be expected to persist for about a week. During that time, Thomas will have severe abdominal pain. The infection presents no threat of death or permanent injury to Thomas. The virus, however, can be treated with a series of injections of a potent, synthetic anti-viral serum. With treatment, Thomas can be expected to be well in two days. The serum has no negative side-effects. Use of the serum has been stated by Church officials to violate the doctrine of the Church of Christian Science.

The Schott Case

Ms. Schott regained consciousness briefly. She was asked to consent to a blood transfusion. She refused consent, stating that it was against her religion. She then lost consciousness.

The Brahma Case

Conrad's condition has improved dramatically after seeing a Rastafarian Faith-Healer. Conrad has been examined by a physician and he appears no longer to be diabetic. Modern medical science has no explanation for the change in Conrad's condition.

The Constanza and Phillips Cases

Mr. Constanza's former wife and the mother of his daughter has been located in England. She refuses to return to the United States or to take custody of her daughter. Members of the Commune have agreed to adopt Mr. Constanza's daughter if he dies.

The infection in Suzy Philip's ear has worsened. It now appears that loss of hearing is almost certain if antibiotics are not administered immediately.

ADDITIONAL DISCUSSION QUESTIONS

The Morgan Case

1. What was the cause of death of Jason Morgan? Of Natalie Morgan? Consider the following:

    (a) Mrs. Morgan's refusal to consent to care;

    (b) Loss of blood/blood products;

    (c) The drunk driver who caused the accident;

    (d) Dr. Reeves' failure to order the life-saving procedures;

    (e) The Jehovah's Witness Church for prohibiting members from utilizing blood products.

Would it be appropriate to charge the drunk driver with the death of Jason and/or Natalie?

2. Was it appropriate to give Mark Morgan a blood transfusion without informing Mrs. Morgan? If so, is it appropriate to allow a 14 year old to consent to treatment but not to refuse treatment?

3. Should treatment be ordered for Mrs. Morgan? Remember, she now has only one dependent who is 14 years old.

The Donovan Case

1. Should Thomas be ordered to undergo the injections to treat his viral infection? What factors should be considered?

2. Should legal recourse be taken against the Donovans if they refuse to allow Thomas to have the injections?

3. How much, if any, weight should be given to the expressed desires of Thomas? Remember that Thomas is five years old and developmentally disabled.

The Schott Case

1. Should a transfusion be ordered for Ms. Schott considering her reiterated refusal? If so, what are the grounds for justifying not honoring her explicit refusal of treatment?

2. Should the fact that Ms. Schott's injuries are the result of an apparent suicide attempt be used as a basis for ignoring her expressed desires regarding refusal of treatment? Consider the case included at Appendix H.

The Brahma Case

1. What is the proper course of action in light of Conrad's diagnosis and prognosis?

2. Should decision-making authority be taken away from Conrad's parents? If so, who should be authorized to make decisions on behalf of Conrad?

The Constanza and Phillips Cases

1. In light of Mr. Constanza's ex-wife refusing to take custody of their daughter, should Mr. Constanza be ordered to undergo the procedure? How much weight should be given to the fact that Commune members are willing to adopt Mr. Constanza's daughter?

2. What should be done in Suzy Phillips' case?

3. Should cases like those of Suzy Phillips and Thomas Donovan, where an ailment exists which is not life-threatening but which may be painful or cause permanent injury, be treated differently than cases in which an ailment or injury threatens the life of a child? If so, what principles should be applied to make treatment decisions in each type of case?

CHAPTER 7

ASSISTED REPRODUCTIVE TECHNOLOGY

THE BUSINESS OF MAKING BABIES

INSTRUCTIONS AND OBJECTIVES

This chapter presents issues arising from use of artificial reproductive technology services offered by the fictitious Beginnings Fertility Clinic. The case study describes services offered by Beginnings Fertility Clinic and sets forth materials used by Beginnings to market its services and solicit sperm and ova donors. Participants are called upon to deal with issues of ethics, law, and public policy, as those issues arise from use of assisted reproductive technologies. Technologies at issue include: artificial insemination; in vitro fertilization; cryogenic preservation of sperm and embryos; sperm and ova donation; and surrogacy arrangements. Issues presented ask participants to balance the rights of individuals against public policy considerations. Additionally, the role assignments include several roles for participants who are seeking to resolve conflicts and the role of an arbitrator who has authority to issue decisions.

THE CASE STUDY

Welcome to Beginnings Fertility Clinic. We strive to provide complete fertility services for individuals and couples faced with reproductive difficulties. The following materials provide information about the services provided by Beginnings Fertility Clinic. Beginnings provides a full range of artificial insemination, in vitro fertilization, and surrogacy services. Beginnings also maintains a catalog of sperm and ova donors and a supply of cryogenically preserved embryos made from donor sperm and ova. The following materials describe the services offered by Beginnings Fertility Clinic.

Artificial Insemination Services

Beginnings provides a panoply of artificial insemination services using your donated sperm, anonymously donated sperm, sperm selected from our catalog of qualified donors, or a mixture of any of those. Artificial insemination is a simple procedure whereby sperm is placed in the vagina with a syringe. This procedure is performed at the time of ovulation to optimize chances of pregnancy. Sperm may be provided by a known donor, such as the recipient woman's husband, or the recipient woman may choose to utilize sperm from our catalog of over 200 qualified donors. All sperm supplied by Beginnings is screened for disease and other abnormalities. Should prenatal testing indicate that a fetus resulting from sperm supplied by Beginnings is genetically or otherwise abnormal, termination services will be provided free of charge regardless of the source of the fetal abnormality (restrictions apply, consult a Beginnings representative for complete details). An excerpt of our catalog of sperm donors is included with this packet of information, but if you don't see what you're looking for, have no fear there are 200 more donors where these came from!

In Vitro Fertilization Services

Beginnings Fertility Clinic provides comprehensive in vitro fertilization ("IVF") services with any combination of supplied or donated sperm and ova. IVF is the process whereby ova are harvested from a woman through aspiration. The ova are then fertilized with sperm in our laboratory. The resulting fertilized ova are then placed in the woman designated to carry the child. If for any reason you or your mate is unable to carry the child, Beginnings provides full surrogacy services. Available options for sperm and ova selection for IVF include:
  1. Your supplied ova can be fertilized with your supplied sperm. This is convenient for couples who would like to cryogenically preserve the resulting fertilized ova for later implantation or for clients utilizing the services of a surrogate.
  2. Your supplied ova can be fertilized with donated sperm. This option is particularly good for the woman who wishes to have a child but who cannot become impregnated by her partner or for the woman who does not have a partner and/or who wishes to hire the services of a surrogate.
  3. Donated ova can be fertilized with your supplied sperm. This plan works well for single men desiring to have children or for couples where the woman cannot supply the ova. Beginnings has an active enrollment of over 100 women willing to donate their ova upon request for this procedure. Unfortunately, due to the deterioration that occurs to unfertilized ova, Beginnings does not maintain a supply of unfertilized, donated ova in stock.
  4. Donated ova can be fertilized with donated sperm. The resulting fertilized ova can then be implanted in you or your partner, implanted in a surrogate, or cryogenically preserved for future use.

Whatever your needs or concerns, one of these plans should be right for you. Please consult the enclosed biographies of Beginnings' highly qualified sperm and ova donors and surrogates for more information.

Surrogacy Services

Beginnings employs a number of highly qualified surrogates. Beginnings' surrogates are all in excellent health and free from communicable diseases. All surrogates retained by Beginnings have children of their own and so they know what to expect from pregnancy and childbirth. All surrogates are contractually bound to remain drug-free at all times and they are required to abstain from drinking alcohol, smoking, and engaging in any risky behavior during pregnancy. All efforts are taken to ensure the success of the pregnancy and the health of the child.

We hope you find what you are looking for, and that in the end you come home to Beginnings because this really is *Where Dreams Are Conceived!*

SAMPLE SPERM DONORS

Sperm donor: "Mark"

Age: 45
Race: African American
Hair: Brown   Eyes: Brown
Height: 6'2"   Weight: 210
Employment: International Tax Attorney
IQ: 162
Interests: Mark enjoys tennis and played football in college. Mark is also an avid traveler, photographer, and an excellent pianist.

Sperm donor: "Dennis"

Age: 19
Race: Caucasian
Hair: Blond   Eyes: Green
Height: 5'10"   Weight: 160
Employment: Student Majoring in Business at an Ivy League university
IQ: Above Average
Interests: Dennis enjoys playing lacrosse. He is Social Chairman of his fraternity and captain of his school's debate team.

Sperm donor: "Kyle"

Age: 21
Race: Caucasian
Hair: Brown   Eyes: Blue
Height: 6'0"   Weight: 180
Employment: Professional Kickboxer
IQ: Average
Interests: Kyle enjoys snowboarding, sky-diving, and riding his motorcycle.

Statement of Sperm Donation Policy. Upon the request of the recipient, and for a set fee, Beginnings will discontinue use of any sperm donor whose donation is used to produce a child. Beginnings does recommend that before you request retirement of a donor, you obtain surplus specimens that can be cryogenically stored for your future use so that all of your children can have the same biological father.

SAMPLE OVA DONORS

Ova donor: "Eve"

Age: 22
Race: Hispanic
Hair: Brown   Eyes: Hazel
Height: 5'5"   Weight: 110
Employment: Student Majoring in Dramatic Arts
IQ: 130
Interests: Eve enjoys singing, dancing, and acting. She is an accomplished flautist and enjoys oil painting in her spare time.

Ova donor: "Rhonda"

Age: 24
Race: Caucasian
Hair: Blond   Eyes: Blue
Height: 5'10"   Weight: 128
Employment: Cheerleader Coach and PE Instructor
IQ: Average
Interests: Rhonda enjoys horseback riding, skiing, and hang-gliding. On the weekends, Rhonda spends her time Salsa dancing and sun-bathing.

Ova donor: "Candace"

Age: 19
Race: Asian
Hair: Black   Eyes: Brown
Height: 5'2"   Weight: 110
Employment: Pre-med Student at U.C. Berkeley
IQ: 168
Interests: Candace is fluent in four languages, proficient at playing the violin, and enjoys painting with watercolors.

SAMPLE SURROGATES

Surrogate: "Mary"

Age: 32
Race: Italian American
Height: 5'9"   Weight: 130
Employment: Kindergarten Teacher
IQ: Above Average
Status: Married for 13 years with four children of her own.
Experience: Mary has acted as a surrogate twice before. On both occasions she delivered healthy babies and experienced no post-partum depression or separation anxiety.
Motivation To Be A Surrogate: Mary wants to share the joy that her children have brought her with other people who are unable to have children on their own.

Surrogate: "Jessica"

Age: 28
Race: Caucasian
Height: 5'8"   Weight: 120
Employment: Artist
IQ: 140
Status: Married for three years with one child of her own.
Experience: Jessica has never been a surrogate before but the birth of her own child was trouble-free and the child was born healthy.
Motivation To Be A Surrogate: Jessica desires to give birth to another child but she and her husband cannot afford another child right now so she wants to give birth for someone else.

Surrogate: "Martha"

Age: 26
Race: African American
Height: 5'9"   Weight: 145
Employment: Stay at home mother
IQ: Average
Status: Married for seven years with four children of her own.
Experience: Martha has served as a surrogate once before and enjoyed the experience very much. All of her births have been trouble-free.
Motivation To Be A Surrogate: Martha simply wishes to be a surrogate to help others have children.

SAMPLE CRYOGENICALLY PRESERVED EMBRYOS

Embryo Number 11572

Embryo sex: Male

Sperm Donor Profile:
"Marcus"
Age: 22
Race: Caucasian
Hair: Blond   Eyes: Blue
Height: 5'11"   Weight: 165
Employment: Medical Student
IQ: 160
Interests: SCUBA diving, ice hockey, and playing guitar.
Marcus' sperm has been used to produce three healthy babies to date.

Ovum Donor Profile:
"Katie"
Age: 26
Race: Caucasian
Hair: Blond   Eyes: Blue
Height: 5'6"   Weight: 118
Employment: Ph.D. Candidate in Molecular Biology
IQ: 165
Interests: Reading, jogging, and travel.
Katie's ova have been used to produce two healthy babies to date.

Embryo Number 11578

Embryo sex: Female

Sperm Donor Profile:
"Jacob"
Age: 45
Race: African American
Hair: Black   Eyes: Brown
Height: 6'0"   Weight: 190
Employment: Newspaper Editor
IQ: 150
Interests: Classical music, horticulture, and old movies.
Jacob's sperm has never been used before but he does have three healthy children of his own.

Ovum Donor Profile:
"Dolorous"
Age: 28
Race: Caucasian
Hair: Brown   Eyes: Brown
Height: 5'5"   Weight: 120
Employment: High School English Teacher
IQ: Average
Interests: Raising angora rabbits, antiques, and vegetarian cuisine.
Dolorous' ova have never been used before and she has no children of her own.

Embryo Number 11590

Embryo sex: Male

Sperm Donor Profile:
"Kevin"
Age: 19
Race: Caucasian
Hair: Brown   Eyes: Green
Height: 6'4"   Weight: 185
Employment: Undergraduate college student studying aeronautical engineering at an Ivy League University
IQ: Considerably above average.
Interests: Kevin likes to sail, travel, and is a jazz aficionado.
Kevin's sperm has been used by approximately 12 couples to produce over 20 healthy babies.

Ovum Donor Profile:
"Susan"
Age: 22
Race: Caucasian
Hair: Blond   Eyes: Blue
Height: 5'10"   Weight: 130
Employment: First year law student
IQ: 150
Interests: Sailing, international travel, and playing saxophone.
Susan's ova have been used to produce one healthy baby.

FLYER DISTRIBUTED BY BEGINNINGS TO SOLICIT SPERM DONORS

Students!

Earn up to $200 per <u>week</u>!

Beginnings Fertility Clinic is actively seeking
Law Students, Medical Students and
Graduate Students
to donate sperm to help couples have children.

100% Confidential
100% Safe

Call 1-800-555-4646 to arrange an appointment.

Pay off your student loans, Pay tuition,
Buy a new car!
It's the easiest money you'll ever make!

FLYER DISTRIBUTED BY BEGINNINGS TO SOLICIT OVA DONORS

Women -- <u>You</u> can Help.

Hundreds of couples can't have children
due to fertility problems.
Now you can help.

Beginnings Fertility Clinic
has the technology to allow you
to help others have the children they can't
have on their own.

Egg donation is safer and easier than ever before.
Call 1-800-555-4747 to find out how you can help.

Monetary compensation is provided.

DISCUSSION QUESTIONS

1. Is the process of artificial insemination ethical? Does the source of the sperm affect the ethical integrity of the act? For example, are the same ethical issues raised by a woman who is artificially inseminated with her husband's sperm as are raised by a woman who is inseminated with donated sperm?

2. Is the process of IVF ethical? What ethical and policy arguments can be raised against IVF? Are those arguments convincing?

3. Is the medical community obligated by the principle of beneficence to provide artificial insemination and IVF services to persons who could not otherwise have children? If so, does the same obligation apply to helping people who could otherwise have children but who elect to utilize one of those procedures for nonmedical purposes, such as convenience?

4. What ethical arguments can be raised against surrogacy? What arguments can be raised in favor of it?

5. Are Beginnings Fertility Clinic's informational materials ethical? Is it acceptable for Beginnings to market its services in this manner?

6. Is it ethical to advertise sperm and ova donors in the ways done by Beginnings? For example, is it ethical for Beginnings to give couples information about the gamete donors and let the recipients pick and choose based on the presumption that the offspring will be similar to their genetic parents? Does this type of marketing degrade the traditional value of biological parenthood?

7. Does a sperm or ova recipient have the right to be fully informed of all characteristics of the gamete donor? What, if any, additional information should be supplied by Beginnings about sperm and ova donors?

8. Is it ethical for Beginnings to provide free services to terminate defective fetuses resulting from donated sperm and/or ova? Can Beginnings ethically guarantee the quality or characteristics of the genetic materials they provide? If so, what recourse should be available if the guarantee is breached before birth? After birth? For example, what legal recourse should be available to a couple receiving a cryogenically preserved embryo from Beginnings if the resulting child born is of a different race or sex than anticipated? What if the child is the carrier of an undesirable genetic characteristic or disorder that could have been, but was not, detected before birth?

9. Is it ethical for Beginnings to maintain a supply of cryogenically preserved embryos for implantation? Can this be distinguished from selling children? If so, how?

10. Are Beginnings' activities consistent with good public policy?

11. Is it ethical for Beginnings to solicit sperm donations from college students? Beginnings mails the flyer included on page 97 to male students attending local universities. Is that ethical? Is it coercive for Beginnings to mail the flyer to male students who are badly in need of money?

12. John, a deeply in debt 19 year old student college student, receives the flyer and visits the clinic for a consultation to donate sperm. What information should be given to John regarding sperm donation? Must John's informed consent be obtained for Beginnings to use his donated sperm in any of the procedures provided by Beginnings?

13. Is it ethical for Beginnings to pay John $400 for two sperm donations and then charge $5,000 to artificially inseminate a woman with John's sperm? Is Beginnings exploiting John?

14. Is it ethical for Beginnings to solicit ova donations with the flyer included at page 98? Is the flyer misleading? Must a woman's informed consent be obtained for Beginnings to use her ova in any the procedures that Beginnings provides?

15. On February 9, 2000, CNN.com reported that a donor recruiting service placed an advertisement in the Stanford University student newspaper offering $100,000 to a suitable ova donor. The advertisement was placed on behalf of a San Francisco couple and stated that the donor must be bright, young, white, and athletic. Are such advertisements ethical? Why or why not?

16. Are ova donation and sperm donation ethically similar acts? What factors should be considered? For example, ova donation is an invasive procedure that causes the donating woman pain, whereas sperm donation is noninvasive and not painful. Does that medical distinction carry any ethical consequences?

17. Does the fact that a woman has a limited number of ova, whereas a man can produce a virtually limitless supply of sperm, distinguish the acts ethically and/or medically?

18. Does the fact that sperm can be cryogenically preserved without deterioration, whereas ova must be fertilized before being cryogenically preserved, ethically distinguish the two acts?

19. Is it ethical to cryogenically preserve fertilized ova? Does permitting that practice constitute good public policy?

20. What should be done with unused fertilized ova? Consider each of the following options:

a. Using the fertilized ova for scientific experimentation;

b. Thawing the fertilized ova and allowing them to deteriorate; and

c. Donating the fertilized ova to infertile couples.

21. Currently no federal law and very little state law exists regulating ova and sperm donation. Should the following activities be regulated:

a. Sperm donation?

b. Ova donation?

c. Cryopreservation of embryos?

d. Surrogacy arrangements?

22. Ms. Black and Mr. Shapiro are both present at today's meeting. Ms. Black is acting as a surrogate for an embryo created with a donated ovum and Mr. Shapiro's sperm. Ms. Black initially agreed to give-up the child for adoption by Mr. Shapiro but she has changed her mind and now wishes to keep the child. How should the Shapiro-Black conflict be resolved?

23. Also present at today's meeting are Ms. McGee and Mr. and Mrs. Smith. Ms. McGee is carrying a fetus created with her ovum and Mr. Smith's sperm. Ms. McGee originally agreed to give birth to the child and then relinquish her rights so that the Smiths could adopt the child, but Ms. McGee has changed her mind. Ms. McGee's change of heart has resulted from the discovery that Mrs. Smith is an alcoholic. Ms. McGee now feels that Mrs. Smith is unfit to be a mother and that the child will be better off with if custody is granted to Ms. McGee. How should the Smith-McGee case be resolved?

24. How are the Smith-McGee and Shapiro-Black conflicts similar? How are they dissimilar?

25. Should assisted reproductive technologies only be made available to married couples? Why or why not? Should the technologies be made available to single persons? To homosexual couples? What public policy issues are raised by each of these questions?

26. Would it be ethical for Beginnings to offer cloning services? Would it be ethical to allow a couple to have a single embryo cloned multiple times so that each of the couple's children was genetically identical but born at different times?

27. What, if any, ethical issues are raised by cloning that are not raised by the other reproductive technologies discussed in this chapter?

28. What are the public policy implications of cloning? Are those implications unique to cloning or are they also raised by use of other reproductive technologies?

SUGGESTED RESEARCH

Internet Research

Recently, there has been a proliferation of sperm banks and fertility clinics advertising their services on-line on the world wide web. A number of those organizations offer catalogs of sperm specimens which provide the physical descriptions of the donors. There has even been discussion of soon being able to order sperm on-line and have it delivered to the buyer's home. The following sites are examples of on-line fertility services:

The Sperm Bank of California: http://www.thespermbankofca.org
Cryos International Sperm Bank Ltd.: http://www.cryos.dk/
The University of California San Francisco IVF Program: http://www.ihr.com/ucsfivf/index.html
Fairfax Cryobank: http://www.fairfaxcryobank.com
Infertility Resources: http://www.ihr.com/infertility

Texts

Annas, George J. *Standard of Care: The Law of American Bioethics*. New York
    City, N.Y.: Oxford University Press, 1993, 61-70.
Munson, Ronald. *Intervention and Reflection: Basic Issues in Medical Ethics*. 4th
    ed. Sudbury, MA: Wadsworth, 1992, 459-519.
Pence, Gregory E. *Classic Cases in Medical Ethics*. 2nd ed. New York City, NY:
    McGraw-Hill, 1995, 93-145.

ROLE ASSIGNMENTS FOR 18 PLUS PARTICIPANTS

1. Mr./Ms. Jefferson, President and CEO of Beginnings
2. Brad Brown, Beginnings Sperm Donor
3. Eric Marx, Beginnings Sperm Donor
4. Nancy Carter, Beginnings Ova Donor
5. Jenny Blake, Beginnings Ova Donor
6. Susan Smith, Potential Beginnings Client
7. Roger Smith, Potential Beginnings Client
8. Whitney Alexander, Potential Beginnings Surrogate
9. Mr./Ms. Hancock, Representative of The Pro-Life Coalition
10. Mr./Ms. Yee, Reproductive Rights Advocate
11. Ms. Black, Pregnant Beginnings Surrogate
12. Mr. Shapiro, Beginnings Client
13. Ms. McGee, Beginnings Surrogate
14. Mr. Smith, Beginnings Client
15. Mrs. Smith, Beginnings Client
16. Willy Ford, Former Beginnings Sperm Donor
17. Mr./Ms. Mitchell, Conceived from Beginnings Services
18. Arbitrator (The role of arbitrator may be assigned to several participants to form
a panel of arbitrators.)

Role Assignment Number 1

Assume the role of Mr./Ms. Jefferson, President and CEO of Beginnings. Argue in
support of the activities of Beginnings Fertility Clinic. Consider the following
propositions:

    1. Beginnings aims to help people have children. Many of the people who come
to Beginnings could not have children without assistance. Most of the people who
criticize the activities of Beginnings are not in need of such services. It is not
equitable to allow reproductively functional people to legislate the morality of those
who need assistance to have children.

    2. To prohibit reproductive assistance breaches the autonomy rights of
individuals to control their own bodies. Such a prohibition also violates the medical
community's duty of beneficence because reproductive assistance is a societal good
to which individuals are entitled.

3. Sperm donation has been accepted for decades as an ethical practice. Without donated sperm, many women and couples would be unable to have children. Furthermore, donated sperm are screened to prevent the spread of disease. Disease prevention not only benefits the prospective parents and children, but society as a whole.

4. Ova donation is the medical equivalent of sperm donation. Arguments against ova donation are sexist and paternalistic.

5. Technology is a tool that enables people to achieve desired ends. Artificial insemination and IVF are examples of technology that should be utilized to aid individuals to have children. Failing to utilize those technologies violates a duty that is owed by the medical profession to those who cannot otherwise have children.

Role Assignment Number 2

Assume the role of Brad Brown, a Beginnings sperm donor. Argue in favor of the activities of Beginnings. Consider the following propositions:

1. You are a graduate student who is desperately short of money. You are paid $200 each time for your weekly donation. That money helps you pay for school. Economically this is a lucrative arrangement.

2. Argue that you a aware of the fact that you may have numerous biological children about whom you have no knowledge but that that is not ethically problematic. You have no responsibility for any of those children and if they bring happiness to others then that justifies the arrangement.

3. Argue that the situation results in no harm to anyone. You get paid and others get the children they want. It is a situation where everyone wins.

4. Argue that because you are healthy, disease free, intelligent, and attractive, society will benefit by you propagating as much as possible.

Role Assignment Number 3

Assume the role of Eric Marx, a Beginnings sperm donor. Argue against the acceptability of sperm donation. Consider the following:

1. Beginnings targeted you for donation by mailing a flyer to your dormitory when you were a sophomore in college. You needed the money so you scheduled an appointment. Beginnings asked questions about your health, the health of your parents, your IQ, and interests. At no time did Beginnings explain to you that your sperm may produce up to hundreds of children that you will never know about. You donated to Beginnings once a week for a year and half before deciding to stop. Beginnings refuses to tell you how many women were fertilized with your sperm or whether your sperm was ever transferred to clinics in other parts of the country.

2. Argue that Beginnings violated your right to be informed when they took your sperm without disclosing the purpose of the donation or the number of times that your sperm might be used.

3. Argue that sperm donation is contrary to good public policy because it produces children who will never know their biological father. That results in people not knowing their medical histories and it frustrates social order. It is possible that you have hundreds of children who do not know their relation to you or to each other. Your unknown children may someday become romantically involved with each other without knowing that they are biologically related to one another. This has clear social and medical consequences

Role Assignment Number 4

Assume the role of Nancy Carter, a Beginnings ova donor. Argue in favor of the activities of Beginnings. Consider the following propositions:

1. Ova donation is the exact equivalent of sperm donation. The extraction process is more invasive and painful but the object harvested is the genetic equivalent of sperm.

2. The principles of autonomy and justice dictate that women should have control over their bodies and their reproductive faculties. To allow sperm donation but disallow ova donation would be sexist and paternalistic. Women must be empowered to determine for themselves whether ova donation is ethically acceptable. It is not the role of government to dictate morality.

3. Reproduction is a fundamental right that cannot be interfered with except in the face of the most pressing legal arguments. Such arguments do not exist in the case of ova donation.

Role Assignment Number 5

Assume the role of Jenny Blake, a former Beginnings ova donor. Argue against the acceptability of ova donation. Consider the following:

1. The pain was horrendous when you donated your ova. Harvesting ova is an invasive, painful procedure that cannot be compared to sperm donation. The processes and experiences of harvesting sperm verses those of harvesting ova differ dramatically. The two processes are medically, ethically, and psychologically distinct. Arguments comparing ova donation to sperm donation should be rejected.

2. Sperm and ova donation are also dissimilar in that men produce sperm throughout their lives, whereas women have only a limited number of ova. With each ova donation up to 8 or 10 ova may be taken. If a woman donates repeatedly she may endanger her future reproductive capacity.

3. Ova donation is not ethically acceptable because it requires the ova to be fertilized before they are stored. Stored ova are often abandoned. The question then

arises as to what to do with the abandoned embryos. To destroy those embryos is the equivalent of abortion on a mass scale.

4. Ova donation is also not acceptable because it most often requires the use of a surrogate. Recent history has shown that surrogacy often results in legal entanglements and custody battles. Those are problems that can be avoided entirely if ova donation is prohibited. Permitting ova donation constitutes bad public policy.

Role Assignment Number 6

Assume the role of Susan Smith, a 42 year old woman who is considering using Beginnings' services. You and your 24 year old husband want very much to have children, but your husband is not ready to accept that responsibility. You fear that if you wait much longer, your own chances of becoming pregnant and successfully carrying a child to term may be jeopardized. You and your husband have, therefore, decided that you want to create several embryos with your ova and your husband's sperm to be cryogenically preserved for future use. In approximately five years, you plan to hire a surrogate to carry two of the embryos to term. You have sought the services of Beginnings to help you accomplish that goal.

Argue that Beginnings provides services that are beneficial to society and to individuals. Also argue that the services that Beginnings provides will become increasingly necessary as more women enter into the workforce and postpone having children so that they can first pursue a career.

Role Assignment Number 7

Assume the role of Roger Smith, a potential Beginnings client. You are a 24 year old man who is married to a 42 year old woman. You and your wife want very much to have children but you are not at point in your life or your career where you want to assume the responsibility of fatherhood. Your wife is worried that if you wait much longer she will not be able to conceive or carry a child to term. You and your wife, therefore, are seeking the services of Beginnings in order to create several embryos with your sperm and your wife's ova. You want those embryos to be cryogenically preserved for your future use. You anticipate hiring a surrogate in about five years to carry two of the embryos to term. You want Beginnings to help you accomplish your goal.

Argue that Beginnings provides services that are valuable to society. Beginnings basically gives people control over their own fertility and allows people to make responsible reproductive choices. Empowering people to take control of their fertility is an objective that individuals should be entitled to pursue without interference from the government or special interest groups. So long as the individuals involved find the services that Beginnings provides to be ethically acceptable, the government, or anyone, else should not interfere.

Role Assignment Number 8

Assume the role of Whitney Alexander, a potential Beginnings surrogate. In making arguments for the acceptability of surrogacy, consider the following:

1. Offering the service of your body to carry a child for someone else is a private decision that you should be able to make without interference from the government or the courts. Attempts of law-makers to regulate surrogacy are sexist and paternalistic.

2. Social good is produced by you carrying a child for someone else. This is because you are in perfect health, you do not smoke, drink, or take drugs. By you carrying the child, rather than someone else who may be less healthy or more prone to destructive behaviors, you are promoting the health of the child and you are saving society money that might otherwise be spent on health care if a less healthy woman carried the child.

3. Even if a woman wants to hire your services for sake of convenience, that is acceptable because it is simply a matter of private contract. So long as all parties freely reach an agreement, the government has no business regulating your private conduct or reproductive choices.

4. You have also volunteered to be an ovum donor, in which case you are willing to be impregnated through artificial insemination and then carry the child to term. Some critics have alleged that this is the equivalent of selling babies, but you see nothing wrong with it. The morality of the act should be determined by the treatment that the child receives. So long as the child is loved and provided for, the arrangement between the parties should not be subject to regulation or scrutiny by uninterested parties.

5. Market forces should be allowed to control the fertility industry. If people think these acts are immoral then they need not take part in them. The law should not interfere with the provision of reproductive services for those who have no ethical problem using them.

Role Assignment Number 9

Assume the role of Mr./Ms. Hancock, a representative of the Pro-Life Coalition. In arguing against the use of technology in reproduction, consider the following propositions:

1. When IVF is used, numerous embryos are created and implanted into the woman. That results in unwanted embryos either in or ex utero. If ex utero, those embryos are often allowed to thaw and then discarded. That is blatant disregard for human life. If the embryos are in utero, unwanted embryos are often selectively terminated. That is abortion. It is disrespectful of the inherent value of human life for the law to condone the use of technology to create and then destroy life. The function of the law should be to preserve the value and sanctity of human life.

2. Social order and the family structure are disrupted by sperm and ova donation. The family structure is the fundamental building block of society. By disrupting formation of the biological family structure, individuals lose their sense of identity. For example, persons created from sperm and ova donation have no knowledge of their family history of disease and, because records are sealed to protect the donors, vital information cannot be obtained. Social order is further disrupted because related individuals who do not know their biological history may become romantically involved with each other later in life. It is reasonably foreseeable that the sperm or ova of one donor will be used to create numerous children who are raised in various families within the same community. Those children may become romantically involved and even have children of their own, not knowing that they are biologically related. That presents the danger of creating genetically inferior children and violating deeply held moral values prohibiting intimate relations among related persons.

3. The fact that some people cannot have children is unfortunate, but social justice does not demand that technology be used to assist them. There is no moral imperative mandating that society, or the medical profession, provide reproductive services that are unnatural and that result in social harm. In fact, the ethical principle of nonmaleficence requires the medical profession to refrain from engaging in harmful activities.

4. Reproductive technologies create enormous risk for errors to be made. Sperm specimens are easily mixed through improper cleaning of laboratory instruments and frozen embryos are easily mismatched or lost. In the past, such errors have resulted in many couples having children produced by sperm or ova other than what they selected. Such errors have even results in parents having children of different races than themselves when that was not their intention.

5. Furthermore, Beginnings' guarantee that they will provide free abortion services to eliminate children with qualities other than those that are planned is socially unacceptable and is the equivalent eugenics.

Role Assignment Number 10

Assume the role of Mr./Ms. Yee, a reproductive rights advocate. Argue in favor of Beginnings' activities. Consider the following propositions:

1. Reproduction is a highly personal activity that is protected as a fundamental right under the U.S. Constitution. As such, reproduction is protected from state intervention except in the case where the state has a compelling interest and where there is no other less restrictive means of achieving the compelling interest except by abridgment of exercise of the fundamental right. Because the activities of Beginnings all concern human reproduction, all of those acts should be given the utmost legal protection.

2. Argue that a utilitarian theory supports the activities of Beginnings. That is because the activities benefit all parties involved. The benefits produced include

children for couples who would otherwise be childless, income for the donors, and a sense of satisfaction for the surrogates. Because all participants are consenting adults, no one can be said to be harmed by the activities.

3. Respect for personal autonomy requires that individuals be allowed to donate sperm, ova, embryos, and surrogacy services.

Role Assignment Number 11

Assume the role of Ms. Black, a pregnant Beginnings surrogate. You are four months pregnant with an embryo that you agreed to carry for Mr. and Mrs. Shapiro. The embryo is the product of Mr. Shapiro's sperm and a donated ovum. In vitro fertilization was used to fertilize the ovum and then it was implanted in you. You signed a contract agreeing to carry the fetus to term and then give it up for adoption by the Shapiros. You have since decided that you would like to keep the child yourself and you have given notice of anticipatory breach of the contract. You are here today to ask the Shapiros to rescind the contract and allow you to keep the infant when it is born. If the Shapiros refuse to rescind the contract, argue that the contract should be declared void. Argue that the contract is fundamentally a contract for the sale of a child and, therefore, inherently unethical and void as against public policy. You have decided that if the contract is found to be valid, you will breach it by aborting the fetus. You certainly cannot be compelled to carry a child against your will--that would be contrary to U.S. case law and your fundamental right to privacy.

Role Assignment Number 12

Assume the role of Mr. Shapiro. You are here today because Ms. Black is a Beginnings surrogate carrying your child. The embryo implanted in Ms. Black was the result of IVF with your sperm and a donated ovum. Ms. Black is here today to seek rescission of the surrogacy contract so that she may keep the child when it is born. Argue that the contract is valid and must be enforced. The child that is being carried is the product of your sperm and the child bears no biological or genetic relation to Ms. Black. Argue that the only relationship Ms. Black has with the fetus is that created by contract. Ms. Black should not be allowed to keep your child. This is a contractual matter and contract law principles must be used to resolve the dispute. Ms. Black should be held to the terms of the contract. If she breaches, she and Beginnings must be held liable for your losses.

Role Assignment Number 13

Assume the role of Ms. McGee, a Beginnings surrogate. You are a Beginnings surrogate who is currently carrying a seven month old fetus. The fetus is the product of your ovum and Mr. Smith's sperm. You were impregnated through artificial insemination. The contractual arrangement between yourself and the Smiths calls for you to relinquish all custody rights upon the birth of the child and allow the Smiths to adopt the child. Since signing the contract you have changed your mind and decided that you want to retain custody of the child. You have made this decision based upon your discovering that Mrs. Smith is an alcoholic. You, therefore, do not believe she is fit to be the mother of your child. Argue that because the child is the product of your own genetic material, you have the same right to custody as does Mr. Smith. Argue that the best interest standard should be applied and that the court should award custody to the parent who will provide for the best interest of the child. Because Mrs. Smith is an alcoholic, she is unfit to take custody.

Role Assignment Number 14

Assume the role of Mr. Smith. You are the biological father of the fetus being carried by Ms. McGee and you and your wife are parties to a surrogacy contract to take custody of the child when it is born. Ms. McGee is here to inform you that she intends to breach the contract and wishes to take custody when the child is born. In addition to being the surrogate, Ms. McGee is also the child's biological mother as she was artificially inseminated with your sperm to create the fetus. Ms. McGee will be arguing that the best interest standard should be applied to award her custody because your wife is an alcoholic. Her argument is basically that because your wife is an alcoholic, it is in the child's best interest to be raised by her instead of by you and your wife. Argue that rather than applying the best interest standard, the court should treat this as it would any other contract case and honor the terms of the contract by awarding you and your wife full custody. Argue that public policy should favor surrogacy in order promote reproductive freedom and, therefore, the terms of surrogacy contracts should be honored and enforced. If Ms. McGee did not want you and your wife to have custody of the child then she should have never entered into the agreement.

Role Assignment Number 15

Assume the role of Mrs. Smith. You are here today because Ms. McGee is carrying a seven month old fetus that was supposed to go to you and your husband upon its birth. Ms. McGee was the ovum donor and is acting as the surrogate. The fetus was created through the artificial insemination of Ms. McGee with your husband's sperm. Ms. McGee now wants to terminate the surrogacy agreement and retain custody of the child when it is born. Ms. McGee argues that because you are an alcoholic, it is in the child's best interest for her to be granted full custody of the child and to raise it herself. Argue that the fact that you have a drinking problem should not be considered because a contractual arrangement exists entitling you and your husband to custody of the child. Argue that the contract terms must be honored. Furthermore, argue that many children have alcoholic parents and that the fact that you have this disease should not be used as a reason to terminate an existing contract or your right to have and raise a child. Also, argue that you have an interest in custody of the child because the child is the product of your husband's sperm. Argue that it would be inconsistent with societal values to award the child to Ms. McGee who is unmarried and who does not have a relationship with the child's biological father. Giving Ms. McGee custody would foster the antiquated notion that biological mothers have greater interests in being with their children than do biological fathers. Such is not the case, and your husband's interest in the child must be given equal weight to that of Ms. McGee. When viewed in light of the custody provisions in the surrogacy contract, it is clear that you and your husband should be granted custody.

Role Assignment Number 16

Assume the role of Willy Ford, a former Beginnings sperm donor. You were recruited as a sperm donor for Beginnings when you were a student in your early twenties. You donated once a week for about eight months but you have not donated in almost six years. Recently, you were diagnosed as having a rare blood disorder that is genetically carried. Because you were placed up for adoption as an infant, you never knew that you were a carrier of the disease due to your adoption records being sealed. You are present at today's meeting to convince Beginnings administrators to inform women who were impregnated with your sperm that their children may be carriers of the disease. You also want Beginnings to destroy any remaining specimens of your sperm that may still be frozen. Also, argue that social order should be preserved whenever possible and that sperm and ova donation inherently frustrate social order and should, therefore, be prohibited.

Role Assignment Number 17

Assume the role of Mr./Ms. Mitchell, the product of a Beginnings embryo. You recently discovered that you were created through use of donated sperm, a donated ovum, and a surrogate. You are present at today's meeting to request that the identities of your genetic parents be revealed to you so that you can obtain the medical history of your biological family. You are also curious as to whether you have any biological siblings or half-siblings. Argue that Beginnings, as a provider of health services, owes you a duty of nonmaleficence and that that duty will be violated if Beginnings refuses to disclose to you your biological family's medical history. That is because you may be genetically predisposed to certain diseases and, thus, be subject to harm if you are not given the information you request.

Role Assignment Number 18

Assume the role of an arbitrator. You are present today to render decisions in the following cases:

1. Who should get custody of the Shapiro-Black baby when it is born? If Ms. Black does not like the custody decision that is rendered, can she be compelled to carry the child to term? If so, what would be the legal and ethical principles relied upon to require her to give birth to the child?

2. Who should get custody of the Smith-McGee baby when it is born? What factors should be considered in making this decision?

3. Should the recipients of Willy Ford's sperm be notified that their children may be carriers of the rare blood disorder? Should Beginnings be ordered to destroy remaining specimens of Mr. Ford's sperm? If it is discovered that Beginnings has frozen embryos in stock that were created with Mr. Ford's sperm, should those embryos be destroyed? If not, should potential recipients be warned that the embryos may carry the disorder?

4. Should Mr./Ms. Mitchell be told who his/her biological parents are? Who his/her biological siblings are? What factors weigh on each side of those issues?

CHAPTER 8

TWINS AND TRANSPLANTS

Choosing Who Lives

INSTRUCTIONS AND OBJECTIVES

This chapter sets forth two highly unusual fact patterns. The first concerns the birth of conjoined twins and raises issues regarding how to evaluate and compare quality of life verses quantity of life considerations. The central issue involves whether the twins can legally and ethically be separated.

The second fact pattern involves a set of twins, both of whom have fatal conditions, but one of whom can be saved by a heart transplant from the other. This fact pattern requires analysis of when, if ever, it is legally and ethically acceptable to hasten the death of one individual to save the life of another.

The case study includes role assignments for ten participants, including two judges who have authority to order or prevent treatment in each case.

THE CASE STUDY

The following two cases are currently under review at University Hospital. Interested parties are present at today's meeting, as are two judges who have authority to order treatment, or issue restraining orders preventing treatment, in each case.

The Williams Case

Last Wednesday, Marsha Williams was admitted to University Hospital for a cesarean section procedure. Mrs. Williams gave birth to conjoined ("Siamese") twins, Laura and Mary. The twins are joined at the abdomen and share a common liver. Both twins suffer from intestinal tract damage. The twins are positioned in such a way that they are essentially facing each other, each looking over the shoulder of the other. If not separated, the twins are predicted to have a 60 percent chance of surviving one year and a 30 percent chance of surviving two years. Doctors predict that it is almost certain that, if not separated, both twins will die before the age of three.

Doctors have determined that if the twins are surgically separated, one of the twins will have a chance of surviving but the other twin will die as a result of the separation procedure. Either twin may be chosen to be the survivor as there is no medical condition demonstrating that either twin would have a better chance of surviving the procedure than the other twin. It is expected that if the separation procedure is successful, the twin selected to live will have a 75 percent chance of living a normal life. The other twin is given no chance of surviving the separation.

The Atherton Case

Margie Atherton endured a high-risk pregnancy with many complications. Mrs. Atherton gave birth to twin boys by cesarean section approximately three hours ago. Jason Atherton was born with hypoplastic left heart syndrome. Doctors have determined that due to the severity of the malformation, Jason will not live more than two weeks. Other than the malformed heart, Jason is developmentally normal and healthy. Andy Atherton was born with anencephaly. Andy is not expected to live more than 72 hours. Andy exhibits minimal brainstem functions, including self-sustained respiration, rocking motions, and occasional sounds. Andy reacts involuntarily when subjected to painful stimuli.

DISCUSSION QUESTIONS

The Williams Case

1. Should the twins be separated? What factors should be considered? Can the separation procedure be ethically justified even though it will necessarily end the life of one of the twins? Can electing not to separate the twins be justified considering the impact that it would have on the twins' quality of life?

2. How should quality of life and quantity of life factors be weighed against each other? For example, can the fact that one twin can be given the opportunity to live a normal life expectancy be used to justify terminating the life of the other twin?

3. Would the separation procedure be ethically acceptable if the twins would live a normal life expectancy if not separated? Remember, the separation procedure will end the life of one the twins. How do quantity of life verses quality of life factors affect your analysis of that situation?

4. Does the bioethical principle of distributive justice require that the twins be left conjoined so that each twin can live her natural life expectancy?

5. Is an ethical duty of nonmaleficence owed to the twin who will not survive the procedure? If so, does performing a surgery that will necessarily kill her violate that duty? If that duty is violated, can the violation be justified?

6. Does a strictly utilitarian approach justify performing the operation? What does a deontological approach dictate?

7. Should the best interest standard be implemented to determine appropriate treatment in this case? If so, whose best interest should be valued most highly?

8. Is the separation procedure legal? Assuming the criminal code provision included at Appendix K to be valid law in this jurisdiction, can the separation procedure be legally performed knowing that it will kill one of the twins?

9. Should the separation procedure be performed?

The Atherton Case

1. If protection from criminal prosecution is guaranteed, and it is determined that the likelihood of success is greatly enhanced if the heart transplant is immediately performed, should the transplant from Andy to Jason be performed before Andy meets the statutory definition of death?

2. Assuming the criminal code provision included at Appendix K to be valid law in this jurisdiction, is conducting the transplant legal knowing that the removal of Andy's heart will hasten his inevitable death?

3. Does Andy have an inviolable right to life regardless of how short that life may be? What weight should be given to the argument that all life, regardless of quantity or quality, is sacred and must not be violated? How does that argument compare with a strictly utilitarian approach in this case?

4. How does this case compare to the Williams case? Are the two sets of twins in analogous situations? Are the proposed procedures analogous? If not, why not? Does adherence to the principle of justice dictate that these two cases be treated similarly?

5. What effect does application of the case *In re T.A.C.P*, included at Appendix L, have on the facts presented?

6. Would your analysis be altered if Jason and Andy were not twins but both of their parents agreed to the transplant?

CASE UPDATES

The Williams Case

Doctors have found no medical criteria indicating that either Mary or Laura would have a better chance at surviving the surgical separation procedure, however, two other conditions have been discovered. First, doctors believe that Mary may be either partially or completely deaf. It is too early to determine the exact extent of Mary's deafness but doctors have determined that her hearing is significantly impaired. Second, Laura has a large birth mark on her face. The birth mark is not medically significant but it may be aesthetically undesirable when Laura gets older.

The Atherton Case

A prominent bioethicist has phoned to suggest that a "double heart transplant" be conducted in which the heart of each twin would be transplanted into the body of the other. This course of action has been suggested because it will give Jason the optimal chance of successfully receiving Andy's heart and living a normal life while not hastening the death of Andy. It is argued that Andy would not be harmed because he would most likely die from complications of anencephaly before he would die from complications due to the malformed heart.

ADDITIONAL DISCUSSION QUESTIONS

The Williams Case

1. Should the fact that Mary is most likely hearing impaired be used as grounds to select Laura as the twin who will live? Should the fact that Laura has a birth mark be used as grounds to select Mary as the twin who will live?

2. Doctors have determined that Mary's hearing impairment is the result of her cochlea not properly developing. Doctors have determined, however, that if Mary is selected to be the surviving twin, they will be able to perform a cochlear transplant after the separation procedure which would transplant Laura's cochlea into Mary. Would it be ethical to perform the cochlear transplant?

3. Doctors have determined that if Laura is chosen to be the surviving twin they can perform a skin graft from Mary to Laura which would eliminate the unsightly birth mark on Laura's face. Would it be ethical for the skin graft to be performed?

4. Given the updated information, what course of action should be taken?

The Atherton Case

1. Is the performance of a double heart transplant ethically acceptable? Is it ethically acceptable to subject Andy to an operation from which he will derive no benefit?

2. In some instances, where an individual is deemed not to have capacity to make a decision on his or her own behalf, the standard of substituted judgment is used. Under that standard, an interested party, such as a parent or a court, will make a treatment decision which is intended to be the decision that the affected party would make if he or she had capacity to make the decision without assistance. The substituted judgment standard is discussed in the case of *Strunk v. Strunk* which is included at Appendix M.

Can the substituted judgment standard be implemented to justify conducting the double heart transplant? Can that standard be used to justify a single heart transplant from Andy to Jason?

3. Is it reasonable to expend resources to transplant Jason's heart into Andy when

it is known that Andy will not live for more than a week? Would such a procedure be medically futile?

4. Should the transplant be attempted? If so, should it be a single transplant or a double transplant?

SUGGESTED RESEARCH

Statutes

Appendix K: Sample Penal Code Statute.

Case Law

Appendix L: *In re T.A.C.P.* 609 So.2d 588 (Fla. 1992).
Appendix M: *Strunk v. Strunk*, 445 S.W. 2d 145 (Ky. Ct. App. 1969).

Texts

Annas, George J. *Standard of Care: The Law of American Bioethics.* New York City, N.Y.: Oxford University Press, 1993, 234-39.
Beauchamp, Tom L. and Childress, James F. *Principles of Biomedical Ethics.* 4th ed. New York City, N.Y.: Oxford University Press, 1994, 45-62 and 193-96.
Pence, Gregory E. *Classic Cases in Medical Ethics.* 2d ed. New York City, NY: McGraw-Hill, 1995, 253-71 and 327-35.

ROLE ASSIGNMENTS FOR TEN PARTICIPANTS

1. Marsha Williams
2. Advocate Representing the Interests of Laura Williams
3. Advocate Representing the Interests of Mary Williams
4. Dr. Browning, the Williams' Pediatrician
5. Judge Burbank
6. Margie Atherton
7. Advocate Representing the Interests of Jason Atherton
8. Advocate Representing the Interests of Andy Atherton
9. Dr. Lucas, the Athertons' Pediatrician
10. Judge Mitchell

Role Assignment Number 1

Assume the role of Marsha Williams. You are present today because you are being faced with an impossible choice. You simply cannot bring yourself to choose which of your children is going to live and, yet, you cannot imagine allowing them to live conjoined. Listen carefully to all arguments and comments made at today's meeting. At the end of the meeting, you will be called on to decide upon a course of action. Be prepared to provide your reasoning and the factors which affect your decision.

Role Assignment Number 2

Assume the role of an advocate representing the interests of Laura Williams. You are present today to represent the best interests of Laura. While participating in today's discussion, consider the following propositions:

1. To allow the twins to live conjoined is effectively the same as choosing to allow both to die. Affording both of the twins the opportunity to live for two or three years does not outweigh the quality and quantity of life that one twin could attain if they are separated.

2. The fact that Mary is deaf will affect her quality of life if she is chosen to be the surviving twin.

3. If Mary is chosen to live, she will likely require the cochlear transplant. That procedure is invasive and may not be successful. It would be futile to expend the resources required to perform the cochlear transplant when those resources could be saved simply by choosing Laura to be the surviving twin. Additionally, if Laura is chosen to be the surviving twin, and the cochlear transplant is not performed, a great deal of resources will be required to teach her and her parents sign language.

4. The fact that Laura has a birth mark on her face is not medically significant and should not be considered as a factor against choosing Laura to survive.

5. Argue that Laura should be chosen to survive and that the skin graft from Mary to Laura should be performed.

Role Assignment Number 3

Assume the role of an advocate representing the interests of Mary Williams. While participating in today's discussion, formulate arguments to protect Mary's best interests. Consider the following propositions:

1. To allow the twins to live conjoined is effectively the same as choosing to allow both to die. Affording both of the twins the opportunity to live for two or three years does not outweigh the quality and quantity of life that one twin could attain if they are separated.

2. Mary's hearing impairment should not be considered as a factor weighing against choosing her to live because it has no bearing on the success of the separation procedure.

3. Mary's hearing impairment can be corrected through the cochlear transplant.

Certainly, Laura would want Mary to be given her cochlea if she was capable of making that decision.

4. To elect to allow Laura to live because Mary is deaf amounts to nothing short of discriminating against Mary because she is hearing impaired.

5. Argue that Mary should be chosen to live and that the cochlear transplant should be performed.

Role Assignment Number 4

Assume the role of Dr. Browning, the Williams' pediatrician. You are present today to attest to the fact that there is no objective medical criteria that indicates that either Laura or Mary would have a better chance of surviving the separation procedure. You are also here to attest to the fact that one of the twins will necessarily die as a result of the separation.

Formulate arguments in favor of leaving the twins conjoined in order for each of them to live out her natural life expectancy. Consider the following propositions:

1. The surgical separation is an invasive procedure that will put both twins at risk. Although doctors have given estimates of the likelihood of the procedure being successful, it is possible that neither twin would survive the procedure.

2. Leaving the twins conjoined would allow each of them to have an opportunity at life. They may even live longer conjoined than doctors have predicted.

3. If the twins are separated, one of them will necessarily be killed. It is not ethically acceptable to kill one twin to save the other.

Role Assignment Number 5

Assume the role of Judge Burbank. You are present today to order treatment, or to issue a restraining order preventing treatment, if you do not agree with the treatment decision made by Mrs. Williams. Carefully listen to all arguments presented at today's meeting and review the materials included in the Appendices. Be prepared to provide your reasoning for either affirming or overruling Mrs. Williams' decision.

Role Assignment Number 6

Assume the role of Margie Atherton. You are present today in order to seek assistance in making the very difficult decision of how to treat your sons. Listen carefully to all arguments and comments made at today's meeting. At the end of the meeting, you will be called on to decide upon a course of action with regard to treating your sons. Be prepared to provide your reasoning and the factors which affect your decision.

Role Assignment Number 7

Assume the role of an advocate representing the best interests of Jason Atherton. Argue in favor of transplanting Andy's heart into Jason's body as soon as possible. Consider the following propositions in formulating your arguments:

1. Removing Andy's heart will not harm Andy because Andy does not manifest the characteristics of human life, or the potential to manifest those characteristics, that generally demand protection. For example, Andy is not now, nor will he ever be, self-conscious or capable of engaging in higher brain activities. Additionally, it is not possible for Andy to survive for any significant length of time. Therefore, removing Andy's heart from his body will not affect his quality of life and it will only minimally affect his quantity of life.

2. Jason's condition can be treated and he can live a normal life if he receives a heart transplant. Because Jason and Andy are twins, Andy is a perfect donor match for Jason. It is likely that Jason will die before a suitable donor heart becomes available if he is placed on an organ recipient waiting list.

3. Application of both the best interest standard and the substituted judgment standard require that Andy's heart be given to Jason. The procedure should be performed as soon as possible, and before Andy is legally dead in order to optimize the chances of success.

Role Assignment Number 8

Assume the role of an advocate representing the best interests of Andy Atherton. Argue that Andy must be respected as a human being and treated with dignity even though he suffers from anencephaly. Consider the following propositions in formulating your arguments:

1. Andy breathes on his own, his eyes are open, he makes involuntary noises, and he moves when subjected to painful stimuli. Andy is alive.

2. Andy's heart should not be removed from his body before Andy is declared legally dead. To do so would be to treat Andy as a means to an end rather than as a human being deserving of respect.

3. A double heart transplant should not be performed. To do so would be to subject Andy to a highly invasive medical procedure that would provide no benefit to Andy.

4. Andy should be allowed to live his life regardless of how short or qualitatively compromised his life may be.

Role Assignment Number 9

Assume the role of Dr. Lucas, the Athertons' pediatrician. You are present today to attest to the medical conditions of Andy and Jason. In your medical opinion, Andy will most likely not live more than 72 hours. Andy will never be capable of higher brain functions because he completely lacks development of a cerebrum and cerebellum. The signs of life that Andy exhibits are all involuntary reflexes.

Jason will likely not live more than two weeks without a heart transplant. With a heart transplant, Jason will potentially live a normal life.

In order for the success of a heart transplant from Andy to Jason to be optimized, the heart must be transplanted as soon as possible. Andy's heart will likely be deteriorated beyond the point of being suitable for transplant if you wait until Andy is legally dead to perform the transplant. You have tested the twins and determined that Andy is a perfect organ donor match for Jason. It is almost certain that Jason will die if he is placed on an organ recipient waiting list.

Role Assignment Number 10

Assume the role of Judge Mitchell. You have authority to order treatment, or to issue a restraining order preventing treatment, in the Atherton case. Carefully listen to all arguments presented and review the materials included in the Appendices. At the end of today's meeting you will be called upon to either affirm or overrule the treatment decision made by Mrs. Atherton. Be prepared to provide the basis for your decision.

CHAPTER 9

FREE ABORTION SERVICES AND
FETAL TISSUE RESEARCH

Freedom of Choice and Coercion

INSTRUCTIONS AND OBJECTIVES

This chapter sets forth and scrutinizes the business activities of the fictitious Freedom America Women's Clinic. The Clinic is engaged in the business of providing free late-term abortion services and selling the abortuses to a laboratory in Central America. The issues raised by the case study are primarily twofold. First, issues are raised concerning whether providing free abortion services, or paying women to have abortions, is ethically acceptable when targeted at vulnerable populations, particularly destitute women. This issue is intensified by the fact that the Clinic profits from use of the abortuses. Second, issues are raised as to whether it is acceptable for fetal tissue to be used for medical experimentation and commercial purposes. This issue is intertwined with the issue of whether it is acceptable to impose U.S. ethical standards on activities that occur in another country or whether so doing constitutes "ethical imperialism."

The issues presented in this case study are of a sensitive nature. Yet, the issues presented are implicit to analysis of issues such as fetal tissue research, the right of individuals to control their own bodies, and treatment of vulnerable populations. The underlying issues all relate, on some level, to the interconnection of law and ethics and instances where legally permissible activities might be deemed ethically unacceptable.

THE CASE STUDY

The American Academy of Legal and Medical Ethics is composed of physicians, attorneys, public policy specialists, and moral philosophers. The purpose of the Academy is to foster open debate on contemporary issues in applied ethics. The topic of today's discussion concerns the recent practices of two affiliated abortion clinics. The controversy caused by the clinics is outlined below.

123

Beginning in October 1998 and continuing to the present, the Freedom America Women's Clinic, with locations in East St. Louis and South Central Los Angeles, has run the following advertisement:

Medical Research Project Seeks Volunteers

The Freedom America Women's Clinic is currently seeking pregnant women who are between three and five months gestation who seek to terminate their pregnancies. The Freedom America Women's Clinic will provide qualifying women with termination services free of charge and appropriate follow-up care. Volunteers must be 18 years of age and in good health. For further information call 555-7362 or visit one of our locations.

Upon investigation of Freedom America, it has been discovered that the clinics provide free abortion services to women who meet three conditions. First, the woman must be at least 18 years of age. Second, the woman must be free of serious medical conditions. Third, the woman must sign the following agreement:

I, _____, understand that Freedom America Women's Clinic will provide abortion services to me free of charge. I understand that Freedom America may, at their election, use biological and genetic materials resulting from the abortion for purposes determined by Freedom America to be in the interest of science or otherwise useful or beneficial. I understand that I may not now, nor at any future time, claim any interest in the scientific or business affairs of Freedom America or any of its associated enterprises.

Signature: _____   Date: _____

Ninety percent of women responding to the advertisement have been found to qualify for free abortion services so long as the agreement is signed. Women volunteers are given free abortions and follow-up care, which often includes one or more hot meals and up to 48 hours clinic stay. A counselor is provided for women who express emotional discomfort after receiving an abortion. Several women have been comforted with statements indicating that science will benefit from their own misfortune.

Women receiving abortions are not informed of the uses to which Freedom America puts the aborted fetuses and placenta. Freedom America has three uses for those materials. The first involves dissection of the fetus and sale of various tissues to laboratories around the world. The laboratories conduct experiments on the tissue and, in some instances, use elements extracted from fetal tissue in the manufacture of medications.

The second use involves the sale of fetal tissue, skin cells in particular, and the placenta to cosmetic companies. The cosmetic companies extract various substances, including proteins, from the placenta for use in manufacturing make-up, anti-aging products, and lotions. The fetal skin tissue is used by cosmetics companies to test skin and hair products for possible irritants and toxins.

The third use involves dissection of the fetus and the preservation in liquid nitrogen of fetal brain cells, pituitary glands, lung and liver cells, and bone marrow. By contractual arrangement, the preserved fetal cells are sold and shipped to a laboratory in the small Central American Republic of Guadaladora. In Guadaladora, treatments are conducted which involve the implantation of the living fetal cells into human beings. The fetal tissue has been used in treatments for Parkinson's disease, Down's syndrome, diabetes, stroke, impotence, and male pattern baldness. The Guadaladoran laboratory caters mostly to wealthy individuals from Europe, Asia, and the Middle East. Treatments cost between $10,000 and $100,000 depending upon the ailment and the type of fetal tissue implantation required. Abortion is strictly prohibited under Guadaladoran law and both the woman aborting and the doctor performing the procedure are subject to fines and imprisonment. Guadaladoran law, however, does not regulate or prohibit the importation of or experimentation on fetal tissue. All activities of the laboratory in Guadaladora are legal under local law, though they would be prohibited from occurring in the United States.

Freedom America has grossed nearly four million dollars to date from the sale of fetal tissue. Plans are currently underway to open additional abortion clinics in Philadelphia, New Orleans, and Detroit.

DISCUSSION QUESTIONS

1. Is the solicitation of women to undergo pregnancy termination ethically acceptable? Is Freedom America encouraging women to abort? Is it coercing women? If Freedom America is encouraging or coercing women, is that ethically acceptable?

2. What are the public policy implications of encouraging women to have abortions?

3. Is Freedom America's advertisement misleading? Are the women really "research volunteers?"

4. Does the fact that the abortion clinics are located in poor and lower middle class areas make the practice ethically suspect? If Freedom America were to admit that poor women are targeted by the advertisements, would that affect the acceptability of the advertisements?

5. Does the fact that Freedom America will only give free services to women who are at least three months pregnant make the practice ethically suspect? Note that Freedom America does not offer free services to women who are less than three months pregnant because such fetuses are not developed to a state that the tissue can be profitably utilized.

6. An important aspect of Freedom America's policy of only providing services to women between three and five months gestation concerns the abortion technique that is utilized. The standard method for performing abortions up to three months gestation is vacuum suction curettage. That procedure takes approximately ten minutes and recovery is fast. There is usually some bleeding and possibly cramps. The abortion method utilized by Freedom America is the evacuation procedure. That method is considered the safest method for aborting after three months gestation. The evacuation procedure involves causing the uterus to contract with a prostaglandin hormone so that the fetus is expelled as in natural labor. That procedure may take up to 12 hours and the woman may be required to stay at the Freedom America clinic for 24 to 48 hours. The time required for the procedure and length of clinic stay afterward depend upon the gestation of the fetus. The evacuation method also incurs greater pain and inconvenience to the woman. Mortality rates for vacuum suction curettage are fewer than 1 per 100,000 procedures. The mortality rate for the evacuation procedure is 3 per 100,000. Freedom America has not had any fatalities resulting from services provided to date.

Is Freedom America's practice of only providing evacuation procedures, and not vacuum suction curettage, ethically acceptable? Does the fact that early-term fetuses cannot be profitably utilized by Freedom America justify the clinic's refusal to terminate those pregnancies? Can the argument be made that Freedom America is putting women through greater pain and greater risk for Freedom America's own financial gain? Is the greater risk justified by the fact that Freedom America does not charge for its services?

7. The St. Louis Freedom America clinic refers women who are less than three months pregnant to other clinics. The Los Angeles clinic generally advises such women that they are welcome to take advantage of Freedom America's free services upon reaching three months gestation. Are either of those practices ethically acceptable? Is the practice of the Los Angeles clinic coercive or exploitive? Does that practice violate the principle of either nonmaleficence or autonomy?

8. Does the use to which the fetal tissue is put affect the ethical integrity of the practice of offering free abortion services? What, if any, ethical distinctions can be made between the following acts:

a. Experimenting on the fetal tissue;
b. Implanting live fetal cells into human recipients;
c. Using fetal by-products to manufacture and test cosmetics; and
d. Disposing of the tissue as medical waste.

Are any of the acts, in themselves, ethically unacceptable? If so, why?

9. Can an act which is ethically suspect be economically justified?

10. Does the act of implanting live fetal cells into a human being have any unique ethical significance? If so, why?

11. Does treating a serious ailment, such as Parkinson's disease, warrant the use of ethically suspect procedures that might not be acceptable for the treatment of a less serious disorder? For example, should a more intense level of ethical scrutiny be

applied to use of fetal tissue to treat male pattern baldness than is used to evaluate use of fetal tissue to treat Parkinson's disease or Down's syndrome?

12. If other noncontroversial treatments are available, should such treatments be preferred over ethically questionable treatments? What if the ethically questionable treatment is less expensive or more readily available to more patients?

13. Do scientists and physicians have an ethical obligation to conduct experiments using fetal tissue if such experiments have a reasonable probability of success?

14. Should women responding to the advertisement be informed of the specific uses to which the fetal tissue is put?

15. Should women be required to give informed consent to the specific uses to which their fetal tissue is put? If so, what are the public policy implications of requiring that informed consent?

16. Do women have a right to know that Freedom America is profiting from use of the fetal tissue? Are the women entitled to any of the profits? Consider application of *Moore v. The Regents of the University of California* included at Appendix N.

17. Would it be ethically acceptable for Freedom America to compensate women for receiving abortions? Freedom America is considering use of the following advertisement. Is it ethically acceptable?

Medical Research Project Seeks Volunteers

Freedom America Women's Clinic seeks fetal tissue for scientific and commercial uses. Qualified women may receive free abortion services and be compensated $25 to $50 for donating the tissue from their unwanted pregnancy. To qualify, women must be at least 18 years of age, in good health, between three and five months pregnant, and wish to terminate their pregnancy. For further information call 555-7362 or visit one of our locations.

18. Can the "donation" of fetal tissue be likened to the donation of blood or sperm, for which compensation is often provided? What factors distinguish donation of fetal tissue from donation of blood or sperm?

19. Freedom America sells the fetal tissue to the laboratory in Guadaladora because implantation of fetal tissue into human beings is illegal in the United States. Is it ethical for Freedom America to collect fetal tissue in the United States for the purpose of using it abroad for uses which are prohibited in the United States?

20. Should U.S. ethical standards prohibiting fetal tissue implantation be used to condemn the activities of the Guadaladoran laboratory? If so, does that constitute ethical imperialism?

SUGGESTED RESEARCH

Case Law

Appendix N: *Moore v. Regents of the University of California*, 793 P.2d 479 (1990).

Texts

Annas, George J. *Standard of Care: The Law of American Bioethics.* New York City, N.Y.: Oxford University Press, 1993, 181-86.
Engelhardt, H. Tristam. *The Foundations of Bioethics.* 2nd ed. New York City, N.Y.: Oxford University Press, 1996, 271-77.
Munson, Ronald. *Intervention and Reflection: Basic Issues in Medical Ethics.* 4th ed. Belmont, CA: Wadsworth, 1992, 47-102.
Pence, Gregory, E. *Classic Cases in Medical Ethics.* 2nd ed. New York City, NY: McGraw-Hill, 1995, 146-73.

ROLES ASSIGNMENTS FOR 15 PARTICIPANTS

1. Dr. White, Owner and Operator of the Freedom America Women's Clinics
2. Mr./Ms. Benjamin, Chief Financial Officer of Freedom America
3. Dr. Molina, M.D., Director of the Guadaladora Clinic
4. Dr. Washington, Director of Fetal Tissue Experimentation at the University of Guadaladora
5. Dr. Ward, Ph.D., Moral Philosopher and Bioethicist
6. Ellen Potts, Former Patient of Freedom America
7. Helen Forest, Former Patient of Freedom America
8. Jessica North, Former Patient of Freedom America
9. Mr./Ms. Birch, Representative of New Day Cosmetics
10. Dr. Abrahms, M.D., Obstetrician/Gynecologist
11. Dr. Warner, M.D., Physician and Clinical Researcher
12. Dr. Thomas, M.D., Primary Care Physician
13. Mr./Ms. Davis, Esq., Attorney in the Public Interest
14. Dr. Forbes, Ph.D., Clinical Researcher
15. Mr./Ms. Font, Representative of the Advocacy Group Ethics in Medicine Now

Role Assignment Number 1

Assume the role of Dr. White, owner and operator of Freedom America Women's Clinic. In defending your clinics and their activities, consider the following propositions:

1. The women that respond to your clinics' advertisements are seeking abortions. Argue that your clinics do not persuade or bribe women to terminate their pregnancies.

2. The fact that the clinics are located in poor areas is justified because they provide free services to those who need them most.

3. The fact that Freedom America gives free services only to women who have reached three months gestation is a simple matter of economics. The only reason Freedom America provides services free of charge is because the fetal tissue can be sold to cover the expense of providing the abortions. If the fetal tissue had no value, as is the case with lesser developed fetuses, then Freedom America would not provide any free services. Like any other business, Freedom America operates to make a profit.

4. The evacuation technique of abortion is safe. Freedom America seeks women who require such a procedure and does not encourage women to postpone receiving an abortion. It is the woman's personal choice whether to wait a few weeks in order to take advantage of the free services. To prevent women from doing so would violate their autonomy rights. The evacuation procedure is medically accepted, therefore, offering that service for free cannot be unethical.

5. Women have no right to be informed of what is done with the fetuses because the fetuses are medical waste. Besides, the agreement signed by the women constitutes informed consent for Freedom America to use the fetuses as Freedom America deems appropriate. The tissue can be used to save and enhance human lives, therefore, it would be unethical to destroy it.

6. Compensating women for their unwanted fetuses is a good way of spreading the wealth derived from a valuable product. Women would have to be crazy to purposely get pregnant and abort for $25, therefore, that amount of compensation will most likely not increase the number of abortions performed. By providing women with that small amount of compensation, Freedom America is abiding by the principle of distributive justice. Because women are contributing to the research, and to the profits, distributive justice dictates that women should be compensated for their contribution. That compensation is in the form of free services and, possibly, up to $50.

Role Assignment Number 2

Assume the role of Mr./Ms. Benjamin, Chief Financial Officer of Freedom America. In defending the practices of Freedom America, consider the following:

1. Freedom America is simply utilizing a product that has potentially significant health benefits and, therefore, carries a substantial market value. If not for Freedom America, the fetuses would be destroyed. It would be unethical to destroy a product that can potentially save thousands of lives. The abortions will be performed regardless of how the product from the abortion is used. To destroy the fetal cells is the equivalent of killing all the people who could be saved through fetal tissue transplants.

2. The advertisements merely inform women of services of which they can take advantage. It is up to the individual woman whether or not she wants to abort and, if so, whether she wants to take advantage of Freedom America's offer.

3. It was your idea to compensate women for donating their unwanted fetuses. Argue that the compensation is for the woman's pain and time. It is certainly not an amount that makes it worth a woman getting pregnant for purposes of being compensated to have an abortion, but it may make it easier for women who must take time off work to access abortion services. Furthermore, the principle of distributive justice requires that the benefits of medical research be distributed to those who undergo the risk and inconvenience required to conduct the research. By providing free services and a small amount of compensation to the women, Freedom America is distributing some of the benefits resulting from the research to the women who make the research possible.

Role Assignment Number 3

Assume the role of Dr. Molina, Director of the Guadaladora clinic. You have personally overseen the purchase of a large amount of fetal tissue from Freedom America. That tissue has been used to make progress in curing Parkinson's disease and it has been used to treat Down's syndrome, impotence, male pattern baldness, stroke, and diabetes. "Fetal surgery," as you call it, is the medical wave of the future and it represents cures and treatments to many of man's most terrible diseases. The world has an abundant supply of fetal tissue that would be destroyed if not for your work.

Argue that destroying fetal tissue is like destroying the rain forests--both represent an infinite number of treatments and medications that have yet to be discovered. So long as abortion is legal, why should the incidental benefits resulting from abortion be denied?

Furthermore, the acts engaged in by the Guadaladora clinic comply with the bioethical standards and laws of Guadaladora. Argue that American standards cannot be imposed upon your clinic. For bioethicists in the United States to demand that U.S. standards be applied in Guadaladora is ethical imperialism. It represents a paternalistic view that the ethical standards of the United States are superior to those of Guadaladora. It must be recognized that Guadaladora is an autonomous country with its own laws and ethical standards which must be respected.

Role Assignment Number 4

Assume the role of Dr. Washington, Director of Fetal Tissue Experimentation at the University of Guadaladora. Argue that there is an ethical duty on the medical community to utilize fetal tissue in any way that might produce medical benefits. So long as abortion is legal, the only ethical question to be considered regarding abortion is at the individual level. So long as the woman freely chooses the abortion, the practice cannot be condemned because both society and the individual condone it. The use to which the fetal tissue is put cannot be ethically suspect because, although the tissue may be alive at the cellular level, it is not in any way sentient or deserving of special treatment. Besides, even if the tissue were deserving of special treatment, it would make no sense to allow the tissue to be thrown in the garbage instead of being used to save lives. The medical profession has a duty to derive any and all possible benefits from experiments using the fetal tissue.

It is also ethical to use fetal tissue for uses that derive economic but not necessarily medical benefits. Argue that abortion clinics should be permitted to sell the products of abortions for any purpose, including the manufacture and testing of cosmetic products.

Role Assignment Number 5

Assume the role of Dr. Ward, Ph.D., professor of philosophy and bioethics. Argue in favor of the use of fetal tissue experimentation and the practices of Freedom America. Consider each of the following propositions:

1. Abortion is legal. The evacuation procedure used by Freedom America is the recommended procedure for late-term abortions. The women in question freely seek to have abortions at Freedom America and are not persuaded to do so. It cannot be maintained that the women are being coerced or pressured into doing something that they find morally objectionable.

2. Freedom America is profiting from the services that they provide. They prepare and preserve the fetal tissue for transport. All abortion clinics inevitably possess a large quantity of fetal tissue. Freedom America simply utilizes the fetal products in a way that demands a market price.

3. Freedom America's sale of fetal products is analogous to hospitals profiting from donated blood. In both instances, a donated biological product is processed and sold for a profit. In both instances, the product only gains value from the processing and the product is of no value if not properly processed.

4. The use of fetal tissue in transplants and experiments creates a direct benefit, either in the form of an immediate good to the individual undergoing the transplant or in the form of gaining scientific knowledge. That good is gained at no one's expense, therefore, it is not ethically suspect.

5. The use of fetal tissue products in the manufacture of cosmetics is also not ethically objectionable. Because the products are not manufactured at the expense of any individual, the products themselves cannot be ethically suspect. The fetal products are sold to cosmetics companies because they demand a market price. If consumers object to the use of fetal products being used in cosmetics testing and manufacturing then consumers should refrain from purchasing such products.

Role Assignment Number 6

Assume the role of Ellen Potts, a former patient of Freedom America. You visited Freedom America when you were 18 weeks pregnant. You were unsure whether you wanted to abort but you really could not afford to have a child. You could not even afford the hospital bills for the delivery. You were out of work and homeless because you had just been evicted. Freedom America promised that they would take care of you and they did. After an hour-long discussion, you agreed to abort. Freedom America told you that if you decided to abort, they would let you stay in the clinic for two days, give you three free hot meals a day, and that they would make sure that your fetus would be donated to science. They said that your fetus might even be used to help find a cure for a horrible disease. Now that you are back on your feet, you realize that Freedom America made abortion so attractive that you really could not turn it down. At that point in your life you would have done almost anything for a warm bed.

Role Assignment Number 7

Assume the role of Helen Forest, a former patient of the Freedom America Clinic. You initially responded to the clinic's advertisement when you were eight weeks pregnant. You decided to wait until you were 12 weeks pregnant to take advantage of Freedom America's free services. You made that decision, however, from your own free will and you are glad that you did. It was worth waiting the extra few weeks to get the free care and you are glad that the fetus was used to help science. The idea that cells from your fetus might be living on in some other person is rather fulfilling. At least some good came from situation. You also do not object to the fact that Freedom America profited from your abortion, but you believe that Freedom America should be required to share their profits with you by paying you for your fetal tissue.

Role Assignment Number 8

Assume the role of Jessica North, a former patient of Freedom America. You have lived in an abandoned building for four years. You have no heat or water and you only eat when the shelter gives you food. You have had two abortions at Freedom America and they always take good care of you. The first time you had an abortion you were scared but Freedom America convinced you that you could never raise a child. They also gave you a turkey dinner with all of the fixings and you even got to take a shower. The second time you got pregnant you knew you would go back to Freedom America. You waited four months and then went to the clinic. The people at the clinic still remembered you and were glad that you went back to them. If you ever get pregnant again you will go back to Freedom America.

Role Assignment Number 9

Assume the role of Mr./Ms. Birch, a representative of New Day Cosmetics. You favor the business engaged in by Freedom America. Placenta tissue provides your company with proteins that enhance the quality of cosmetics and anti-aging products. Those products have a market value that is determined by consumers. Currently, consumers buy millions of dollars of products each year that contain substances derived from human placental tissue. If the public felt that your company's activities were ethically objectionable then consumers would voice their opinions by not buying your products. That has not happened.

Also argue that it makes sense to use human fetal tissue for testing cosmetics. Results from tests performed on human tissue are more accurate than results of tests performed on animal tissue. In fact, human tissue can be used instead of animal tissue so fewer rabbits and dogs will have to be used. Unlike the animals, fetal tissue is not sentient and it cannot feel pain. Fetal tissue is also ideal because there is such an abundant supply.

Role Assignment Number 10

Assume the role of Dr. Abrahms, an obstetrician/gynecologist. In arguing against the practices of Freedom America, consider the following propositions:

1. By offering free services, free clinic stays, and free hot meals, Freedom America is making it advantageous for lower income and poor women to have abortions. Freedom America is basically luring in poor women so that it can profit from convincing those women to abort. In short, Freedom America is exploiting its patients.

2. If Freedom America wants to act in the public interest, they should provide free services to all women and encourage women to undergo the least invasive and safest abortion procedure possible. Freedom America has an ethical obligation to provide early-term abortions and encourage women seeking abortions to abort as early as possible. Freedom America is causing women to incur greater health risks and increased pain and inconvenience by encouraging them to postpone pregnancy termination. The evacuation procedure also causes a greater financial loss to the women because it requires them to take more time off work. That clearly violates the principle of nonmaleficence.

3. The use to which the fetal tissue is put does affect the ethical integrity of the act of abortion because the tissue is being used without obtaining the informed consent of the women. A woman may believe that it is morally reprehensible for the living tissue of her fetus to be injected into another person. If so, such a woman has the right to object to a part of her own body being exploited in that way. To not allow a woman to refuse consent violates the principle of autonomy.

4. Compensating women for the fetal products is ethically unacceptable because it encourages destitute women to abort. Women must be able to make their own

reproductive decisions without outside influences. Paying women to abort is against public policy and contrary to the health interests of the women.

Role Assignment Number 11

Assume the role of Dr. Warner, a physician and clinical researcher. In arguing against the practices of Freedom America, consider the following propositions:

1. It is well established that the earlier an abortion is performed, the less risk there will be to the woman's health and the less pain and suffering that will be involved. By only providing free later term abortions, Freedom America is putting its own financial interests ahead of the health interests of its patients.

2. Use of fetal tissue has not been proved to effectively treat or cure any disease. The research conducted in Guadaladora is suspect and the profit margins of the Freedom America and Guadaladora clinics are staggering. The "research" being conducted by the Guadaladoran clinic is motivated only by profit and not by public interest. If Freedom America was truly concerned with women's health issues, it would not put its own interests ahead of the health of its patients.

3. Compensating women to abort is ethically unacceptable. That is because it encourages women to incur a risk to their own health for money, and because it will inevitably lead to women being treated as fetus factories. Some women seeking Freedom America's services are so poor that it is conceivable that they would intentionally become pregnant for the purpose of aborting, regardless of the amount of compensation provided. For some women, a warm bed and a couple of hot meals might even be enough to persuade them to abort.

Role Assignment Number 12

Assume the role of Dr. Thomas, a primary care physician and public health researcher. You operate a clinic near the Los Angeles Freedom America Clinic. You have performed some research and found the information set forth below to be true of Freedom America patients. Your study included a random sampling of 100 women who received abortions at the Los Angeles Freedom America Clinic. Of those 100 women, the following is a breakdown by ethnicity:

Ethnicity	Number of Women
African American	41
Hispanic	32
Caucasian/White	19
Asian American	7
Other/Unknown	1

Of the 100 women, the following is a breakdown by income distribution:

Income Distribution Information	
Percentage on welfare/public assistance	63
Percentage living below the poverty line	77
Percentage homeless	13

Based on the foregoing, you believe that Freedom America's practices and advertisements are clearly targeted at underprivileged women who may be easily manipulated and coerced to either have abortions or postpone abortions until after the third month gestation to take advantage of Freedom America's offer of free services. You also found that 25 percent of women surveyed were repeat patients of the Freedom America Clinic.

Argue that some of the Freedom America clients are so desperate that they would become pregnant for purposes of "donating" their fetal tissue in return for even minimal compensation.

Role Assignment Number 13

Assume the role of Mr./Ms. Davis, a attorney acting in the public interest. You and Dr. Thomas share results of a study that you did regarding women who receive services from Freedom America. Your study included a random sampling of 100 women who received abortions at the Los Angeles Freedom America Clinic. Of those 100 women, the following is a breakdown by ethnicity:

Ethnicity	Number of Women
African American	41
Hispanic	32
Caucasian/White	19
Asian American	7
Other/Unknown	1

Of the 100 women, the following is a breakdown by income distribution:

Income Distribution Information	
Percentage on welfare/public assistance	63
Percentage living below poverty line	77
Percentage homeless	13

In arguing against Freedom America's practices, consider the following:

1. Freedom America has targeted low income women. That is because such women are less likely to sue if they are harmed and because they are more easily manipulated. The offer of a free bed for a night and a couple of hot meals is enough to convince many desperate women to wait another month before aborting. That is especially true if the women have no knowledge that waiting will increase the potential health risks. For Freedom America to fail to inform women of the increased risks associated with postponing an abortion violates the woman's right to be informed.

2. The advertisement being considered by Freedom America is outrageous. The term "donating fetal tissue" is misleading because it infers that a fetus is not being destroyed, that the woman is helping science, and that no risk exists to the woman. Women are entitled to know the use to which their fetal tissue is put.

3. Women have a right to know that a part of their bodies is being sold and used in the manufacture of cosmetics. The waiver that is signed is meaningless because it does not inform the women of the use being made of their fetal tissue. The presumption of women seeking abortions is that the fetus will be destroyed. That presumption must be fulfilled in the absence of clear notification to the contrary.

Role Assignment Number 14

Assume the role of Dr. Forbes, a clinical researcher. Freedom America is essentially creating a market for human biological and genetic products. Such a market already exist for sperm and blood, but that is different because the donation of sperm or blood carries no risk to the donor and sperm and blood are manufactured involuntarily without any effort on the part of the donor. Furthermore, the donation of sperm and blood are not invasive procedures and they involve only minutes of time and minimal, if any, pain. If Freedom America is allowed to sell human fetuses, that will lead to the eventual acceptance of organ sales.

It must also be remembered that a fetus is a potential human being. Even if the law does not recognize a fetus as deserving of full legal protection, the law must at least prevent the deliberate exploitation of fetuses.

It must also be realized that Freedom America is collecting fetal tissue for experiments and procedures that are prohibited by U.S. law and bioethical standards. The fact that the transplants take place abroad does not eliminate the fact that the tissue is collected in the United States where U.S. laws and standards do apply.

Role Assignment Number 15

Assume the role of Mr./Ms. Font, a representative of the bioethics advocacy group Ethics in Medicine Now. Argue against the actions of Freedom America for the following reasons:

1. Freedom America is devaluing the human fetus by encouraging women to abort. Argue that by turning abortion into "fetal tissue donation," Freedom America

is desensitizing women to the seriousness of abortion and its possible health effects. The benefits gained from the research done at the Guadaladora clinic do not justify the exploitation of women by Freedom America.

2. Freedom America represents itself as acting in the public interest but they are not truly acting to promote women's health. That is because Freedom America's main motive is financial. Freedom America should fully disclose its financial interests in the fetuses to all women considering "fetal tissue donation." Women cannot give truly informed consent without obtaining full disclosure by Freedom America.

3. Freedom America is violating its ethical duty to its patients by operating for the purpose of making a profit. The clinic cannot act both for the sake of women's health and for the purpose of making a profit because those two goals conflict with one another. For example, the interest of women's health requires that elective abortions be performed as early as possible to minimize the potential adverse health effects to the woman. The interest of profit, however, requires Freedom America to encourage women to wait until later in their pregnancy to abort. Those two interests conflict and cannot be reconciled.

CHAPTER 10

PROPERTY RIGHTS, BODY PARTS, AND
REPRODUCTION

Who Owns the Human Body?

INSTRUCTIONS AND OBJECTIVES

Chapter 10 sets forth five fact patterns, each of which raises issues concerning an individual's ownership interest, if any, in his or her biological material. Each of the fact patterns sets forth concerns of varying complexity, both at the individual and policy levels. By using the fact patterns in conjunction with one another, participants are called upon to analyze the characteristics that distinguish between apparently simple issues and more complex issues. The common questions that intertwine each of the fact patterns is whether an individual should be granted a property interest in a particular body part or reproductive material and whether the individual's motive for requesting ownership should be questioned by hospital officials.

The case study is set in a meeting of hospital administration and includes role assignments for 16 or more participants. The role assignments include one or more adjudicators who may be called upon at the end of the discussion to make decisions with regard to disposition of the requests made in each of the five fact patterns.

THE CASE STUDY

It has come to the attention of the administration at County General Hospital that policy determinations must be made concerning the rights of patients over their body parts, products, and reproductive and genetic materials. The Hospital is concerned with what, if any, legal and ethical duties are owed by the hospital and its physicians to patients with regard to ownership of, or property interests in, such items. The Hospital's concern has been spawned by five cases that are summarized below.

Numerous parties are present at today's meeting, representing the interests at issue in each case. Each party will have the opportunity to speak before the members of the County General Hospital Adjudication and Policy Board who are present today. At the end of today's meeting, the Board members will vote to resolve the issues presented in each case. It is the aim of today's meeting to not only resolve the cases at hand but to establish policy guidelines that can be used to help resolve and avoid future conflicts.

The Anderson Case

Mrs. Anderson first sought medical attention at County General Hospital during her seventh month of pregnancy when she began having acute, recurring pains and bleeding. Mrs. Anderson had not had prior prenatal care. Numerous tests were conducted and two conditions were discovered. First, it was discovered that the Anderson fetus suffered from anencephaly. Second, it was discovered that Mrs. Anderson's medical condition was not sound and that for her to proceed with her pregnancy would endanger her health and possibly threaten her life. Upon consultation with her physician and a hospital counselor, Mr. and Mrs. Anderson decided to abort the pregnancy. That was a painstaking decision for the Andersons because of their desire for a child and because of their religious convictions. However, Mrs. Anderson's pregnancy was terminated and Mr. and Mrs. Anderson are present today to request possession of the fetal corpse so that they can have a funeral and bury the fetus at their family cemetery plot.

The Bonitas Case

Mr. and Mrs. Bonitas have a seven year-old daughter who suffers from a rare blood disorder, treatment of which requires a bone marrow transplant. All of the Bonitas family members have been tested and none is a suitable donor. Physicians have advised that in cases such as this, the highest likelihood of finding a donor match is from a sibling. Mrs. Bonitas has become pregnant for the specific purpose of producing a bone marrow donor to save her daughter's life. Mr. and Mrs. Bonitas, however, do not wish to raise another child and have inquired as to whether the bone marrow can be taken from the fetus and the fetus then aborted. Such a procedure has been used on an experimental basis in Europe and proved successful in clinical trials when performed at the fifth month gestation. Mr. and Mrs. Bonitas have made a formal request that County General Hospital provide for extraction of bone marrow from the fetus at the fifth month of pregnancy so that Mrs. Bonitas can then abort the fetus.

The Carnap Case

Ms. Carnap is a 39 year-old, single attorney who desires to have children. Due to difficulty conceiving, Ms. Carnap has been taking fertility drugs and has been artificially inseminated with donated sperm. Ms. Carnap is now pregnant with seven embryos. Through use of genetic testing, doctors have determined that four of the embryos are male and three are female. Ms. Carnap does not wish to have seven children, nor does she wish to incur the health risks to herself and the unborn children that often accompany multiple births. Ms. Carnap would like to have three children, but no more than two at one time. Ms. Carnap is also only interested in having sons. It is possible that embryos may be terminated in utero but only if located near the abdominal wall. If not located near the abdominal wall, the embryos must first be removed and then be destroyed ex utero. It is also possible, through use of advanced technology, to remove the embryos and cryogenically preserve them for future use. The configuration of Ms. Carnap's embryos is as follows:

Embryo Number	Sex	Located near the abdominal wall?	Ms. Carnap's request.
1	M	No	Carry to term.
2	M	Yes	Remove and preserve for future use.
3	F	No	Remove and terminate.
4	M	No	Carry to term.
5	F	No	Remove and terminate.
6	M	Yes	Remove and preserve for future use.
7	F	Yes	Terminate in utero

The Dewey Case

Dr. Dewey is a medical researcher. He has been admitted to County General Hospital in need of a splenectomy. It is common knowledge that due to a rare medical condition, cells taken from Dr. Dewey's spleen after removal may be of great use in medical experimentation. It is also possible that research performed on Dr. Dewey's spleen cells may be highly profitable. Dr. Dewey will only consent to performance of the splenectomy at County General Hospital if it is agreed that his spleen will be preserved and returned to him after the surgery. Further, Dr. Dewey has requested that a contract be drafted that will forfeit all property interests in the spleen that County General or any of its physicians may claim after the surgery.

The Ellis Case

Ernest Ellis is fourteen years old. Ernest excels at science and he dreams of someday becoming a famous physician. Ernest has just had his tonsils removed at County General Hospital and wants to know if he can take them home in a jar of formaldehyde.

DISCUSSION QUESTIONS

The Anderson Case

1. What are the arguments for and against granting the Andersons possession of the fetal corpse? If possession is granted, what, if any, policy precedent is set?

2. How will treating the fetus as a person (i.e., by conducting a funeral) affect hospital policy regarding abortion? Regarding miscarriage? Does the fact that the Anderson fetus was seven months old distinguish it from a fetus aborted during the first trimester? If a woman received an abortion at County General Hospital during her eighth week of pregnancy and then requested possession of the abortus, would the hospital's decision in the Anderson case affect how the hospital should respond in that case? Why or why not? How can the cases be distinguished?

3. Should a patient's motive for seeking possession of the abortus affect the hospital's response?

4. Should the abortus be considered the property of the Andersons? How does the abortus compare to an organ or tumor that is removed from an individual?

The Bonitas Case

1. If there was a 100 percent chance that bone marrow extracted from a five month old fetus produced by Mr. and Mrs. Bonitas could save the life of their seven year old daughter, but the procedure to save the life of the daughter would necessarily terminate the fetus, would it be ethical for the Bonitases to produce the fetus for that purpose? Would it violate any duty owed by the Bonitases to their daughter if the Bonitases did not produce the fetus? Is a greater duty owed to the fetus or to the daughter?

2. Assuming that abortion is legal on demand up to the sixth month gestation in this jurisdiction, is there an ethical problem with the Bonitas' request? If so, what is the ethical problem? Consider each of the following acts:

   a. The act of abortion;

   b. The act of creating a fetus with no intention of ever giving birth;

   c. The act of allowing the fetus to grow for five months before performing an inevitable abortion; and

   d. The motive of destroying a fetus to save a child.

3. Would it be ethical for Mrs. Bonitas to carry the fetus to term, deliver the

child, remove the necessary bone marrow, and then place the child up for adoption?

4. A new technology has been developed whereby the embryo in Mrs. Bonitas can be injected with a chemical that will prevent development of the embryo's nervous system. The fetus will otherwise develop normally but with no chance of ever surviving ex utero. Would it be ethical for that technology to be used in order to extract the bone marrow at five months and then abort the fetus? Does the destruction of a fetus with no potential to survive as a person ex utero differ ethically from the destruction of a developmentally normal fetus? If so, does it make a difference if the lack of brain development is caused intentionally verses naturally?

5. Assuming it be technologically possible, would it be ethically acceptable for doctors to remove the embryo from Mrs. Bonitas' body and grow it in a laboratory until viable bone marrow is produced with the intent of destroying the embryo after removal of the bone marrow? Does growing the embryo in a laboratory make its destruction more or less ethically acceptable than destroying the embryo by abortion?

6. Does the physician performing the abortion have any claim to either conduct experiments upon the abortus or sell the abortus for purposes of experimentation?

The Carnap Case

1. Should Ms. Carnap's request be carried out? If not, why not? Consider the following:

a. Ms. Carnap can destroy all of the embryos by electing to have an abortion;

b. If Ms. Carnap decides to remove the female embryos and store them, she has no legal obligation to ever carry them to term; and

c. If all of the embryos are left in place, doctors have predicted that, at most, five will survive full-term and they will most likely be developmentally disabled.

2. Does the fact that Ms. Carnap wishes to only have sons affect the ethical integrity of her choices? If Ms. Carnap were not on fertility drugs but could become pregnant without aide, would it be ethically acceptable for her to repeatedly get pregnant and abort each time the fetus was female?

3. If gender did not matter to Ms. Carnap but intelligence did, would it be ethically acceptable for her to abort all of the embryos with potential IQs below 140? What if Ms. Carnap only wanted children with blue eyes or who would grow to be at lest six feet tall?

4. Does the manner in which the embryos are destroyed affect the ethical integrity of the act of destruction? In other words, does it make any difference whether the embryos are destroyed in utero verses ex utero?

5. Is it to be ethically acceptable for Ms. Carnap to choose to preserve the male embryos which could easily be destroyed (embryo numbers 2 and 6), while choosing to destroy the female embryos which could more easily be carried to term (embryo number 2 and 5)? What if Ms. Carnap's election to only keep the male embryos places her health at greater risk than if she chose to only keep the female embryos?

6. Does the physician removing the embryos that Ms. Carnap wishes to destroy

have any claim to those embryos after removal? Does he have any claim to the genetic components of the embryos that remain after termination? If the physician chooses to experiment on the embryos, does he have an ethical obligation to obtain Ms. Carnap's informed consent?

The Dewey Case

1. Should Dr. Dewey be granted possession of his spleen? Upon what grounds, if any, can the surgeon removing the spleen refuse to return it to Dr. Dewey after its removal?

2. If Dr. Dewey's surgeon knows that he might profit from Dr. Dewey's spleen, is it ethical for him to refuse to return it to Dr. Dewey? Does Dr. Dewey's surgeon have an ethical or legal obligation to disclose to Dr. Dewey that profits might be made from research performed on the spleen? If the surgeon retains possession of the spleen and makes profits from it, is the surgeon ethically obligated to share the profits with Dr. Dewey? Consider application of *Moore v. Regents of the University of California* included at Appendix N.

3. If Dr. Dewey is granted possession of his spleen and makes large profits from conducting research using the spleen cells, does Dr. Dewey have an ethical duty to share those profits with the surgeon who removed the spleen?

4. What if removal of Dr. Dewey's spleen is not medically necessary but Dr. Dewey wants to have it removed solely for the purpose of using it in research? Should the hospital and physicians agree to remove the spleen under such circumstances?

The Ellis Case

1. Should Ernest be given his tonsils?

2. How, if at all, does Ernest's case differ from Dr. Dewey's?

3. Assume that Ernest is given his tonsils. If Ernest performs an experiment on the tonsils, does Earnest's surgeon have any claim to profits made from the experiment?

4. Should the Anderson fetal corpse, the Bonitas fetus, the Carnap embryos, the Dewey spleen, and the Ellis tonsils be treated differently from one another? Can and should each of those things be distinguished from the others based on whether it is reproductive material verses a body part? Why or why not?

SUGGESTED RESEARCH

Texts

Annas, George J. *Standard of Care: The Law of American Bioethics.* New York City, N.Y.: Oxford University Press, 1993, 167-77.

Case Law

Appendix N: *Moore v. Regents of The University of California*, 793 P.2d 479 (Cal. 1990).

ROLE ASSIGNMENTS FOR 16 PLUS PARTICIPANTS

1. Mr./Mrs. Anderson
2. Mr./Mrs. Bonitas
3. Ms. Carnap
4. Dr. Dewey
5. Ernest Ellis
6. Mrs. Anderson's Physician
7. Mrs. Bonitas' Physician
8. Bonitas' Family Physician
9. Ms. Carnap's Fertility Specialist
10. Dr. Dewey's Surgeon
11. Ernest Ellis' Physician
12. Director of County General Hospital Medical Research Department
13. Attorney Representing Property Interests in Human Organs
14. Pro-Choice Advocate
15. Pro-Life Advocate
16. Member of County General Hospital Adjudication and Policy Board (This role assignment may be assigned to more than one participant.)

Role Assignment Number 1

Assume the role of Mr./Mrs. Anderson. You and your husband/wife have named your child Adam. According to your religious and moral convictions, you believe that aborting your child was wrong. You believe that fetal life is human life and that, as such, it is sacred. Faced with the circumstances, you were forced to make an extremely difficult decision but you believe that you had no option. All you want now is to be granted possession of Adam's body so that you can bury him at your family's cemetery plot. As far as you are concerned, there is no difference between Adam's death at seven months gestation and the death of a newborn infant. Surely the hospital would allow you to have possession of Adam's body if he died after he was born. You had been trying for three years to have a child and you are determined that your son will receive a proper burial.

Role Assignment Number 2

Assume the role of Mr./Mrs. Bonitas. You believe that life begins at birth. You have a seven year-old daughter who will die if she does not receive a bone marrow transplant from the fetus. The law allows you to abort up until the sixth month gestation and you intend to abort the fetus at that time regardless of whether the doctors extract the needed bone marrow. Quite simply, you cannot afford and you do not desire to have another child. If the doctors refuse to perform the extraction of the bone marrow, you consider them to be blackmailing you into giving birth to a child that you do not want to have. The purpose of creating the fetus was to save the life of your daughter.

Argue that the same legal and ethical protections that are given to a person cannot be afforded to the fetus and that your daughter's interests must be given priority over those of the fetus. Further argue that the doctors should not be able to play God by deciding whether your daughter will live or die simply because they do not like your motivations for creating the fetus or your reasons for electing to abort it. You are paying the doctors to do a job, not to judge your morality. The ethical issue at hand has nothing to with abortion or with your reasons for creating the fetus, rather it has only to with whether the hospital will save your daughter's life.

You have also done some research and, although you are grateful for the concern that your gynecologist has for your/your wife's health, you have learned that the risk of death from an abortion at the fifth month gestation is only 3 in 100,000 compared to 1 in 100,000 if the abortion is performed right now and 9 in 100,000 if the fetus is carried to term and delivered. Therefore, there is no argument to be made that having an abortion at the fifth month gestation will create an increased danger that would not exist if you carried the fetus to term.

Role Assignment Number 3

Assume the role of Ms. Carnap. Argue that the embryos you are carrying are your property. Argue that because you may legally destroy all of the embryos by having an abortion, the embryos should be viewed as your property to do with as you please. Accordingly, no one should be able to tell you how many or which ones to keep. Doctors have informed you that if you carry all seven embryos to term, probably no more than five of the embryos will survive. You have also been informed that with the addition of each surviving fetus there will be an increase in the likelihood of birth defects and complications, including Down's syndrome and low birth weights. You have also been informed that the higher the number of fetuses surviving full term, the greater the risk of injury to your own health.

You have decided that you want three sons, two now and one at a later date. You do not want daughters and you are not paying your doctors to convince you otherwise. The argument that the fetuses that are easiest to terminate should be terminated and that the others should be carried to term is meaningless because technology exists to enable you to choose the embryos you want and to preserve or destroy the others. The embryos are your genetic material and they are a part of your body to do with as you choose.

Role Assignment Number 4
Assume the role of Dr. Dewey. Argue that the bottom line is that the spleen is your spleen regardless of whether it is inside or outside of your body. You know that research performed using cells from your spleen may be profitable because you carry a rare disorder. As a medical doctor, you have the knowledge to exploit that profitability and you see no reason why anyone should have a stronger claim to possession of your spleen than you do. Distinguish your case from the facts presented in *Moore v. Regents of the University of California*, included at Appendix N, by arguing that you have knowledge prior to the removal of your spleen that it may be profitable and you have the medical training to exploit that profitability. Mr. Moore had neither of those things.

If the doctors will not agree to sign a contract relinquishing all claims to possession and use of the spleen, argue that you will have the spleen removed somewhere else. If no one else is willing to abide by your terms, you will remove the spleen yourself.

Role Assignment Number 5
Assume the role of Ernest Ellis. All you want is your tonsils so that you can show them to your biology class. That seems pretty simple to you. After all, they are your tonsils. Argue that your tonsils are your property and that you should have the right to do with them as you please.

Role Assignment Number 6
Assume the role of Mrs. Anderson's physician. You witnessed what a difficult decision it was for the Andersons to choose to abort the fetus but, in the end, they had no choice. They believed that they were killing their child. The abortion was long and complicated. You believe that the Andersons have the sincerest intentions but you also know that releasing the fetal corpse to the Andersons will set a dangerous precedent. It could mean that all women seeking abortions would be entitled to possession of the abortus and some of those other women might not have sincere intentions. You feel that it is best if the hospital establishes a policy that it will retain and disposes of all abortuses, including the Andersons'. Carried to the extreme, a policy granting possession of the fetus to the Andersons could lead to women taking possession of their abortuses and selling them to researchers or even cosmetics company who might want substances that can be extracted from human fetuses. Policy concerns dictate that no property interest should be created in the product of an abortion. All abortuses should be treated as medical waste.

Role Assignment Number 7

Assume the role of Mrs. Bonitas' physician. You are aware of and support a woman's right to control her fertility but you strongly object to a woman becoming pregnant for any purpose other than to have a child. Argue that by waiting until the fifth month to abort, Mrs. Bonitas is incurring three times the risk of mortality to herself than if she immediately aborted. An abortion at the fifth month will take several hours and Mrs. Bonitas will have to stay in the hospital overnight. The procedure will have to be performed by inducing contraction of the uterus with an injection of a prostaglandin hormone, rather than by vacuum aspiration which is the usual procedure for an early term abortion.

There is also no guarantee that the bone marrow transplant from the fetus will work to save the life of the Anderson's daughter. In fact, studies show that there is less than a 50 percent chance of the procedure being successful. You might agree to perform the procedure if there was a greater degree of certainty that it would be successful, but given the experimental nature of the procedure you do not believe that the risk to be incurred to Mrs. Bonitas' health justifies performance of the procedure.

Furthermore, argue that performing the procedure sets a bad policy precedent because it condones women becoming pregnant for purposes other than the creation of a child. If such a precedent is set, where will it stop? Argue that setting such a precedent could lead to women getting pregnant to produce donor organs and body parts to sell to the parents of children in need. The end result could be that women will be treated as factories for the production of fetal parts. Allowing the procedure to be performed may also extend the time boundaries during which abortions are deemed acceptable because the older a fetus, the more useable parts it has for transplant. Will we soon accept performance of abortions at nine months gestation if they produce parts that are in high demand?

Role Assignment Number 8

Assume the role of the Bonitas' family physician who cares for their daughter. You have a great deal of faith in the procedure to extract the bone marrow from the fetus. There is a 50 percent chance that it will save the daughter's life. You have informed Mrs. Bonitas that she is incurring only minimal risk to herself by having the procedure performed and that the benefit to her daughter may be the gift of life. The procedure in question has been performed twelve times, six of which were successful. You do not understand how the hospital could even consider turning down the Bonitas' request. After all, Mrs. Bonitas is already pregnant and she is determined that she will abort at the fifth month regardless of whether the procedure is performed. Also, argue that performing the procedure, even if not successful, could lead to advancements in medical knowledge which could be used to help other people. Everything involved is perfectly legal. So long as the Bonitases have no moral problems with their actions, neither should anyone else.

Role Assignment Number 9

Assume the role of Ms. Carnap's physician and a fertility specialist. Argue that Ms. Carnap has the right to control her fertility but argue that the choices she wants to make are not justified. Maintain the position that Ms. Carnap should not be allowed to choose the sex of which embryos to carry. You believe that to allow that would set a very dangerous precedent. In the near future, technology will be available to determine innumerable genetic traits and characteristics of embryos. Where will we draw the line in meeting parental requests? Will we destroy embryos because they will develop into people who will be too short, have the wrong color eyes, or not have a high enough IQ? This is the first step towards eugenics and genetic cleansing. Society does not condone the practice of eugenics that occurred in Nazi Germany and society should not permit the practice of eugenics in its hospitals.

You also do not think that Ms. Carnap should be allowed to destroy the female embryos if they are removed. Your position on that issue stems from purely practical considerations. Time and resources were devoted to creating those embryos and Ms. Carnap may one day decide to that she would like to have a daughter. Cryogenically storing the embryos will incur very little cost and it will not give rise to a duty on Ms. Carnap to ever have the embryos implanted. Besides, those embryos may be the last embryos that can ever be created using the same donor sperm.

Role Assignment Number 10

Assume the role of Dr. Dewey's surgeon. Argue that by removing Dr. Dewey's spleen, you contribute to the profitability of the spleen. No one will make any money off the organ if it stays in Dr. Dewey. In fact, not removing the spleen would most likely cause Dr. Dewey's death. By removing the organ you are providing a service that is contributing to whatever findings are made from research that is performed on the organ. Therefore, you should be entitled to some of the profits derived from that research. If Dr. Dewey does not agree with you then he can have someone else remove his spleen or even attempt to remove it himself as he has threatened. If Dr. Dewey is allowed to keep the spleen, where will the line be drawn in future cases? Research demands that hospitals and physicians have organs and tissue upon which to experiment. If a property right is found in human organs, where will researchers obtain human tissue? Granting Dr. Dewey a property interest in the spleen could lead to property rights being granted in possession of other organs. The inevitable conclusion would be that people would be permitted to sell body parts for a profit. That would constitute bad public policy as poor people may be lead to sell kidneys and bone marrow just to pay their bills.

Role Assignment Number 11

Assume the role of Ernest Ellis' physician. You feel bad that you cannot give Ernest the tonsils but when the hospital removes a body part, the hospital must maintain control over the removed part and make sure that it is either properly disposed of or used in appropriate medical research. Ernest is not going to do anything bad with the tonsils but granting possession of the tonsils to Ernest would set a bad precedent. What if someone comes into the hospital and has a kidney removed just so they can gain possession of it and sell on the black market? Once a body part is removed from the body, it must become the property of the hospital. Any other course of action would set a bad public policy precedent.

Role Assignment Number 12
Assume the role of Director of the County General Hospital Medical Research Department. Whenever a body part is removed, you generally have the option to use it in research. The research that you perform leads to medical advancements that may save thousands of lives. Argue that once a body part has been removed from an individual it should be used for medical research. It is just like when an individual dies in the hospital, it is not uncommon to see interns practicing procedures on the corpse. Such experimentation causes no harm and is necessary in order for medical advancements to be made. Besides, setting a policy that all removed body parts shall be used for research purposes establishes a clear rule that is easily followed. Once that rule is deviated from, issues will be confused and research will suffer.

Role Assignment Number 13
Assume the role of an attorney present to argue for individuals' property rights in bodily parts and products. Argue that since there is now a pecuniary interest in human anatomical parts and products, it only makes sense that the pecuniary interest should belong to the person from whom the anatomical part or product is removed. People are often remunerated for blood donations, men may be paid for sperm, and individuals often receive stipends for participating in clinical trials. It makes no sense that people should be prohibited from profiting from research conducted on their body parts after removal. Argue that hospitals and physicians should be forced to recognize the ownership rights of individuals in their own bodily parts and products. Propose that the hospital initiate a new policy that would presume all bodily parts and products removed from an individual to be the property of that individual. The hospital could then acquire the property rights from the person through the individual donating his or her parts or through use of a fixed   fee schedule. For example, the hospital could adopt a policy that they would pay $20 for a spleen, $30 for a kidney, etc. If the individual having the organ removed does not wish to sell or donate the organ to research, then the burden and cost of proper disposal could be passed on to that individual. Such a policy would provide a high level of certainty as to an individual's ownership interests in his body parts and it would help to prevent disputes, such as those presented at today's meeting.

Role Assignment Number 14
Assume the role of a pro-choice advocate. In participating in today's discussion,

consider the following:

1. Mrs. Anderson should be denied possession of the fetal corpse. It is not a baby, it is a fetus. The abortus is medical waste and should be treated as such.

2. Mrs. Bonitas should not only be allowed but encouraged to have the bone marrow extracted and then abort the fetus. She does not want to raise another child. The fact that she has inconvenienced herself to get pregnant to save her daughter is admirable. Mrs. Bonitas has already said that she will abort regardless of whether the procedure is performed. Why should we waste the bone marrow and condemn her daughter to death?

3. Ms. Carnap should be allowed to do whatever she wishes with her embryos. Abortion is legal in this country and Ms. Carnap should be allowed to terminate whichever embryos she wishes for whatever reason. Ms. Carnap's motivation for choosing selective termination is personal and should not be judged by hospital administrators or anyone else. The fact that Ms. Carnap does not want to preserve the female embryos is justified and her wishes should be honored. She should be entitled to control her own reproductive choices.

Role Assignment Number 15

Assume the role of a pro-life advocate. Argue for the sanctity of human life, born or unborn. Affirm the proposition that life begins at conception. In formulating your arguments, consider the following:

1. The Andersons should be granted possession of the corpse. The body is that of their child and they should be free to bury him as they deem appropriate. To deny them that right is to substitute the hospital's religious and spiritual beliefs for those of the Andersons.

2. Mrs. Bonitas' threat to have an abortion should not be used to justify the creation and subsequent destruction of one human life to save another. If the child is born, he or she could be a bone marrow donor and then live a normal life. If the Bonitases do not wish to raise another child, they should put it up for adoption. Why destroy two lives when both can be saved? The unborn child is deserving of the same dedication and love that Mr. and Mrs. Bonitas have shown for their daughter.

3. Ms. Carnap should not be permitted to pick and choose which of her children shall live and which shall die. Ms. Carnap assumed the risk that she would become pregnant with multiple pregnancies when she decided to take fertility drugs. Ms. Carnap must assume the obligation of giving birth and caring for what she has created. Even if Ms. Carnap is allowed to selectively terminate, she should not be allowed to do so based on the sex or any other characteristics of the embryos. To allow selective termination based on such characteristics is nothing short of allowing parents to practice eugenics.

Role Assignment Number 16

Assume the role of a member of the County General Hospital Adjudication and Policy Board. Your role today is to listen to all arguments presented, act as an arbitrator, and ask questions. Challenge the points that you think are weak and propose arguments that are not made by others. At the end of today's meeting you will be asked to cast a vote as to what to do in each of the five cases. Your vote, along with those of the other Board members (if any), will determine whether to grant or deny the requests of each patient. You may modify or partially grant requests, but in order for any course of action to be taken, it must be agreed upon by a majority of voting administrators. In making your final decisions, consider the effect that it will have on the people present today, as well as the policy that it will establish and how that policy will affect future patients who may have different motives or different situations.

CHAPTER 11

OUTBREAK IN AMERICA

The Policy of Public Verses Private Interests

INSTRUCTIONS AND OBJECTIVES

Chapter 11 is set in a meeting of the Four Corners Virology Task Force. This fictitious government body has been assembled to determine appropriate treatment protocols to govern outbreak of the newly discovered Hanta II virus. This case study asks participants to consider societal verses individual interests as they converge in the face of a threat to the public health. Issues such as the scope of informed consent, research interests verses autonomy concerns, community verses individual rights, and treatment of vulnerable populations are raised. Issues are presented that require analysis with reference to the bioethical principles of autonomy, beneficence, nonmaleficence, and, particularly, social justice.

The case study includes role assignments for 15 or more participants, including individuals with authority to render decisions with regard to issues presented.

THE CASE STUDY

Eight weeks ago, Brian French was taken by his parents to the emergency department at the Casper City Hospital in Casper, Wyoming. Brian was suffering from hemorrhagic fever with renal syndrome. Physicians at Casper City Hospital diagnosed Brian as having Hanta virus disease resulting from infection with the Hanta virus. Brian and his family had been vacationing at a national park in the Four Corners area where Arizona, New Mexico, Colorado, and Utah border. That region has been the flashpoint of Hanta virus outbreaks in the past. Physicians at Casper City Hospital notified the Centers for Disease Control ("CDC") and followed the normal course of treatment. Prior Hanta virus infections have been successfully treated, but even with treatment approximately 40 percent of cases are fatal. Physicians at Casper City Hospital had no reason to believe that Brian's case differed from prior Hanta virus cases. No available evidence indicated Hanta virus to be airborne.

Four days later, while Brian was still being treated at Casper City Hospital, three members of the Navajo Nation living on a reservation in New Mexico became ill with identical symptoms. Again, Hanta virus was identified as the causal agent and routine care was administered.

Brian and the three infected individuals in New Mexico all died within ten days of onset of symptoms. In the past six weeks, 47 individuals in Casper have reported symptoms similar to those of Brian French. Thirteen (28 percent) of symptomatic individuals have died. Of the 34 symptomatic individuals in Casper, 29 (85 percent) have been symptomatic less than ten days. Similarly, in the past six weeks, 83 members of the Navajo Nation in New Mexico have become symptomatic. Twenty-eight (34 percent) of the symptomatic persons in New Mexico have died. Of the 55 symptomatic persons still living, 48 (84 percent) have been symptomatic for less than ten days.

Officials from the CDC have confirmed that the cause of the hemorrhagic fever and renal syndrome is a viral agent closely related to Hanta virus. The agent has been named Hanta II. Hanta II has been determined to be a mutated form of the Hanta virus.

Very little is known about Hanta II as it was only discovered two months ago. Hanta II resembles the Hanta virus when viewed under the micron microscope but Hanta II is far more virulent. Hanta II has a mortality rate of approximately 65 percent. In 90 percent of cases in which Hanta II is fatal, the infected individual dies within ten days of the onset of symptoms. The mode of transmission between individuals is not known but the virus appears to be airborne. No other explanation accounts for the disease spreading so quickly or for the pattern of infection.

In Casper, there are currently 34 individuals reporting Hanta II symptoms. Twenty-seven of those persons are receiving care at the Casper City Hospital. The remaining infected persons have refused admission to the hospital and are scattered throughout Casper.

In New Mexico, elders of the Navajo Nation have advised the 55 infected persons to remain on the reservation but some have been uncooperative and have been leaving the reservation on occasion. The whereabouts of three infected individuals are unknown.

No serum for Hanta virus exists. Traditional Hanta virus treatments have been administered on a limited basis in Casper but without apparent effect on Hanta II. Two pharmaceutical companies have been independently developing treatments for Hanta virus but neither has been fully tested. Treatment proposals from each of these pharmaceutical companies are included below. Because Hanta II has only recently been discovered, no data exists as to whether each of the experimental Hanta virus treatments might be effective against Hanta II.

Additionally, the Navajo Nation is concerned about the possibility of continuing infection from rodent feces on the Reservation. Hanta virus can be spread from rodent droppings to humans and it is presumed that Hanta II can as well. Because the rodent population has boomed this year due to heavy rains last summer, Elders of the Navajo Nation are concerned that new infections are not only resulting from person to person contact but also from environmental exposure. A proposal has been made that aerial spraying be conducted over the Reservation in order to eliminate the rodent population and kill any Hanta II virus that is present in the environment.

TREATMENT PROTOCOL SUBMITTED BY
SILOCHEM PHARMACEUTICAL CORPORATION

Silochem Pharmaceutical Corporation has been developing an anti-viral agent to combat Hanta virus. The development has been proceeding for 18 months, during which time the drug Athanol has been found to be effective in destroying Hanta virus in deer mice, rats, rabbits, and other small mammals and rodents identified as natural reservoirs of the virus. Athanol has been tested on human subjects in phase one clinical trials. In those trials, Athanol was tested on 30 individuals and found to cause kidney and liver damage due to toxicity. Those effects, however, can be controlled through careful dosing and monitoring.

In deer mice, Athanol has been found to be 58 percent effective in destroying Hanta virus. Approximately 37 percent of Hanta infected mice receiving a moderate dose of Athanol have died from toxicity related complications. At lower levels, Athanol has not been effective at eradicating Hanta virus. A board of independent reviewers make the following predictions as to the effects of Athanol if used on human subjects infected with Hanta II:

Estimated Hanta II cure rate	55 to 85 percent
Estimated Hanta II fatality rate	5 to 35 percent
Estimated fatalities due to Athanol toxicity	10 to 30 percent

Silochem Pharmaceutical Corporation proposes that Athanol be used on a universal basis in Casper and in a double-blind research study in New Mexico, where one-half of infected persons would be given Athanol and the other half would be given a placebo. Silochem recommends that the double-blind research study be conducted in New Mexico because the cases of Hanta II are all contained on the Navajo Reservation, which is a homogenous population in a geographic area with clearly defined boundaries. It is proposed that all subjects in New Mexico who are given Athanol be started on low doses. Doses may be gradually increased until desirable effects are observed. All patients treated with Athanol may likewise be monitored for kidney and liver failure and dosages may be lowered if effects of toxicity become evident. If drug doses are lowered before significant liver or kidney damage occurs, permanent side-effects will not likely be incurred by the subjects.

Use of the double-blind research method will allow Silochem and the American public to more fully understand the effectiveness of Athanol and it will allow, in hindsight, for the natural course of Hanta II to be more fully understood. For the study to be successful, all members of the Navajo Nation who are infected, or who have potentially been exposed to Hanta II, must be confined to the Reservation.

Silochem recommends that Athanol be used on a universal mandatory basis in Casper. That protocol is justified because residents of Casper have a greater chance of spreading the virus beyond geographical confines, therefore, the most aggressive approach must be taken to stop the virus at that location. Silochem maintains that the risk to individuals of incurring side-effects from mandatory use of Athanol is justified by the benefit bestowed upon society from reducing the rate of infecting third parties.

Requiring all infected persons in Casper to take Athanol may impede upon personal choice but Silochem is convinced that once infected persons are given the data they will understand the urgency of the situation. This situation may be likened to requiring tuberculosis testing of school children or requiring compulsory vaccinations for infectious diseases. Mandatory use of Athanol is similar to those other compulsory public health measures because both require only minimal infringements upon autonomy while reaping great benefits for society as a whole.

TREATMENT PROTOCOL SUBMITTED BY
PHARMCORP PHARMACEUTICAL RESEARCH

Pharmcorp has been developing an anti-viral serum over the past four years. That serum, Zorfanide, has been tested for effectiveness against HIV, Hanta virus, viral hepatitis A, and rabies. The serum boasts a 94 percent success rate at eliminating Hanta virus in primates. The serum has not been tested on human subjects, but it is predicted that Zorfanide will be equally effective in humans. Animal fatalities associated with Zorfanide have been negligible at less than one percent. Reliable dosage guidelines are available based on Zorfanide testing on baboons and chimpanzees. Zorfanide has, however, been found to cause total body paralysis in eight percent of primate subjects. The eight percent of test subjects that have become paralyzed are cured of Hanta virus infection. The paralysis results from the tendency of Zorfanide to accumulate and cause deterioration in the spinal column of primates. Other possible long term side-effects on humans are not known but no other side-effects have been observed in any animal tests.

Pharmcorp proposes making Zorfanide available on a compulsory basis to all Hanta II sufferers. It is the position of Pharmcorp that Zorfanide presents the only viable, medically sound treatment option for Hanta II sufferers. Additionally, public health concerns necessitate an aggressive approach to eradicate Hanta II. Zorfanide has the highest cure rate of any proposed treatment and Zorfanide has been extensively tested on primates for four years. Pharmcorp proposes mandatory Zorfanide treatment in order to stop the spread of Hanta II. Accordingly, all Hanta II sufferers must be quarantined and treated with Zorfanide. That course of action will save 52 lives within the next two weeks if immediately initiated. The long-term benefits of mandatory Zorfanide treatment will be immeasurable.

At the request of the Elders of the Navajo Nation, Pharmcorp is prepared to spray the populated areas of the reservation with an agent that will kill all rodents and eradicate all Hanta II virus present in the environment. There is a possibility that the

Hanta II virus is incubating in rodent feces that are already scattered throughout the Reservation. Aerial spraying may effectively eliminate that potential source of infection. Aerial spraying is proposed to take place at night so as not to inconvenience residents of the Reservation. It is possible that after spraying, some individuals may experience nausea, vomiting, and loss of appetite. All outdoor areas with which individuals have close contact, such as outdoor drinking fountains, child play areas, and picnic tables, must be thoroughly washed after the spraying to prevent prolonged human illness. Any human health effect caused by the spraying will be temporary.

DATA SUMMARY

Table 1. Number of persons currently infected with Hanta II

Casper, Wyoming	34
New Mexico	55
Total	89

Table 2. Fatalities to date

Casper, Wyoming	13
New Mexico	28
Total	41

Table 3. Predicted fatalities among currently infected cases if not treated

Casper, Wyoming	22
New Mexico	36
Total	58

Table 4. Predicted fatalities among currently infected cases if Athanol is used universally

Deaths resulting from Hanta II	18
Deaths resulting from Athanol toxicity	22
Total deaths	40

Table 5. Predicted fatalities and side-effects among currently infected cases if Zorfanide is used universally

Deaths resulting from Hanta II	5
Deaths resulting from Zorfanide	1
Total Deaths	6
Number of individuals paralyzed	7

Table 6. Total fatalities predicted within two months if no action is taken

Casper, Wyoming	180
New Mexico	320
Total	500

DISCUSSION QUESTIONS

1. What duty is owed to the individuals who are currently infected with Hanta II? What duty is owed to persons who are at risk of becoming infected?

2. Must all possibly successful treatments be disclosed to infected persons in order for informed consent to treatment to be obtained from those individuals? Do infected persons have a legal or ethical claim to access experimental treatments such as Athanol and Zorfanide?

3. Must infected persons be allowed to choose for themselves which treatment to utilize? If people are allowed to decide for themselves, are their decisions truly informed given the lack of information about Hanta II and the limited amount of information available about Athanol and Zorfanide use in humans?

4. Are persons infected with Hanta II competent to make decisions regarding which treatment to utilize? Is there a risk that, out of fear of dying, infected persons will make unwise choices? If so, does that warrant allowing a physician or government official to choose treatment on behalf of infected persons?

5. Does the scientific community have enough information about either drug to make either available for human use? If either, or both, drugs are made available, should their use be considered experimentation, innovative therapy, or research? What is the difference? What level of safety and effectiveness must a drug promise to be considered acceptable for human use? Does the severity of the disease make a difference?

6. Assuming that the numbers predicted in the tables above are accurate, what course of action would a purely utilitarian approach mandate? What protocol would a deontological approach mandate?

7. Is it ethically acceptable to quarantine infected individuals? Is it legally acceptable under the state statutes included at Appendix O?

8. Is it ethically acceptable to require an infected individual to be treated with either Athanol or Zorfanide?

9. Is it reasonable to compare compulsory treatment of infected individuals with Athanol or Zorfanide to requiring children to be vaccinated against contagious diseases? Why or why not? How much weight should be given to the risk incurred by the individual from a treatment or procedure in determining whether to require the intervention? How should the benefit and risk to the individual be weighed against the benefit to society?

10. Is a double-blind study ethically appropriate? Can participation in such a study be required in order to receive treatment?

11. Should the same protocol be implemented at both locations? If it were determined that research would benefit most if Athanol were used at one location and Zorfanide at the other, would that be ethically acceptable?

12. Should aerial spraying be utilized? What criteria should be used to make that determination? If a vote were taken among members of the Navajo Nation in favor of the spraying, would that constitute a reasonable basis for exposing those who voted against the spraying to the harm incurred from the spraying?

13. Can there ever be such a thing as "community consent?" Can a community consent to mandatory treatment of all of its members who are infected with Hanta II? How might community consent be obtained? Would a vote at a town hall meeting be sufficient? Would the consent of elected officials or tribal leaders suffice?

14. What protocol(s) should be implemented?

SUGGESTED RESEARCH

Statutes

Appendix O: Wyoming Statutes, Title 35, Sections 4-103 and 4-105 and New
    Mexico Statutes, Section 24-1-3.

Texts

Annas, George J. *Standard of Care: The Law of American Bioethics*. Oxford
    University Press: New York City, N.Y., 1993, 132-44.
Munson, Ronald. *Intervention and Reflection: Basic Issues in Medical Ethics*. 4th
    ed. Belmont, CA: Wadsworth, 1992, 311-81.
Pence, Gregory E. *Classic Cases in Medical Ethics*. 2nd ed. New York City, NY:
    McGraw-Hill, 1995, 225-52.
Veatch, Robert M. *Medical Ethics*. 2nd ed. Sudbury, MA: Jones and Bartlett, 1997,
    135-84 & 185-208.

ROLE ASSIGNMENTS FOR 15 PLUS PARTICIPANTS

1. Mr./Ms. Hurley, Esq. an Advocate for Hanta II Infected Persons
2. Mr./Mrs. French, Bryan's Parent

3. Mr./Ms. Hemet, Representative of the Infected Members of the Navajo Nation
4. Dr. Reilly, Chief of Staff at Casper City Hospital
5. Dr. Beggs, a Clinical Researcher
6. Dr. Lyman, Director of Medical Services for the Navajo Nation
7. Governor Williams, Governor of New Mexico
8. Dr. Jacobs, Bioethicist Specializing in Research Ethics
9. Mr./Ms. Kraft, Esq., Attorney Representing Casper City Hospital
10. Governor Washington, Governor of Wyoming
11. Mr./Ms. Banks, Pharmcorp Pharmaceutical Representative
12. Mr./Ms. Markowicz, Silochem Pharmaceutical Representative
13. Dr. Rankin, CEO of Casper City Hospital
14. Mr./Ms. Fry, Risk Manager at Casper City Hospital
15. Members of the Four Corners Virology Task Force (This role is suitable for assignment to multiple participants.)

Role Assignment Number 1

Assume the role of Mr./Ms. Hurley, Esq., an advocate for Hanta II infected persons. You are interested in protecting the rights of Hanta II sufferers.

Argue that both Athanol and Zorfanide must be made available for elective use after full disclosure of all known risks. Those drugs represent the only possible treatments for Hanta II. To withhold either of those drugs from infected persons is unethical.

Argue for full disclosure of all risks and benefits anticipated with use of each drug and the likelihood of incurring each of those risks and benefits. Individual autonomy must be preserved and fully informed consent must be obtained for any treatment to be utilized. Any mandatory treatment or use of double-blind studies is unethical because it would violate the principles of autonomy and nonmaleficence.

Assert that aerial spraying should be used because it presents only minimal risk and it is not invasive. The benefits gained from the spraying far out weigh any risk that might be incident to it.

Argue for quarantine measures to be instituted to protect all persons. Quarantine will protect uninfected persons by preventing them from being exposed to Hanta II and it will protect infected persons by insuring that their whereabouts are known so that they can be treated. Quarantine will also protect persons who are unknowingly infected from spreading the disease or from reaching a remote area and becoming ill.

Role Assignment Number 2

Assume the role of Mr./Mrs. French, the parent of Brian French. While Brian was ill, you became symptomatic and suffered from Hanta II disease. You are one of the small percentage of infected persons who are lucky enough to survive without treatment. The disease was terrible but it did not kill you. You believe that the experimental treatments will only give false hope and, worse yet, they may actually kill some patients who might otherwise survive without treatment. You also believe that the pharmaceutical companies are only thinking of their own interests. Using drugs on a human population without first thoroughly testing them for safety amounts to nothing short of human experimentation.

You are here to advocate your position that the disease should be allowed to run its course until a proven cure is found that does not have drastic and unpredictable side-effects. It is unfortunate that 65 percent of infected persons may die, but the experts here today really have very little knowledge of what effect the drugs will have on humans. Had you taken Zorfanide you would have risked a chance of permanent paralysis for nothing. We do not know enough about Zorfanide or Athanol to risk using them on people.

Role Assignment Number 3

Assume the role of Mr./Ms. Hemet, an elder of the Navajo Nation. You have seen many threats to the Navajo Nation come and go. You are here today to defend the sovereignty of the Navajo Nation and fight for your right to be free from being treated as guinea pigs by the big pharmaceutical companies and government officials.

Argue for Athanol and Zorfanide to be made available at the discretion of the Navajo Elders. It should be up to the leaders of the Navajo Nation to decide whether those treatments warrant use by your people. Under no circumstances will you allow a double-blind research study to be conducted and you will not allow any compulsory treatments. It is important to you that the Navajo elders be able to explain the risks and benefits of all treatment options to individual members of the Navaho Nation. It must be left to the infected individuals to consent or not consent to treatment after being fully informed of all potential risks and benefits.

Argue against any effort made, such as quarantine, which might restrict the liberty rights of members of the Navajo Nation. Such restrictions are unacceptable because they would treat your people like animals to be caged. Scientists have not proven that the Hanta II virus is airborne. Until such proof is made, individual liberty must not be abridged.

Also, you oppose use of aerial spraying because it would subject individuals to unconsented harm. Even if a vote were taken among the Navajo citizens approving the spraying, such a vote would not constitute individual consent. Failure to obtain individual informed consent would be unethical.

Role Assignment Number 4

Assume the role of Dr. Reilly, Chief of Staff at Casper City Hospital. Your primary concern is curing your infected patients. Argue that the best means of doing that is to use Zorfanide on a universal basis. Propose that Zorfanide be presented to patients as the only treatment option for Hanta II. Patients should be informed of the risk of paralysis but they should also be informed that the risk of paralysis is minimal compared to the likelihood of death if Hanta II is left untreated. If patients refuse consent to Zorfanide treatment, argue that they should be quarantined until all signs of infection disappear or until death, whichever occurs first. Hanta II can be eradicated with aggressive Zorfanide treatment. The persons who may become paralyzed during the course of treatment will at least be alive. If any other course of action is taken, Hanta II may claim the lives of hundreds, or even thousands, of people. Treatment must be quick and aggressive.

Furthermore, the urgency of the situation does not warrant a double-blind study. Formulating a research control strategy would only cause administrative delays. If infected persons consent to treatment with Zorfanide, Zorfanide is exactly what they should receive and not a placebo.

Role Assignment Number 5

Assume the role of Dr. Beggs, a clinical researcher. Argue in support of the following propositions:

1. A double-blind study should be used to determine the feasibility of both Athanol and Zorfanide. Because the effects of either drug on humans are not thoroughly understood, a double-blind study should be conducted with each drug in order to determine the effectiveness of each and to discover unknown side-effects that each drug may cause. Receiving a placebo is not necessarily bad because the effects of the drugs are not known. It may turn out that people who receive the placebo are the lucky ones, but that cannot be determined until a double-blind study is completed.

2. The drugs should not be made available outside the studies. If individuals are given the option of entering the study or taking the drug outside the study, people will not participate in the study because of the possibility of receiving a placebo. The truth is that even the experts do not know enough about either drug to adequately inform infected persons of the risks and benefits. If people cannot be adequately informed, they cannot give effective consent. If consent is not meaningfully informed then there is no reason to seek it. Participation in the study should, therefore, be mandatory. Subjects should not be informed that they are in a study or that they may be given a placebo.

3. Athanol should be used on one population and Zorfanide on the other, each in a double-blind study. This will simplify administration of the studies.

4. All persons infected with Hanta II should be deemed eligible for the studies.

5. The benefits to science and to society from conducting the double-blind studies will be immeasurable if another Hanta II outbreak ever occurs. The studies will also allow scientists to study the natural course of the Hanta II virus.

Role Assignment Number 6

Assume the role of Dr. Lyman, Director of Medical Services for the Navajo Nation. Your primary concern is that members of the Navajo Nation be treated the same as infected persons in Casper. It is your opinion that infected persons on the Reservation already have a mistrust of the federal government. The outrage would be enormous if any course of action were adopted that even appeared to provide inadequate treatment to the Navajo community. Accordingly, you believe that autonomy must be valued above all else in making decisions regarding the Navajo people. Care must be taken to avoid any appearance of paternalism.

You firmly oppose the use of a double-blind study on the Reservation. Although a double-blind study might be appropriate in some circumstances, this is an emergency situation. Infected persons will most likely die if they are given a placebo. You want both Athanol and Zorfanide to be made available for elective use and you want all infected persons to be fully informed of the potential risks and benefits of each drug.

Formulate arguments in support of advising all individuals to stay on the Reservation but adamantly oppose any quarantine restrictions. Such restrictions will only cause resentment among the population. Furthermore, quarantine restrictions would be impossible to enforce because of the enormous size of the Reservation and the numerous means of coming and going.

Aerial spraying should be presented as an option to the Navajo people. If they vote in favor of it, then it should be utilized. If they reject it, then it should not be used.

Role Assignment Number 7

Assume the role of Governor Williams, Governor of New Mexico. Argue in support of the following propositions:

1. Above all, Hanta II is a threat to the public health. The results will be disastrous if Hanta II spreads to the general population. Accordingly, argue in favor of strict and aggressive quarantine measures. Argue in support of the immediate closure and armed patrol of the Reservation borders. Individuals on the Reservation should be monitored by public health workers for signs of Hanta II infection. The community center and medical clinic on the Reservation should be turned into quarantine centers. Individuals should be confined to the quarantined areas upon presentation of symptoms indicating infection. Persons not infected with the virus should be restricted to their homes and not be permitted to enter quarantined areas.

2. Because Zorfanide appears to have the greatest effectiveness against Hanta virus, it should be used on all infected persons on a compulsory basis. The goal of mandatory treatment is to stop the spread of the virus. There is no time to seek individual consent from every individual.

3. Infected persons should not be informed of the possibility of paralysis from Zorfanide. That risk has not been confirmed to exist in humans and, even if it does,

there is no reason to cause further anxiety among infected individuals. A person is better off paralyzed than dead.

4. Aerial spraying should be conducted immediately. Even though the benefits of aerial spraying may be small, those benefits outweigh the risks.

5. Research concerns are not important at this point. Scientists will be able to review the data in hindsight and determine the efficacy of Zorfanide use on future outbreaks. The concern right now is saving lives and protecting the uninfected population.

Role Assignment Number 8

Assume the role of Dr. Jacobs, a bioethicist specializing in research ethics. Consider the following propositions:

1. Any compulsory treatment violates the autonomy of the individual. It is settled law in the United States that an individual may refuse medical treatment even if that refusal of care results in his or her own death. The autonomy of the individual must be respected and treatment cannot be mandatory. This is especially the case if the individual incurs risks from the treatment. In this case, both Athanol and Zorfanide have known risks and it is reasonable to assume that both have unknown side-effects.

2. If experimental drugs are made available to infected persons, special precautions must be taken to ensure the adequacy of consent. Because infected persons have a high likelihood of fatality, they will be susceptible to consenting to any drug that is presented to them without fully understanding that the drug may be harmful. For this reason, written consent of all individuals should be obtained after they have been informed of the risks and benefits of all possible protocols. Full disclose of risks and benefits should include: notice that the drugs have not been thoroughly tested on humans; disclosure of the possibility that Zorfanide may cause paralysis; disclosure of the fact that Athanol may cause kidney and liver failure; all statistical estimates as to likelihood of cure, side-effects and death, both with treatment and without; and notice that the individual has the right to refuse treatment.

3. If a double-blind study is undertaken, enrollment in the study must be on a strictly voluntary basis. No person should be required to take part in a study in order to receive treatment. To do so would violate the autonomy of the individual. A duty of nonmaleficence is owed to every individual infected with Hanta II. If a double blind study is conducted without the informed consent of the subjects, the subjects receiving the placebo will be harmed by not receiving the treatment to which they believe they have consented.

4. Both Zorfanide and Athanol should be made available to all persons on a strictly voluntary basis. Withholding a potentially promising treatment from infected persons is not ethical.

5. Aerial spraying should not be approved unless voted on and unanimously approved by affected persons. If the vote is not unanimous, then the persons voting

against the spraying would be subjected to unconsented harm.

Role Assignment Number 9

Assume the role of Mr./Ms. Kraft, Esq., an attorney representing Casper City Hospital. Your utmost concern is protecting Casper City Hospital from liability. In arguing for a protocol that will minimize hospital liability, consider each of the following:

   1. The hospital may incur liability by not fully informing patients of risks associated with each treatment. The hospital will likely incur liability if it knowingly withholds information regarding the possibility of renal failure or paralysis resulting from use of Athanol and the risk of paralysis resulting from use of Zorfanide.

   2. If both treatments are deemed viable, then both should be made available for elective use by all patients. Liability may result if the hospital only offers one of the treatments and it is later discovered that the other treatment is more effective.

   3. Patients must be told that the treatments are experimental. Patients must be informed of all known risks and of the possibility that unknown side-effects may occur.

Role Assignment Number 10

Assume the role of Governor Washington, the Governor of Wyoming. You sympathize with scientists wanting to turn this outbreak into an opportunity to experiment, but you believe that use of a double-blind study is inappropriate from a public policy point of view. Argue that the only goal should be to eradicate Hanta II. Ordinarily, you would honor the principle of informed consent but in this situation there simply is not enough time to gain consent from every individual and you do not believe that enough information is known about either drug for a lay person's consent to be truly informed. Therefore, recommend universal, mandatory treatment with Athanol. You support use of Athanol because it will significantly lower the fatality rate, its side-effects are more predictable and controllable than those of Zorfanide, and it may be the case that many people would view total body paralysis as a fate worse than death. You also support treating all infected persons the same so there can be no charges of favoritism or prejudice. If, after a few weeks, Athanol is not giving favorable results, treatment procedures can be reevaluated.

Role Assignment Number 11

Assume the role of Mr./Ms. Banks, a representative of Pharmcorp Pharmaceutical Research Corporation. You are here to lobby for use of Zorfanide. Argue that Zorfanide is clearly the treatment of choice because it has the highest cure rate and produces negligible fatalities. The aim here is to eliminate Hanta II. Zorfanide is more effective than Athanol at eradicating Hanta virus, therefore, it will most likely be more effective at eradicating Hanta II. Zorfanide is also a better treatment choice because Zorfanide has been tested for a longer period of time, even though it has not been tested on humans. Paralysis may not occur in humans and, even if it does occur, it is likely to only occur in eight percent of cases. That number is negligible considering that Athanol toxicity will kill more patients than Zorfanide will paralyze. Science cannot progress without taking risks. Now is the time to take those risks because there is really nothing to lose. Zorfanide should be used on a universal, mandatory basis.

Role Assignment Number 12

Assume the role of Mr./Ms. Markowicz, a representative of Silochem Pharmaceutical Corporation. You are here to lobby for universal, mandatory use of Athanol. Athanol will significantly reduce fatality rates without causing the horrible side-effects that Zorfanide is likely to cause. Because Zorfanide has not been tested on humans, it may cause numerous unknown side-effects. With Zorfanide, the treatment may be worse than the disease. Unlike Zorfanide, Athanol has been tested on humans, therefore, its side-effects are more easily predicted. Athanol is also superior to Zorfanide because Athanol toxicity levels are easily monitored and controlled. It is also possible that Athanol will have a much higher cure rate in humans than it has had in animals. Use of Athanol should be mandatory because Athanol presents the only truly viable option for treating Hanta II without incurring horrendous side-effects.

Role Assignment Number 13

Assume the role of Dr. Rankin, CEO of Casper City Hospital. In forming your arguments, consider each of the following propositions:

1. The hospital may incur liability if it does not fully disclose the risks associated with each of the available treatments. All risks and benefits should be disclosed to infected persons.

2. Public health concerns require that aggressive action be taken to stop the spread of Hanta II. The best way of preventing the spread of the virus is to cure infected persons. The most effective cure available is Zorfanide. The basic issue concerning use of Zorfanide calls for balancing the number of lives saved by using Zorfanide against the number of persons whose quality of life will be compromised because of paralysis. In this case, lowering the quality of life of the seven persons

who will be paralyzed from mandatory Zorfanide use is warranted because 53 other person's lives will be saved.

3. Argue for universal, mandatory use of Zorfanide after full disclosure of all risks. If an individual strenuously objects to treatment then it might be possible to put him in a strict quarantine to allow the virus to run its course.

Role Assignment Number 14

Assume the role of Mr./Ms. Fry, Esq., Risk Manager at Casper City Hospital. Argue for not permitting use of either medication. Consider the following propositions:

1. The risks associated with Zorfanide, particularly total body paralysis, are too great to incur. People go to hospitals to be cured, not to be paralyzed. Eight percent is a significant number and it is possible that the paralysis rate in humans will be higher than in primates.

2. Athanol is predicted to have a cure rate of 55 to 85 percent, but the possibility exists that the medication itself will kill up to 30 percent of those who use it. It would not do anyone any good to take a medication that cures the disease but kills the patient. Use of Athanol could conceivably increase the fatality rate.

3. Use of either of the medications would be human experimentation. There is no evidence that the risks incurred by either drug would be outweighed by any likely benefit.

4. The only ethical course of action is to strictly enforce quarantine measures to prevent further infection and allow the virus to run its course. All infected individuals should be quarantined at the first sign of symptoms. Uninfected persons should be confined to their homes. If the virus is confined, it will be eliminated through its natural course and the hospital will not incur any liability nor uselessly expend any resources.

5. To prevent hysteria resulting from rumors of cures, news of Athanol and Zorfanide should not be released.

Role Assignment Number 15

Assume the role of a member of the Four Corners Virology Task Force, a government agency assembled to determine a treatment protocol. At the end of today's meeting you and the other members of the Task Force (if any) will vote to decide upon an appropriate treatment protocol to implement. Listen to all arguments presented and ask questions that you believe to be pertinent.

When voting, consider each of the following treatment protocol options (as well as any others that may be proposed):

1. Use both drugs in mandatory double-blind studies;

2. Use Athanol at Casper City and Zorfanide on the Reservation (or vice versa) in mandatory protocols;

3. Make Athanol optional at Casper City and Zorfanide optional at the Reservation (or vice versa);

4. Make both drugs optional at both locations;

5. Make one of the drugs available at one location and no drug available at the other; or

6. Make neither drug available at either location.

Also, determine which, if any, of the following quarantine protocols is appropriate:

1. Quarantine all infected persons and restrict all uninfected persons to their homes;

2. Quarantine all infected persons but do not restrict the freedom of uninfected persons; or

3. Do not restrict the freedom of any individuals whether infected or not.

Finally, determine whether aerial spraying should be conducted on the Reservation.

Be prepared to provide the reasoning behind each of your decisions.

CASE UPDATE

The Zorfanide Hanta II cure rate has been determined to be 99 percent with 33 percent of the cured individuals experiencing paralysis. The mortality rate from Hanta II among persons treated with Zorfanide is one percent.

The Athanol cure rate is 40 percent. Sixty percent of persons treated with Athanol die, either from Hanta II or from Athanol toxicity.

The mortality rate of Hanta II, if left untreated, has declined to about 50 percent.

Zorfanide is in short supply. There is only enough Zorfanide to treat one third of current Hanta II cases. Athanol is in ample supply.

ADDITIONAL DISCUSSION QUESTIONS

1. How does the update information alter the treatment protocol that was agreed upon earlier?

2. How should Zorfanide be allocated if demand exceeds supply? Would it be ethical for Pharmcorp to distribute the remaining supply of Zorfanide by auctioning it to the highest bidders? By lottery?

3. Does the principle of distributive justice dictate that Zorfanide should first be made available to the population upon which it was initially tested?

4. In determining allocation of Zorfanide, how should quality of life and quantity of life factors be weighed? Specifically, how should the high risk of paralysis be weighed against the high rate of cure?

APPENDIX A

CONFIDENTIALITY OF HIV TEST RESULTS

*California Health and Safety Code
Sections 120975 Through 121020*

INTRODUCTORY NOTE

California law, like the law of most states, provides heightened confidentiality protections for the results of an HIV test. The statutes in this Appendix have been enacted in California to provide confidentiality protections to HIV test results that are in addition to the general confidentiality protections that apply to other medical information contained in the patient's medical record.

THE STATUTE

California Health and Safety Code § 120975

To protect the privacy of individuals who are the subject of blood testing for antibodies to the probable causative agent of acquired immune deficiency syndrome (AIDS) the following shall apply:

[Except as specifically required by law,] no person shall be compelled in any state, county, city, or other local civil, criminal, administrative, legislative, or other proceedings to identify or provide identifying characteristics that would identify any individual who is the subject of a blood test to detect antibodies to the probable causative agent of AIDS.

California Health and Safety Code § 120980

(a) Any person who negligently discloses results of an HIV test to any third party, in a manner that identifies or provides identifying characteristics of the person to whom the test results apply, except pursuant to a written authorization, as described in subdivision (g), or except as provided in [. . .] any other statute that expressly provides an exemption to this section, shall be assessed a civil penalty in an amount not to exceed one thousand dollars ($1,000) plus court costs, as determined by the court, which penalty and costs shall be paid to the subject of the test.

(b) Any person who willfully discloses the results of an HIV test to any third party, in a manner that identifies or provides identifying characteristics of the person to whom the test results apply, except pursuant to a written authorization, as described in subdivision (g), or except as provided in [. . .] any other statute that expressly provides an exemption to this section, shall be assessed a civil penalty in an amount not less than one thousand dollars ($1,000) and not more than five thousand dollars ($5,000) plus court costs, as determined by the court, which penalty and costs shall be paid to the subject of the test.

(c) Any person who willfully or negligently discloses the results of an HIV test to a third party, in a manner that identifies or provides identifying characteristics of the person to whom the test results apply, except pursuant to a written authorization, as described in subdivision (g), or except as provided in [. . .] any other statute that expressly provides an exemption to this section, that results in economic, bodily, or psychological harm to the subject of the test, is guilty of a misdemeanor, punishable by imprisonment in the county jail for a period not to exceed one year or a fine of not to exceed ten thousand dollars ($10,000) or both.

(d) Any person who commits any act described in subdivision (a) or (b) shall be liable to the subject for all actual damages, including damages for economic, bodily, or psychological harm that is a proximate result of the act.

(e) Each disclosure made in violation of this chapter is a separate and actionable offense.

(f) [. . .]

(g) "Written authorization," as used in this section, applies only to the disclosure of test results by a person responsible for the care and treatment of the person subject to the test. Written authorization is required for each separate disclosure of the test results, and shall include to whom the disclosure would be made.

(h) Nothing in this section limits or expands the right of an injured subject to recover damages under any other applicable law.

(i) Nothing in this section imposes liability or criminal sanction for disclosure of an HIV test [. . .] in accordance with any reporting requirement for a diagnosed case of AIDS by the department or the Centers for Disease Control under the United States Public Health Service.

(j) [. . .]

(k) "Disclosed," as used in this section, means to disclose, release, transfer, disseminate, or otherwise communicate all or any part of any record orally, in writing, or by electronic means to any person or entity.

(l) When the results of an HIV test [. . .] are included in the medical record of the patient who is the subject of the test, the inclusion is not a disclosure for purposes of this section.

California Health and Safety Code § 120985

(a) Notwithstanding Section 120980 [above], the results of an HIV test that identifies or provides identifying characteristics of the person to whom the test results apply may be recorded by the physician who ordered the test in the test subject's medical record or otherwise disclosed without written authorization of the subject of the test [. . .] to the test subject's providers of health care [. . .] for purposes of diagnosis, care, or treatment of the patient, except that for purposes of this section "providers of health care" does not include a health care service plan.

(b) Recording or disclosure of HIV test results pursuant to subdivision (a) does not authorize further disclosure unless otherwise permitted by law.

California Health and Safety Code § 120990

(a) Except in the case of a person treating a patient, no person shall test a person's blood for evidence of antibodies to the probable causative agent of AIDS without the written consent of the subject of the test [. . .] and the person giving the test shall have a written statement signed by the subject or conservator or other [legally authorized] person [. . .] confirming that he or she obtained the consent from the subject. In the case of a physician and surgeon treating a patient, the consent required under this subdivision shall be informed consent, by the patient, conservator, or other [legally authorized] person.

California Health and Safety Code § 121010

Notwithstanding Section 120975 or 120980, the results of a blood test to detect antibodies to the probable causative agent of AIDS may be disclosed to any of the following persons without written authorization of the subject of the test:

(a) To the subject of the test or the subject's legal representative, conservator, or to any person authorized to consent to the test.

(b) To a test subject's provider of health care [. . .] except that for purposes of this section, "provider of health care" does not include a health care service plan.

(c) To an agent or employee of the test subject's provider of health care who provides direct patient care and treatment.

(d) To a provider of health care who procures, processes, distributes, or uses a human body part donated pursuant to the Uniform Anatomical Gift Act.

California Health and Safety Code § 121015

(a) Notwithstanding Section 120980 or any other provision of law, no physician and surgeon who has the results of a confirmed positive test to detect infection by the probable causative agent of acquired immune deficiency syndrome of a patient under his or her care shall be held criminally or civilly liable for disclosing to a person reasonably believed to be the spouse, or to a person reasonably believed to be a sexual partner or a person with whom the patient has shared the use of hypodermic needles, or to the county health officer, that the patient has tested positive on a test to detect infection by the probable causative agent of acquired immune deficiency syndrome, except that no physician and surgeon shall disclose any identifying information about the individual believed to be infected.

(b) No physician and surgeon shall disclose the information described in subdivision (a) unless he or she has first discussed the test results with the patient and has offered the patient appropriate educational and psychological counseling, that shall include information on the risks of transmitting the human immunodeficiency virus to other people and methods of avoiding those risks, and has attempted to obtain the patient's voluntary consent for notification of his or her contacts. The physician and surgeon shall notify the patient of his or her intent to notify the patient's contacts prior to any notification. When the information is disclosed to a person reasonably believed to be a spouse, or to a person reasonably believed to be a sexual partner, or a person with whom the patient has shared the use of hypodermic needles, the physician and surgeon shall refer that person for appropriate care, counseling, and follow-up. This section shall not apply to disclosures made other than for the purpose of diagnosis, care, and treatment of persons notified pursuant to this section, or for the purpose of interrupting the chain of transmission.

(c) This section is permissive on the part of the attending physician [. . .] . No physician has a duty to notify any person of the fact that a patient is reasonably believed to be infected by the probable causative agent of acquired immune deficiency syndrome.

(d) The county health officer may alert any persons reasonably believed to be a spouse, sexual partner, or partner of shared needles of an individual who has tested positive on a test to detect infection by the probable causative agent of acquired immune deficiency syndrome about their exposure, without disclosing any identifying information about the individual believed to be infected or the physician making the report, and shall refer any person to whom a disclosure is made pursuant to this subdivision for appropriate care and follow-up. Upon completion of the county health officer's efforts to contact any person pursuant to this subdivision, all records regarding that person maintained by the county health officer pursuant to this subdivision, including but not limited to any individual identifying information, shall be expunged by the county health officer.

(e) The county health officer shall keep confidential the identity and the seropositivity status of the individual tested and the identities of the persons contacted, as long as records of contacts are maintained.

(f) [Except as specifically required by law,] no person shall be compelled in any state, county, city, or local civil, criminal, administrative, legislative, or other proceedings to identify or provide identifying characteristics that would identify any individual reported or person contacted pursuant to this section.

California Health and Safety Code § 121020

(a)(1) When the subject of an HIV test is not competent to give consent for the test to be performed, written consent for the test may be obtained from the subject's parents, guardians, conservators, or other person lawfully authorized to make health care decisions for the subject. For purposes of this paragraph, a minor shall be deemed not competent to give consent if he or she is under 12 years of age.

(2) [. . .]

(b) Written consent shall only be obtained for the subject pursuant to subdivision (a) when necessary to render appropriate care or to practice preventative measures.

(c) The person authorized to consent to the test pursuant to subdivision (a) shall be permitted to do any of the following:

(1) [R]eceive the results of the test on behalf of the subject without written authorization.

(2) Disclose the test results on behalf of the subject in accordance with Sections 120975 and 120980.

(3) Provide written authorization for the disclosure of the test results on behalf of the subject in accordance with Sections 120975 and 120980.

APPENDIX B

HEALTH CARE PROFESSIONALS AND HIV

Texas Health and Safety Code Section 58.204

INTRODUCTORY NOTE

Many states have enacted statutory provisions that affect the ability of an HIV-positive health care worker to render medical services. The following Texas statute is an example.

THE STATUTE

Texas Health and Safety Code Section 58.204 Modification of Practice

(a) Except as provided by subsections (b) and (c), a health care worker who is infected with HIV or who is infected with hepatitis B virus and is HBeAG positive may not perform an exposure-prone procedure.

(b)(1) A health care worker who is infected with HIV or who is infected with hepatitis B virus and is HBeAG positive may perform an exposure-prone procedure only if the health care worker has sought counsel from an expert review panel and been advised under what circumstances, if any, the health care worker may continue the exposure-prone procedure.

(2) An expert review panel should include the health care worker's personal physician and experts with knowledge of infectious diseases, infection control, the epidemiology of HIV and hepatitis B virus, and procedures performed by the health care worker.

(3) All proceedings and communications of the expert panel are confidential and release of information relating to a health care worker's HIV status shall comply [with applicable law].

(4) Health professional associations and health facilities should develop guidelines for expert review panels and identify exposure-prone procedures, as defined by this subchapter.

(c) A health care worker who performs an exposure-prone procedure as provided under Subsection (b) shall notify a prospective patient of the health care worker's seropositive status and obtain the patient's consent before the patient undergoes an exposure-prone procedure, unless the patient is unable to consent.

(d) To promote the continued use of the talents, knowledge, and skills of a health care worker whose practice is modified because of the worker's HIV or hepatitis B virus infection status, the worker should:

(1) be provided opportunities to continue practice act ivies, if practicable, and

(2) receive career counseling and job retraining.

[. . .]

(f) A health care worker who is infected with HIV or who is infected with hepatitis B virus and HBeAG positive who performs invasive procedures not identified as exposure-prone should not have his or her practice restricted, provided the infected health care worker adheres to the standards of infection control. [. . .]

APPENDIX C

TARASOFF v. THE REGENTS OF THE UNIVERSITY OF CALIFORNIA

Supreme Court of California
131 Cal.Rptr. 14, 17 Cal.3d 425, 551 P.2d 334 (1976)

INTRODUCTORY NOTE

Tarasoff v. The Regents of the University of California was a controversial decision which has had far-reaching implications for physicians and mental health professionals. *Tarasoff* was the first major court decision which placed an affirmative duty on health care professionals to warn reasonably foreseeable third parties of potential harm from a patient. This duty has become known as the "duty to warn."

In practice, meeting that duty requires health care professionals to balance confidentiality concerns against the likelihood that a patient will carry out a threat of harm to a third party. California, and other states, have subsequently enacted statues which provide limited guidance to health care professionals and, in some instances, provide health care professionals with immunity against allegations of breach of patient confidentiality when a patient makes a threat of harm against a reasonably foreseeable victim. One application of *Tarasoff* and its progeny which remains unsettled is with regard to a patient threatening to spread HIV to another person.

THE CASE

On October 27, 1969, Prosenjit Poddar killed Tatiana Tarasoff. Plaintiffs, Tatiana's parents, allege that two months earlier Poddar confided his intention to kill Tatiana to Dr. Lawrence Moore, a psychologist employed by the Cowell Memorial Hospital at the University of California at Berkeley. They allege that on Moore's request, the campus police briefly detained Poddar, but released him when he appeared rational. They further claim that Dr. Harvey Powelson, Moore's superior, then directed that no further action be taken to detain Poddar. No one warned plaintiffs of Tatiana's peril.

177

Concluding that these facts set forth causes of action against neither therapists and policemen involved, nor against the Regents of the University of California as their employer, the superior court sustained defendants' demurrers to plaintiffs' second amended complaints without leave to amend. This appeal ensued.

Plaintiffs' complaints predicate liability on two grounds: defendants' failure to warn plaintiffs of the impending danger and their failure to bring about Poddar's confinement pursuant to the Lanterman-Petris-Short Act. [Citation omitted.]
[. . .]

1. Plaintiffs' complaints.

[. . .]

Plaintiffs' first cause of action, entitled 'Failure to Detain a Dangerous Patient,' alleges that on August 20, 1969, Poddar was a voluntary outpatient receiving therapy at Cowell Memorial Hospital. Poddar informed Moore, his therapist, that he was going to kill an unnamed girl, readily identifiable as Tatiana, when she returned home from spending the summer in Brazil. Moore, with the concurrence of Dr. Gold, who had initially examined Poddar, and Dr. Yandell, Assistant to the director of the department of psychiatry, decided that Poddar should be committed for observation in a mental hospital. Moore orally notified Officers Atkinson and Teel of the campus police that he would request commitment. He then sent a letter to Police Chief William Beall requesting the assistance of the police department in securing Poddar's confinement.

Officers Atkinson, Brownrigg, and Halleran took Poddar into custody, but, satisfied that Poddar was rational, released him on his promise to stay away from Tatiana. Powelson, director of the department of psychiatry at Cowell Memorial Hospital, then asked the police to return Moore's letter, directed that all copies of the letter and notes that Moore had taken as therapist be destroyed, and 'ordered no action to place Prosenjit Poddar in 72-hour treatment and evaluation facility.'

Plaintiffs' second cause of action, entitled 'Failure to Warn On a Dangerous Patient,' incorporates the allegations of the first cause of action, but adds the assertion that defendants negligently permitted Poddar to be released from police custody without 'notifying the parents of Tatiana Tarasoff that their daughter was in grave danger from Posenjit Poddar.' Poddar persuaded Tatiana's brother to share an apartment with him near Tatiana's residence; shortly after her return from Brazil, Poddar went to her residence and killed her.

[. . .] In analyzing this issue, we bear in mind that legal duties are not discoverable facts of nature, but merely conclusory expressions that, in cases of a particular type, liability should be imposed for damage done. As stated in *Dillon v. Legg* [citation omitted]: "The assertion that liability must . . . be denied because defendant bears no 'duty' to plaintiff 'begs the essential question--whether the plaintiff's interests are entitled to legal protection against the defendant's conduct. . . (Duty) is not sacrosanct in itself, but only an expression of the sum total of those considerations of policy which lead the law to say that the particular plaintiff is entitled to protection." [Citation omitted.]

In the landmark case of *Rowland v. Christian* [citation omitted], Justice Peters recognized that liability should be imposed 'for an injury occasioned to another by his want of ordinary care or skill' as expressed in section 1714 of the Civil Code. Thus, Justice Peters, quoting from *Heaven v. Pender* [citation omitted] stated: "whenever one person is by circumstances placed in such a position with regard to another . . . that if he did not use ordinary care and skill in his own conduct . . . he would cause danger of injury to the person or property of the other, a duty arises to use ordinary care and skill to avoid such danger."

We depart from 'this fundamental principle' only upon the 'balancing of a number of considerations'; major ones 'are the foreseeability of harm to the plaintiff, the degree of certainty that the plaintiff suffered injury, the closeness of the connection between the defendant's conduct and the injury suffered, the moral blame attached to the defendant's conduct, the policy of preventing future harm, the extent of the burden to the defendant and consequences to the community of imposing a duty to exercise care with resulting liability for breach, and the availability, cost and prevalence of insurance for the risk involved.'

The most important of these considerations in establishing duty is foreseeability. As a general principle, a 'defendant owes a duty of care to all persons who are foreseeably endangered by his conduct, with respect to all risks which make the conduct unreasonably dangerous.' [Citations omitted.] As we shall explain, however, when the avoidance of foreseeable harm requires a defendant to control the conduct of another person, or to warn of such conduct, the common law has traditionally imposed liability only if the defendant bears some special relationship to the dangerous person or to the potential victim. Since the relationship between a therapist and his patient satisfies this requirement, we need not here decide whether foreseeability alone is sufficient to create a duty to exercise reasonable care to protect a potential victim of another's conduct.

Although, as we have stated above, under the common law, as a general rule, one person owed no duty to control the conduct of another [citations omitted], nor to warn those endangered by such conduct [citation omitted], the courts have carved out an exception to this rule in cases in which the defendant stands in some special relationship to either the person whose conduct needs to be controlled or in a relationship to the foreseeable victim of that conduct. [Citation omitted.] Applying this exception to the present case, we note that a relationship of defendant therapists to either Tatiana or Poddar will suffice to establish a duty of care; as explained in section 315 of the Restatement Second of Torts, a duty of care may arise from either '(a) a special relation . . . between the actor and the third person which imposes a duty upon the actor to control the third person's conduct, or (b) a special relation . . . between the actor and the other which gives to the other a right of protection.'

Although plaintiffs' pleadings assert no special relation between Tatiana and defendant therapists, they establish as between Poddar and defendant therapists the special relation that arises between a patient and his doctor or psychotherapist. Such a relationship may support affirmative duties for the benefit of third persons. Thus, for example, a hospital must exercise reasonable care to control the behavior of a patient which may endanger other persons. A doctor must also warn a patient if the patient's condition or medication renders certain conduct, such as driving a car, dangerous to others.

Although the California decisions that recognize this duty have involved cases in which the defendant stood in a special relationship both to the victim and to the person whose conduct created the danger, we do not think that the duty should logically be constricted to such situations. Decisions of other jurisdictions hold that the single relationship of a doctor to his patient is sufficient to support the duty to exercise reasonable care to protect others against dangers emanating from the patient's illness. The courts hold that a doctor is liable to persons infected by his patient if he negligently fails to diagnose a contagious disease [citation omitted], or, having diagnosed the illness, fails to warn members of the patient's family. [Citations omitted.]

Since it involved a dangerous mental patient, the decision in *Merchants Nat. Bank & Trust Co. of Fargo v. United States* [citation omitted] comes closer to the issue. The Veterans Administration arranged for the patient to work on a local farm, but did not inform the farmer of the man's background. The farmer consequently permitted the patient to come and go freely during nonworking hours; the patient borrowed a car, drove to his wife's residence and killed her. Notwithstanding the lack of any 'special relationship' between the Veterans Administration and the wife, the court found the Veterans Administration liable for the wrongful death of the wife.

In their summary of the relevant rulings Fleming and Maximov conclude that the 'case law should dispel any notion that to impose on the therapists a duty to take precautions for the safety of persons threatened by a patient, where due care so requires, is in any way opposed to contemporary ground rules on the duty relationship. On the contrary, there now seems to be sufficient authority to support the conclusion that by entering into a doctor-patient relationship the therapist becomes sufficiently involved to assume some responsibility for the safety, not only of the patient himself, but also of any third person whom the doctor knows to be threatened by the patient.' [Citation omitted.]

Defendants contend, however, that imposition of a duty to exercise reasonable care to protect third persons is unworkable because therapists cannot accurately predict whether or not a patient will resort to violence. In support of this argument amicus representing the American Psychiatric Association and other professional societies cites numerous articles which indicate that therapists, in the present state of the art, are unable reliably to predict violent acts; their forecasts, amicus claims, tend consistently to overpredict violence, and indeed are more often wrong than right. Since predictions of violence are often erroneous, amicus concludes, the courts should not render rulings that predicate the liability of therapists upon the validity of such predictions.

The role of the psychiatrist, who is indeed a practitioner of medicine, and that of the psychologist who performs an allied function, are like that of the physician who must conform to the standards of the profession and who must often make diagnoses and predictions based upon such evaluations. Thus the judgment of the therapist in diagnosing emotional disorders and in predicting whether a patient presents a serious danger of violence is comparable to the judgment which doctors and professionals must regularly render under accepted rules of responsibility.

We recognize the difficulty that a therapist encounters in attempting to forecast whether a patient presents a serious danger of violence. Obviously we do not require that the therapist, in making that determination, render a perfect performance; the therapist need only exercise 'that reasonable degree of skill, knowledge, and care ordinarily possessed and exercised by members of (that professional specialty) under similar circumstances.' [Citations omitted.] Within the broad range of reasonable practice and treatment in which professional opinion and judgment may differ, the therapist is free to exercise his or her own best judgment without liability; proof, aided by hindsight, that he or she judged wrongly is insufficient to establish negligence.

In the instant case, however, the pleadings do not raise any question as to failure of defendant therapists to predict that Poddar presented a serious danger of violence. On the contrary, the present complaints allege that defendant therapists did in fact predict that Poddar would kill, but were negligent in failing to warn. [. . .] The risk that unnecessary warnings may be given is a reasonable price to pay for the lives of possible victims that may be saved. We would hesitate to hold that the therapist who is aware that his patient expects to attempt to assassinate the President of the United States would not be obligated to warn the authorities because the therapist cannot predict with accuracy that his patient will commit the crime.

Defendants further argue that free and open communication is essential to psychotherapy [and] that 'Unless a patient . . . is assured that . . . information (revealed by him) can and will be held in utmost confidence, he will be reluctant to make the full disclosure upon which diagnosis and treatment . . . depends.' [Citation omitted.] The giving of a warning, defendants contend, constitutes a breach of trust which entails the revelation of confidential communications.

We recognize the public interest in supporting effective treatment of mental illness and in protecting the rights of patients to privacy [citations omitted] and the consequent public importance of safeguarding the confidential character of psychotherapeutic communication. Against this interest, however, we must weigh the public interest in safety from violent assault.

[. . .] We realize that the open and confidential character of psychotherapeutic dialogue encourages patients to express threats of violence, few of which are ever executed. Certainly a therapist should not be encouraged routinely to reveal such threats; such disclosures could seriously disrupt the patient's relationship with his therapist and with the persons threatened. To the contrary, the therapist's obligations to his patient require that he not disclose a confidence unless such disclosure is necessary to avert danger to others, and even then that he do so discreetly, and in a fashion that would preserve the privacy of his patient to the fullest extent compatible with the prevention of the threatened danger. [Citations omitted.]

The revelation of a communication under the above circumstances is not a breach of trust or a violation of professional ethics; as stated in the Principles of Medical Ethics of the American Medical Association (1957), section 9: 'A physician may not reveal the confidence entrusted to him in the course of medical attendance . . . Unless he is required to do so by law or unless it becomes necessary in order to protect the welfare of the individual or of the community.' (Emphasis added.) We conclude that the public policy favoring protection of the confidential character of patient-psychotherapist communications must yield to the extent to which disclosure is essential to avert danger to others. The protective privilege ends where the public peril begins.

Our current crowded and computerized society compels the interdependence of its members. In this risk-infested society we can hardly tolerate the further exposure to danger that would result from a concealed knowledge of the therapist that his patient was lethal. If the exercise of reasonable care to protect the threatened victim requires the therapist to warn the endangered party or those who can reasonably be expected to notify him, we see no sufficient societal interest that would protect and justify concealment. The containment of such risks lies in the public interest. For the foregoing reasons, we find that plaintiffs' complaints can be amended to state a cause of action against defendants Moore, Powelson, Gold, and Yandell and against the Regents as their employer, for breach of a duty to exercise reasonable care to protect Tatiana.

APPENDIX D

THE RIGHTS OF MINORS TO CONSENT TO HEALTH CARE

CALIFORNIA FAMILY CODE SECTIONS 6903 THROUGH 6929

INTRODUCTORY NOTE

In most states, a minor does not have legal capacity to consent to medical treatment on his own behalf and a health care provider must obtain the consent of the minor's parent or guardian in order to provide care to the minor. Generally, persons under the age of 18 are considered minors. However, state statutes often provide exceptions to the general rule and enumerate specific instances when a minor is legally authorized to consent to treatment for himself. In the absence of a statutory provision to the contrary, a minor is generally afforded medical confidentiality with regard to any services to which he has legal capacity to consent. The following statutes are effective in California.

THE STATUTE

California Family Code §6903

"Parent or guardian" means either parent if both parents have legal custody, or the parent or person having legal custody, or the guardian, of a minor.

California Family Code *§ 611*

(a)Upon application by a minor, the court may summarily grant consent for medical care or dental care or both for the minor if the court determines all of the following:

(1) The minor is 16 years of age or older and resides in this states.

California Family Code § 6920

Subject to the limitations provided in this chapter, notwithstanding any other provision of law, a minor may consent to the matters provided in this chapter, and the consent of the minor's parent or guardian is not necessary.

California Family Code § 6921

A consent given by a minor under this chapter is not subject to disaffirmance because of minority.

California Family Code § 6922

(a) A minor may consent to the minor's medical care or dental care if all of the following conditions are satisfied:

(1) The minor is 15 years of age or older.

(2) The minor is living separate and apart from the minor's parents or guardian, whether with or without the consent of a parent or guardian and regardless of the duration of the separate residence.

(3) The minor is managing the minor's own financial affairs, regardless of the source of the minor's income.

(b) The parents or guardian are not liable for medical care or dental care provided pursuant to this section.

(c) A physician and surgeon or dentist may, with or without the consent of the minor patient, advise the minor's parent or guardian of the treatment given or needed if the physician and surgeon or dentist has reason to know, on the basis of the information given by the minor, the whereabouts of the parent or guardian.

California Family Code § 6924

(a) [omitted]

(b) A minor who is 12 years of age or older may consent to mental health treatment or counseling on an outpatient basis, or to residential shelter services, if both of the following requirements are satisfied:

(1) The minor, in the opinion of the attending professional person, is mature enough to participate intelligently in the outpatient services or residential shelter services.

(2) The minor (A) would present a danger of serious physical or mental harm to self or to others without the mental health treatment or counseling or residential shelter services, or (B) is the alleged victim of incest or child abuse.

(c) [omitted]

(d) The mental health treatment or counseling of a minor authorized by this section shall include involvement of the minor's parent or guardian unless, in the opinion of the professional person who is treating or counseling the minor, the involvement would be inappropriate. The professional person who is treating or counseling the minor shall state in the client record whether and when the person attempted to contact the minor's parent or guardian, and whether the attempt to contact was successful or unsuccessful, or the reason why, in the professional person's opinion, it would be inappropriate to contact the minor's parent or guardian.

(e) The minor's parents or guardian are not liable for payment for mental health treatment or counseling services provided pursuant to this section unless the parent or guardian participates in the mental health treatment or counseling, and then only for services rendered with the participation of the parent or guardian.

California Family Code § 6925

(a) A minor may consent to medical care related to the prevention or treatment of pregnancy.

(b) This section does not authorize a minor:

(1) To be sterilized without the consent of the minor's parent or guardian.

(2) To receive an abortion without the consent of a parent or guardian other than as provided in Section 123450 of the Health and Safety Code.

California Family Code § 6926

(a) A minor who is 12 years of age or older and who may have come into contact with an infectious, contagious, or communicable disease may consent to medical care related to the diagnosis or treatment of the disease, if the disease or condition is one that is required by law or regulation adopted pursuant to law to be reported to the local health officer, or is a related sexually transmitted disease, as may be determined by the State Director of Health Services.

(b) The minor's parents or guardian are not liable for payment for medical care provided pursuant to this section.

California Family Code § 6927

A minor who is 12 years of age or older and who is alleged to have been raped may consent to medical care related to the diagnosis or treatment of the condition and the collection of medical evidence with regard to the alleged rape.

California Family Code § 6928

(a) [omitted]

(b) A minor who is alleged to have been sexually assaulted may consent to medical care related to the diagnosis and treatment of the condition, and the collection of medical evidence with regard to the alleged sexual assault.

(c) The professional person providing medical treatment shall attempt to contact the minor's parent or guardian and shall note in the minor's treatment record the date and time the professional person attempted to contact the parent or guardian and whether the attempt was successful or unsuccessful. This subdivision does not apply if the professional person reasonably believes that the minor's parent or guardian committed the sexual assault on the minor.

California Family Code § 6929

(a) [omitted]

(b) A minor who is 12 years of age or older may consent to medical care and counseling relating to the diagnosis and treatment of a drug or alcohol related problem.

(c) The treatment plan of a minor authorized by this section shall include the involvement of the minor's parent or guardian, if appropriate, as determined by the professional person or treatment facility treating the minor. The professional person providing medical care or counseling to a minor shall state in the minor's treatment record whether and when the professional person attempted to contact the minor's parent or guardian, and whether the attempt to contact the parent or guardian was successful or unsuccessful, or the reason why, in the opinion of the professional person, it would not be appropriate to contact the minor's parent or guardian.

(d) The minor's parents or guardian are not liable for payment for any care provided to a minor pursuant to this section, except that if the minor's parent or guardian participates in a counseling program pursuant to this section, the parent or guardian is liable for the cost of the services provided to the minor and the parent or guardian.

(e) [omitted]

(f) It is the intent of the Legislature that the state shall respect the right of a parent or legal guardian to seek medical care and counseling for a drug- or alcohol-related problem of a minor child when the child does not consent to the medical care and counseling, and nothing in this section shall be construed to restrict or eliminate this right.

(g) Notwithstanding any other provision of law, in cases where a parent or legal guardian has sought the medical care and counseling for a drug- or alcohol-related problem of a minor child, the physician shall disclose medical information concerning such care to the minor's parents or legal guardian upon their request, even if the minor child does not consent to disclosure, without liability for such disclosure.

APPENDIX E

FEDERAL DRUG AND ALCOHOL ABUSE
CONFIDENTIALITY REGULATIONS

Title 42 Code of Federal Regulations Part 2

INTRODUCTORY NOTE

Federal regulations provide heightened confidentiality protections for information and records pertaining to an individual's counseling or treatment for alcohol or drug abuse. The federal regulations generally preempt state confidentiality laws unless the state laws set forth confidentiality protections which are stricter than the federal regulations, in which case both sets of requirements apply.

In sections not included in this Appendix, the federal regulations provide that protected information may be released without the written consent of the patient only in the event of a medical emergency, as necessary to conduct audits or evaluations, and as need for authorized research activities

THE REGULATIONS

Section 2.11 Definitions

For purposes of these regulations:
Alcohol abuse means the use of an alcoholic beverage which impairs the physical, mental, emotional, or social well-being of the user.
Drug abuse means the use of a psychoactive substance for other than medicinal purposes which impairs the physical, mental, emotional, or social well-being of the user.
Diagnosis means any reference to an individual's alcohol or drug abuse or to a condition which is identified as having been caused by that abuse which is made for the purpose of treatment or referral for treatment.
Disclose or *disclosure* means a communication of patient identifying information, the affirmative verification of another person's communication of patient identifying

information, or the communication of any information from the record of a patient who has been identified.

[. . .]

Patient means any individual who has applied for or been given diagnosis or treatment for alcohol or drug abuse at a federally assisted program and includes any individual who, after arrest on a criminal charge, is identified as an alcohol or drug abuser in order to determine that individual's eligibility to participate in a program.

[. . .]

Program means:

(a) An individual or entity (other than a general medical care facility) who holds itself out as providing, and provides, alcohol or drug abuse diagnosis, treatment or referral for treatment; or

(b) An identified unit within a general medical facility which holds itself out as providing, and provides, alcohol or drug abuse diagnosis, treatment or referral for treatment; or

(c) Medical personnel or other staff in a general medical care facility whose primary function is the provision of alcohol or drug abuse diagnosis, treatment or referral for treatment and who are identified as such providers.

[. . .]

Records means any information, whether recorded or not, relating to a patient received or acquired by a federally assisted alcohol or drug program.

[. . .]

Treatment means the management and care of a patient suffering from alcohol or drug abuse, a condition which is identified as having been caused by that abuse, or both, in order to reduce or eliminate the adverse effects upon the patient.

[. . .]

Section 2.13 Confidentiality restrictions

(a) *General.* The patient records to which these regulations apply may be disclosed or used only as permitted by these regulations and may not otherwise be disclosed or used in any civil, criminal, administrative, or legislative proceedings conducted by any Federal, State, or local authority. Any disclosure made under these regulations must be limited to that information which is necessary to carry out the purpose of the disclosure.

(b) *Unconditional compliance required.* The restrictions on disclosure and use in these regulations apply whether the holder of the information believes that the person seeking the information already has it, has other means of obtaining it, is a law enforcement or other official, has obtained a subpoena, or asserts any other justification for a disclosure or use which is not permitted by these regulations.

(c) *Acknowledging the presence of patients: Responding to requests.*

(1) The presence of an identified patient in a facility or component of a facility which is publicly identified as a place where only alcohol or drug abuse diagnosis, treatment, or referral is provided may be acknowledged only if the

patient's written consent is obtained in accordance with [. . .] these regulations or if an authorizing court order is entered in accordance with [. . .] these regulations. The regulations permit acknowledgment of the presence of an identified patient in a facility or part of a facility if the facility is not publicly identified as only an alcohol or drug abuse diagnosis, treatment or referral facility, and if the acknowledgment does not reveal that the patient is an alcohol or drug abuser.

(2) Any answer to a request for a disclosure of patient records which is not permissible under these regulations must be made in a way that will not affirmatively reveal that an identified individual has been, or is being diagnosed or treated for alcohol or drug abuse. An inquiring party may be given a copy of these regulations and advised that they restrict the disclosure of alcohol or drug abuse patient records, but may not be told affirmatively that the regulations restrict the disclosure of the records of an identified patient. The regulations do not restrict a disclosure that an identified individual is not and never has been a patient.

Section 2.14 Minor patients

(a) *Definition of minor.* As used in these regulations the term "minor" means a person who has not attained the age of majority specified in the applicable State law, or if no age of majority is specified in the applicable State law, the age of eighteen years.

(b) *State law not requiring parental consent to treatment.* If a minor patient acting alone has the legal capacity under the applicable State law to apply for and obtain alcohol or drug abuse treatment, any written consent for disclosure authorized under [. . .] these regulations may be given only by the minor patient. This restriction includes, but is not limited to, any disclosure of patient identifying information to the parent or guardian of a minor patient for the purpose of obtaining financial reimbursement. These regulations do not prohibit a program from refusing to provide treatment until the minor patient consents to the disclosure necessary to obtain reimbursement, but refusal to provide treatment may be prohibited under a State or local law requiring the program to furnish the service irrespective of ability to pay.

(c) *State law requiring parental consent to treatment.*

(1) Where State law requires consent of a parent, guardian, or other person for a minor to obtain alcohol or drug abuse treatment, any written consent for disclosure authorized under [. . .] these regulations must be given by both the minor and his or her parent, guardian, or other person authorized under State law to act in the minor's behalf.

(2) Where State law requires parental consent to treatment the fact of a minor's application for treatment may be communicated to the minor's parent, guardian, or other person authorized under State law to act in the minor's behalf only if:

(i) The minor has given written consent to the disclosure in accordance with [. . .] these regulations or

(ii) The minor lacks the capacity to make a rational choice regarding such consent as judged by the program director under paragraph (d) of this section.

(d) *Minor applicant for services lacks capacity for rational choice.* Facts relevant to reducing a threat to the life or physical well-being of the applicant or any other individual may be disclosed to the parent, guardian, or other person authorized under State law to act in the minor's behalf if the program director judges that:

(1) A minor applicant for services lacks capacity because of extreme youth or mental or physical condition to make a rational decision on whether to consent to a disclosure under [. . .] these regulations to his or her parent, guardian, or other person authorized under State law to act in the minor's behalf, and

(2) The applicant's situation poses a substantial threat to the life or physical well being of the applicant or any other individual which may be reduced by communicating relevant facts to the minor's parent, guardian, or other person authorized under State law to act in the minor's behalf.

Section 2.31 Form of written consent

(a) *Required elements.* A written consent to a disclosure under these regulations must include:

(1) The specific name or general designation of the program or person permitted to make the disclosure.

(2) The name or title of the individual or the name of the organization to which disclosure is to be made.

(3) The name of the patient.

(4) The purpose of the disclosure.

(5) How much and what kind of information is to be disclosed.

(6) The signature of the patient and, when required for a patient who is a minor, the signature of a person authorized to give consent under Section 2.14.

(7) The date on which the consent is signed.

(8) A statement that the consent is subject to revocation at any time except to the extent that the program or person which is to make the disclosure has already acted in reliance on it. Acting in reliance includes the provision of treatment services in reliance on a valid consent to disclose information to a third party payer.

(9) The date, event, or condition upon which the consent will expire if not revoked before. This date, event, or condition must insure that the consent will last no longer than reasonably necessary to serve the purpose for which it is given.

(b) *Sample consent form.* The following form complies with paragraph (a) of this section, but other elements may be added.

1.   I (name of patient) Request/Authorize:

---

2. (name or general designation of program which is to make the disclosure)

---

3. To disclose: (kind and amount of information to be disclosed)

---

4. To: (name or title of the person or organization to which disclosure is to be made)

_____

5. For (purpose of the disclosure)

_____

6. Date (on which this consent is signed)

_____

7. Signature of patient

_____

8. Signature of parent or guardian (where required)

_____

9. Signature of person authorized to sign in lieu of the patient (where required)

_____

10. This consent is subject to revocation at any time except to the extent that the program which is to make the disclosure has already taken action in reliance on it. If not previously revoked, this consent will terminate upon: (specific date, event, or condition).

(c) *Expired, deficient, or false consent.* A disclosure may not be made on the basis of a consent which:

(1) Has expired;

(2) On its face substantially fails to conform to any of the requirements set forth in paragraph (a) of this section;

(3) Is known to have been revoked; or

(4) Is known, or through a reasonable effort could be known, by the person holding the records to be materially false.

APPENDIX F

CHILD ABUSE REPORTING LAWS

California Penal Code Sections 11164 Through 11166

INTRODUCTORY NOTE

Generally, communications that occur between a health practitioner and a patient during the course of rendering health services are statutorily protected as confidential. This is often the case even if the patient is a minor, so long as the minor has legal capacity to consent to the care being rendered. In certain instances, however, state legislatures have carved out exceptions to medical confidentiality when a competing public policy interest requires confidentiality to be breached. One such instance is the case of reporting suspected child abuse. In most states, health practitioners are required by law to report suspected child abuse to law enforcement officials. Such reporting requirements often put health practitioners in the difficult situation of having to balance patient confidentiality against the need to investigate the suspected abuse and protect the suspected victim. The following statute is California's mandatory child abuse reporting statute.

THE STATUTE

California Penal Code Section 11164

(a) This article shall be known and may be cited as the Child Abuse and Neglect Reporting Act.

(b) The intent and purpose of this article is to protect children from abuse. In any investigation of suspected child abuse, all persons participating in the investigation of the case shall consider the needs of the child victim and shall do whatever is necessary to prevent psychological harm to the child victim.

California Penal Code Section 11165

As used in this article "child" means a person under the age of 18 years.

California Penal Code Section 11165.6

As used in this article, "child abuse" means a physical injury which is inflicted by other than accidental means on a child by another person. "Child abuse" also means the sexual abuse of a child [. . .]. [. . .] "Child abuse" does not mean a mutual affray between minors. "Child abuse" does not include an injury caused by reasonable and necessary force used by a peace officer acting within the course and scope of his or her employment as a peace officer.

California Penal Code Section 11165.8

As used in this article, "health practitioner" means any of the following:

(a) A physician and surgeon, psychiatrist, psychologist, dentist, resident, intern, podiatrist, chiropractor, licensed nurse, dental hygienist, optometrist, marriage, family and child counselor, clinical social worker, or any other person who is currently licensed under [. . .] the Business and Professions Code.

(b) [. . .]

(c) A psychological assistant [. . .].

(d) A marriage, family and child counselor trainee [. . .].

[. . .]

California Penal Code Section 11166

(a) Except as provided in subdivision (b), any [. . .] health practitioner [. . .] who has knowledge of or observes a child, in his or her professional capacity or within the scope of his or her employment, whom he or she knows or reasonably suspects has been the victim of child abuse, shall report the known or suspected instance of child abuse to a child protective agency immediately or as soon as practically possible by telephone and shall prepare and send a written report thereof within 36 hours of receiving the information concerning the incident. [. . .] For the purposes of this article, "reasonable suspicion" means that it is objectively reasonable for a person to entertain a suspicion, based upon facts that could cause a reasonable person in a like position, drawing, when appropriate, on his or her training and experience, to suspect child abuse. For the purpose of this article, the pregnancy of a minor does not, in and of itself, constitute a basis of reasonable suspicion of sexual abuse.

(b) Any [. . .] health practitioner [. . .] who has knowledge of or who reasonably suspects that mental suffering has been inflicted upon a child or that his or her emotional well-being is endangered in any other way, may report the known or suspected instance of child abuse to a child protective agency.

(c) [. . .]

(d) [. . .]

(e) [. . .]

(h) The reporting duties under this section are individual, and no supervisor or administrator may impede or inhibit the reporting duties, and no person making a report shall be subject to any sanction for making the report. However, internal procedures to facilitate reporting and apprise supervisors and administrators of reports may be established provided that they are not inconsistent with this article. The internal procedures shall not require any employee required to make reports pursuant to this article to disclose his or her identity to the employer.
(i) [. . .]

APPENDIX G

CRUZAN v. DIRECTOR, MISSOURI DEPARTMENT OF HEALTH

United States Supreme Court
497 U.S. 261(1990)

INTRODUCTORY NOTE

The *Cruzan* case is an often cited and somewhat controversial decision. It is worth noting that after the U.S. Supreme Court case set forth below was decided, the Missouri trial court heard new evidence provided by Nancy Cruzan's friends and colleagues that she had made explicit and unambiguous statements that clearly and convincingly evidenced that she would not wish to continue receiving life-sustaining treatment. The trial court thereafter authorized, without opposition from the Missouri State Attorney General, Ms. Cruzan's parents to order termination of Ms. Cruzan's nutrition and hydration.

THE CASE

Chief Justice Rehnquist delivered the opinion of the Court.

Petitioner Nancy Beth Cruzan was rendered incompetent as a result of severe injuries sustained during an automobile accident. Copetitioners Lester and Joyce Cruzan, Nancy's parents and coguardians, sought a court order directing the withdrawal of their daughter's artificial feeding and hydration equipment after it became apparent that she had virtually no chance of recovering her cognitive faculties. The Supreme Court of Missouri held that, because there was no clear and convincing evidence of Nancy's desire to have life-sustaining treatment withdrawn under such circumstances, her parents lacked authority to effectuate such a request.

We granted certiorari and now affirm.

On the night of January 11, 1983, Nancy Cruzan lost control of her car as she traveled down Elm Road in Jasper County, Missouri. The vehicle overturned, and Cruzan was discovered lying face down in a ditch without detectable respiratory or cardiac function. Paramedics were able to restore her breathing and heartbeat at the accident site, and she was transported to a hospital in an unconscious state. An attending neurosurgeon diagnosed her as having sustained probable cerebral contusions compounded by significant anoxia (lack of oxygen). The Missouri trial court in this case found that permanent brain damage generally results after 6 minutes in an anoxic state; it was estimated that Cruzan was deprived of oxygen from 12 to 14 minutes. She remained in a coma for approximately three weeks, and then progressed to an unconscious state in which she was able to orally ingest some nutrition. In order to ease feeding and further the recovery, surgeons implanted a gastrostomy feeding and hydration tube in Cruzan with the consent of her then husband. Subsequent rehabilitative efforts proved unavailing. She now lies in a Missouri state hospital in what is commonly referred to as a persistent vegetative state: generally, a condition in which a person exhibits motor reflexes but evinces no indications of significant cognitive function. The State of Missouri is bearing the cost of her care.

After it had become apparent that Nancy Cruzan had virtually no chance of regaining her mental faculties, her parents asked hospital employees to terminate the artificial nutrition and hydration procedures. All agree that such a removal would cause her death. The employees refused to honor the request without court approval. The parents then sought and received authorization from the state trial court for termination. The court found that a person in Nancy's condition had a fundamental right under the State and Federal Constitutions to refuse or direct the withdrawal of "death prolonging procedures." The court also found that Nancy's "expressed thoughts at age twenty-five in somewhat serious conversation with a housemate friend that, if sick or injured, she would not wish to continue her life unless she could live at least halfway normally suggests that, given her present condition, she would not wish to continue on with her nutrition and hydration."

The Supreme Court of Missouri reversed by a divided vote. [. . .]

We granted certiorari to consider the question of whether Cruzan has a right under the United States Constitution which would require the hospital to withdraw life-sustaining treatment from her under these circumstances.

At common law, even the touching of one person by another without consent and without legal justification was a battery. Before the turn of the century, this Court observed that "[n]o right is held more sacred, or is more carefully guarded by the common law, than the right of every individual to the possession and control of his own person, free from all restraint or interference of others, unless by clear and unquestionable authority of law." [Citation omitted.] This notion of bodily integrity has been embodied in the requirement that informed consent is generally required for medical treatment. Justice Cardozo, while on the Court of Appeals of New York, aptly described this doctrine: "Every human being of adult years and sound mind has a right to determine what shall be done with his own body, and a surgeon who performs an operation without his patient's consent commits an assault, for which he is liable in damages." [Citation omitted.] The informed consent doctrine has become firmly entrenched in American tort law. [Citation omitted.]

The logical corollary of the doctrine of informed consent is that the patient generally possesses the right not to consent, that is, to refuse treatment. [R]ecently, [. . .] with the advance of medical technology capable of sustaining life well past the point where natural forces would have brought certain death in earlier times, cases involving the right to refuse life-sustaining treatment have burgeoned. [Citation omitted.]

[. . .]

The Fourteenth Amendment provides that no State shall "deprive any person of life, liberty, or property, without due process of law." The principle that a competent person has a constitutionally protected liberty interest in refusing unwanted medical treatment may be inferred from our prior decisions. In *Jacobson v. Massachusetts*, for instance, the Court balanced an individual's liberty interest in declining an unwanted smallpox vaccine against the State's interest in preventing disease. Decisions prior to the incorporation of the Fourth Amendment into the Fourteenth Amendment analyzed searches and seizures involving the body under the Due Process Clause and were thought to implicate substantial liberty interests. [Citation omitted.]

[. . .]

But determining that a person has a "liberty interest" under the Due Process Clause does not end the inquiry; "whether respondent's constitutional rights have been violated must be determined by balancing his liberty interests against the relevant state interests." [Citation omitted.]

Petitioners insist that, under the general holdings of our cases, the forced administration of life-sustaining medical treatment, and even of artificially-delivered food and water essential to life, would implicate a competent person's liberty interest. Although we think the logic of the cases discussed above would embrace such a liberty interest, the dramatic consequences involved in refusal of such treatment would inform the inquiry as to whether the deprivation of that interest is constitutionally permissible. But for purposes of this case, we assume that the United States Constitution would grant a competent person a constitutionally protected right to refuse lifesaving hydration and nutrition.

Petitioners go on to assert that an incompetent person should possess the same right in this respect as is possessed by a competent person. [. . .]

The difficulty with petitioners' claim is that, in a sense, it begs the question: an incompetent person is not able to make an informed and voluntary choice to exercise a hypothetical right to refuse treatment or any other right. Such a "right" must be exercised for her, if at all, by some sort of surrogate. Here, Missouri has in effect recognized that, under certain circumstances, a surrogate may act for the patient in electing to have hydration and nutrition withdrawn in such a way as to cause death, but it has established a procedural safeguard to assure that the action of the surrogate conforms as best it may to the wishes expressed by the patient while competent. Missouri requires that evidence of the incompetent's wishes as to the withdrawal of treatment be proved by clear and convincing evidence. The question, then, is whether the United States Constitution forbids the establishment of this procedural requirement by the State. We hold that it does not.

Whether or not Missouri's clear and convincing evidence requirement comports with the United States Constitution depends in part on what interests the State may properly seek to protect in this situation. Missouri relies on its interest in the protection and preservation of human life, and there can be no gainsaying this interest. As a general matter, the States - indeed, all civilized nations - demonstrate their commitment to life by treating homicide as serious crime. Moreover, the majority of States in this country have laws imposing criminal penalties on one who assists another to commit suicide. We do not think a State is required to remain neutral in the face of an informed and voluntary decision by a physically able adult to starve to death

But in the context presented here, a State has more particular interests at stake. The choice between life and death is a deeply personal decision of obvious and overwhelming finality. We believe Missouri may legitimately seek to safeguard the personal element of this choice through the imposition of heightened evidentiary requirements. It cannot be disputed that the Due Process Clause protects an interest in life as well as an interest in refusing life-sustaining medical treatment. Not all incompetent patients will have loved ones available to serve as surrogate decisionmakers. And even where family members are present, "[t]here will, of course, be some unfortunate situations in which family members will not act to protect a patient." [Citation omitted.] A State is entitled to guard against potential abuses in such situations. Similarly, a State is entitled to consider that a judicial proceeding to make a determination regarding an incompetent's wishes may very well not be an adversarial one, with the added guarantee of accurate factfinding that the adversary process brings with it. [Citation omitted.] Finally, we think a State may properly decline to make judgments about the "quality" of life that a particular individual may enjoy, and simply assert an unqualified interest in the preservation of human life to be weighed against the constitutionally protected interests of the individual.

In our view, Missouri has permissibly sought to advance these interests through the adoption of a "clear and convincing" standard of proof to govern such proceedings. "The function of a standard of proof, as that concept is embodied in the Due Process Clause and in the realm of factfinding, is to `instruct the factfinder concerning the degree of confidence our society thinks he should have in the correctness of factual conclusions for a particular type of adjudication.'" [Citation omitted.] "This Court has mandated an intermediate standard of proof - `clear and convincing evidence' - when the individual interests at stake in a state proceeding are both `particularly important' and `more substantial than mere loss of money.'"

[. . .]

We think it self-evident that the interests at stake in the instant proceedings are more substantial, both on an individual and societal level, than those involved in a run-of-the-mine civil dispute. But not only does the standard of proof reflect the importance of a particular adjudication, it also serves as "a societal judgment about how the risk of error should be distributed between the litigants." [Citation omitted.] The more stringent the burden of proof a party must bear, the more that party bears the risk of an erroneous decision. We believe that Missouri may permissibly place an increased risk of an erroneous decision on those seeking to terminate an incompetent individual's life-sustaining treatment. An erroneous decision not to terminate results in a maintenance of the status quo; the possibility of subsequent developments such as advancements in medical science, the discovery of new evidence regarding the patient's intent, changes in the law, or simply the unexpected death of the patient despite the administration of life-sustaining treatment, at least create the potential that a wrong decision will eventually be corrected or its impact mitigated. An erroneous decision to withdraw life-sustaining treatment, however, is not susceptible of correction. In *Santosky*, one of the factors which led the Court to require proof by clear and convincing evidence in a proceeding to terminate parental rights was that a decision in such a case was final and irrevocable. The same must surely be said of the decision to discontinue hydration and nutrition of a patient such as Nancy Cruzan, which all agree will result in her death.

[. . .]

In sum, we conclude that a State may apply a clear and convincing evidence standard in proceedings where a guardian seeks to discontinue nutrition and hydration of a person diagnosed to be in a persistent vegetative state. [. . .]

The Supreme Court of Missouri held that, in this case, the testimony adduced at trial did not amount to clear and convincing proof of the patient's desire to have hydration and nutrition withdrawn. In so doing, it reversed a decision of the Missouri trial court, which had found that the evidence "suggest[ed]" Nancy Cruzan would not have desired to continue such measures, but which had not adopted the standard of "clear and convincing evidence" enunciated by the Supreme Court. The testimony adduced at trial consisted primarily of Nancy Cruzan's statements, made to a housemate about a year before her accident, that she would not want to live should she face life as a "vegetable," and other observations to the same effect. The observations did not deal in terms with withdrawal of medical treatment or of hydration and nutrition. We cannot say that the Supreme Court of Missouri committed constitutional error in reaching the conclusion that it did.

Petitioners alternatively contend that Missouri must accept the "substituted judgment" of close family members even in the absence of substantial proof that their views reflect the views of the patient. [W]e do not think these cases support their claim. In *Michael H.*, we upheld the constitutionality of California's favored treatment of traditional family relationships; such a holding may not be turned around into a constitutional requirement that a State must recognize the primacy of those relationships in a situation like this. And in *Parham*, where the patient was a minor, we also upheld the constitutionality of a state scheme in which parents made certain decisions for mentally ill minors. Here again, petitioners would seek to turn a decision which allowed a State to rely on family decisionmaking into a constitutional requirement that the State recognize such decisionmaking. But constitutional law does not work that way.

No doubt is engendered by anything in this record but that Nancy Cruzan's mother and father are loving and caring parents. If the State were required by the United States Constitution to repose a right of "substituted judgment" with anyone, the Cruzans would surely qualify. But we do not think the Due Process Clause requires the State to repose judgment on these matters with anyone but the patient herself. Close family members may have a strong feeling - a feeling not at all ignoble or unworthy, but not entirely disinterested, either - that they do not wish to witness the continuation of the life of a loved one which they regard as hopeless, meaningless, and even degrading. But there is no automatic assurance that the view of close family members will necessarily be the same as the patient's would have been had she been confronted with the prospect of her situation while competent. All of the reasons previously discussed for allowing Missouri to require clear and convincing evidence of the patient's wishes lead us to conclude that the State may choose to defer only to those wishes, rather than confide the decision to close family members.

The judgment of the Supreme Court of Missouri is Affirmed.

APPENDIX H

BOUVIA v. SUPERIOR COURT

California Court of Appeals
179 Ca.App.3d 1127, 225 Cal.Rptr. 297 (1986)

INTRODUCTORY NOTE

The *Bouvia* case excerpted below provides a thorough discussion of the conflict that often arises between the right of an individual to determine his or her own destiny and the interests of the government in promoting and protecting life. Various attempts to get a rehearing at the Court of Appeal or certiorari from the California Supreme Court failed. Strong support for the appellate court decision set forth below may demonstrate a social consensus that neither the government nor any other third party should be able to trump the right of a competent individual to refuse medical care, even when that choice results in death.

THE CASE

BEACH, Associate Justice.

Petitioner, Elizabeth Bouvia, a patient in a public hospital seeks the removal from her body of a nasogastric tube inserted and maintained against her will and without her consent by physicians who so placed it for the purpose of keeping her alive through involuntary forced feeding. Petitioner has here filed a petition for writ of mandamus and other extraordinary relief after the trial court denied her a preliminary injunction requiring that the tube be removed and that the hospital and doctors be prohibited from using any other similar procedures. We issued an alternative writ. We have heard oral argument from the parties and now order issuance of a peremptory writ, granting petitioner, Elizabeth Bouvia, the relief for which she prayed.

[...]

2. Factual Background.

Petitioner is a 28-year-old woman. Since birth she has been afflicted with and suffered from severe cerebral palsy. She is quadriplegic. She is now a patient at a public hospital maintained by one of the real parties in interest, the County of Los Angeles. Other parties are physicians, nurses and the medical and support staff employed by the County of Los Angeles. Petitioner's physical handicaps of palsy and quadriplegia have progressed to the point where she is completely bedridden. Except for a few fingers of one hand and some slight head and facial movements, she is immobile. She is physically helpless and wholly unable to care for herself. She is totally dependent upon others for all of her needs. These include feeding, washing, cleaning, toileting, turning, and helping her with elimination and other bodily functions. She cannot stand or sit upright in bed or in a wheelchair. She lies flat in bed and must do so the rest of her life. She suffers also from degenerative and severely crippling arthritis. She is in continual pain. Another tube permanently attached to her chest automatically injects her with periodic doses of morphine which relieves some, but not all of her physical pain and discomfort. She is intelligent, very mentally competent. She earned a college degree. She was married but her husband has left her. She suffered a miscarriage. She lived with her parents until her father told her that they could no longer care for her. She has stayed intermittently with friends and at public facilities. A search for a permanent place to live where she might receive the constant care which she needs has been unsuccessful. She is without financial means to support herself and, therefore, must accept public assistance for medical and other care.

She has on several occasions expressed the desire to die. In 1983 she sought the right to be cared for in a public hospital in Riverside County while she intentionally "starved herself to death." A court in that county denied her judicial assistance to accomplish that goal. She later abandoned an appeal from that ruling. Thereafter, friends took her to several different facilities, both public and private, arriving finally at her present location. Efforts by the staff of real party in interest County of Los Angeles and its social workers to find her an apartment of her own with publicly paid live-in help or regular visiting nurses to care for her, or some other suitable facility have proved fruitless.

Petitioner must be spoon fed in order to eat. Her present medical and dietary staff have determined that she is not consuming a sufficient amount of nutrients. Petitioner stops eating when she feels she cannot orally swallow more, without nausea and vomiting. As she cannot now retain solids, she is fed soft liquid-like food. Because of her previously announced resolve to starve herself, the medical staff feared her weight loss might reach a life-threatening level. Her weight since admission to real parties' facility seems to hover between 65 and 70 pounds. Accordingly, they inserted the subject tube against her will and contrary to her express written instructions.

Petitioner's counsel argue that her weight loss was not such as to be life threatening and therefore the tube is unnecessary. However, the trial court found to the contrary as a matter of fact, a finding which we must accept. Nonetheless, the point is immaterial, for, as we will explain, a patient has the right to refuse any medical treatment or medical service, even when such treatment is labeled "furnishing nourishment and hydration." This right exists even if its exercise creates a "life threatening condition."

3. The Right to Refuse Medical Treatment

"[A] person of adult years and in sound mind has the right, in the exercise of control over his own body, to determine whether or not to submit to lawful medical treatment." [Citation omitted.] It follows that such a patient has the right to refuse any medical treatment, even that which may save or prolong her life. [. . .] [T]he County and its medical staff contend that for reasons unique to this case, Elizabeth Bouvia may not exercise the right available to others. Accordingly, we again briefly discuss the rule in the light of real parties' contentions.

The right to refuse medical treatment is basic and fundamental. It is recognized as a part of the right of privacy protected by both the state and federal constitutions. [Citations omitted.] Its exercise requires no one's approval. It is not merely one vote subject to being overridden by medical opinion. [. . .] It is indisputable that petitioner is mentally competent. She is not comatose. She is quite intelligent, alert and understands the risks involved.

4. The Claimed Exceptions to the Patient's Right to Choose are Inapplicable.

As in *Bartling* the real parties in interest, a county hospital, its physicians and administrators, urge that the interests of the State should prevail over the rights of Elizabeth Bouvia to refuse treatment. Advanced by real parties under this argument are the State's interests in (1) preserving life, (2) preventing suicide, (3) protecting innocent third parties, and (4) maintaining the ethical standards of the medical profession, including the right of physicians to effectively render necessary and appropriate medical service and to refuse treatment to an uncooperative and disruptive patient. Included, whether as part of the above or as separate and additional arguments, are what real parties assert as distinctive facts not present in other cases, i.e., (1) petitioner is a patient in a public facility, thereby making the State a party to the result of her conduct, (2) she is not comatose, nor incurably, nor terminally ill, nor in a vegetative state, all conditions which have justified the termination of life-support system in other instances, (3) she has asked for medical treatment, therefore, she cannot accept a part of it while cutting off the part that would be effective, and (4) she is, in truth, trying to starve herself to death and the State will not be a party to a suicide.

[. . .]

At bench the trial court concluded that with sufficient feeding petitioner could live an additional 15 to 20 years; therefore, the preservation of petitioner's life for that period outweighed her right to decide. In so holding the trial court mistakenly attached undue importance to the amount of time possibly available to petitioner, and failed to give equal weight and consideration for the quality of that life; an equal, if not more significant, consideration.

All decisions permitting cessation of medical treatment or life-support procedures to some degree hastened the arrival of death. In part, at least, this was permitted because the quality of life during the time remaining in those cases had been terribly diminished. In Elizabeth Bouvia's view, the quality of her life has been diminished to the point of hopelessness, uselessness, unenjoyability and frustration. She, as the patient, lying helplessly in bed, unable to care for herself, may consider her existence meaningless. She cannot be faulted for so concluding. If her right to choose may not be exercised because there remains to her, in the opinion of a court, a physician or some committee, a certain arbitrary number of years, months, or days, her right will have lost its value and meaning. Who shall say what the minimum amount of available life must be? Does it matter if it be 15 to 20 years, 15 to 20 months, or 15 to 20 days, if such life has been physically destroyed and its quality, dignity and purpose gone? As in all matters lines must be drawn at some point, somewhere, but that decision must ultimately belong to the one whose life is in issue.

Here Elizabeth Bouvia's decision to forego medical treatment or life-support through a mechanical means belongs to her. It is not a medical decision for her physicians to make. Neither is it a legal question whose soundness is to be resolved by lawyers or judges. It is not a conditional right subject to approval by ethics committees or courts of law. It is a moral and philosophical decision that, being a competent adult, is hers alone.

[. . .]

Here, if force fed, petitioner faces 15 to 20 years of a painful existence, endurable only by the constant administrations of morphine. Her condition is irreversible. There is no cure for her palsy or arthritis. Petitioner would have to be fed, cleaned, turned, bedded, toileted by others for 15 to 20 years! Although alert, bright, sensitive, perhaps even brave and feisty, she must lie immobile, unable to exist except through physical acts of others. Her mind and spirit may be free to take great flights but she herself is imprisoned and must lie physically helpless subject to the ignominy, embarrassment, humiliation and dehumanizing aspects created by her helplessness. We do not believe it is the policy of this State that all and every life must be preserved against the will of the sufferer. It is incongruous, if not monstrous, for medical practitioners to assert their right to preserve a life that someone else must live, or, more accurately, endure, for "15 to 20 years." We cannot conceive it to be the policy of this State to inflict such an ordeal upon anyone.

It is, therefore, immaterial that the removal of the nasogastric tube will hasten or cause Bouvia's eventual death. Being competent she has the right to live out the remainder of her natural life in dignity and peace. It is precisely the aim and purpose of the many decisions upholding the withdrawal of life-support systems to accord and provide as large a measure of dignity, respect and comfort as possible to every patient for the remainder of his days, whatever be their number. This goal is not to hasten death, though its earlier arrival may be an expected and understood likelihood.

Real parties assert that what petitioner really wants is to "commit suicide" by starvation at their facility. The trial court in its statement of decision said: "It is fairly clear from the evidence and the court cannot close its eyes to the fact that [petitioner] during her stay in defendant hospital, and for some time prior thereto, has formed an intent to die. She has voiced this desire to a member of the staff of defendant hospital. She claims, however, she does not wish to commit suicide. On the evidence, this is but a semantic distinction. The reasonable inference to be drawn from the evidence is that [petitioner] in defendant facility has purposefully engaged in a selective rejection of medical treatment and nutritional intake to accomplish her objective and accept only treatment which gives her some degree of comfort pending her demise. Stated another way, [petitioner's] refusal of medical treatment and nutritional intake is motivated not by a bona fide exercise of her right of privacy but by a desire to terminate her life.... [p] Here [petitioner] wishes to pursue her objective to die by the use of public facilities with staff standing by to furnish her medical treatment to which she consents and to refrain from that which she refuses."

Overlooking the fact that a desire to terminate one's life is probably the ultimate exercise of one's right to privacy, we find no substantial evidence to support the court's conclusion. [. . .] Moreover, the trial court seriously erred by basing its decision on the "motives" behind Elizabeth Bouvia's decision to exercise her rights. If a right exists, it matters not what "motivates" its exercise. We find nothing in the law to suggest the right to refuse medical treatment may be exercised only if the patient's motives meet someone else's approval. It certainly is not illegal or immoral to prefer a natural, albeit sooner, death than a drugged life attached to a mechanical device.

It is not necessary to here define or dwell at length upon what constitutes suicide. Our Supreme Court [has dealt with the matter,] declaring that the State has an interest in preserving and recognizing the sanctity of life [and observing] that it is a crime to aid in suicide. But it is significant that the instances and the means there discussed all involved affirmative, assertive, proximate, direct conduct such as furnishing a gun, poison, knife, or other instrumentality or usable means by which another could physically and immediately inflict some death producing injury upon himself. Such situations are far different than the mere presence of a doctor during the exercise of his patient's constitutional rights. [. . .] No criminal or civil liability attaches to honoring a competent, informed patient's refusal of medical service.

We do not purport to establish what will constitute proper medical practice in all other cases or even other aspects of the care to be provided petitioner. We hold only that her right to refuse medical treatment even of the life-sustaining variety, entitles her to the immediate removal of the nasogastric tube that has been involuntarily inserted into her body. The hospital and medical staff are still free to perform a substantial, if not the greater part of their duty, i.e., that of trying to alleviate Bouvia's pain and suffering. Petitioner is without means to go to a private hospital and, apparently, real parties' hospital as a public facility was required to accept her. Having done so it may not deny her relief from pain and suffering merely because she has chosen to exercise her fundamental right to protect what little privacy remains to her.

Personal dignity is a part of one's right of privacy.

APPENDIX I

FAITH HEALING STATUTES

Ohio State Code Section 2151.03

INTRODUCTORY NOTE

Many state codes make special provisions to allow parents to seek unconventional means of treatment for their children when such methods of treatment are mandated by religious beliefs. Many times, the state statutes must balance the parents' right to exercise their religious freedom against the need to protect the welfare of children. The following statute is law in the state of Ohio.

THE STATUTE

Ohio State Code Section 2151.03. Neglected child defined; failure to provide medical care for religious reasons

(A) As used in this chapter, "neglected child" includes a child:

(1) Who is abandoned by his parents, guardian, or custodian;

(2) Who lacks proper parental care because of the faults or habit of his parents, guardian, or custodian;

(3) Whose parents, guardian, or custodian neglects or refuses to provide him with proper or necessary subsistence, education, medical or surgical care or treatment, or other care necessary for his health, morals, or well-being;

(4) Whose parents, guardian, or custodian neglects or refuses to provide him with the special care made necessary by his mental condition;

(5) [. . .]

(6) Who, because of the omission of his parents, guardian, or custodian, suffers physical or mental injury that harms or threatens to harm the child's health or welfare;

[. . .]

(B) Nothing in this chapter shall be construed as subjecting a parent, guardian, or custodian of a child to criminal liability when, solely in the practice of his religious beliefs, he fails to provide adequate medical or surgical care or treatment for the child. [. . .]

APPENDIX J

IN RE DUBREUIL

Supreme Court of Florida
629 So.2nd 819 (1994)

INTRODUCTORY NOTE

The case set forth below illustrates the decision-making process and the legal and social factors that a court will consider in balancing the right of a competent adult to exercise her religious freedom against the state's interests in preserving and promoting life. The case below examines that potential conflict in the context of a Jehovah's Witness refusing to undergo a potentially life-saving blood transfusion. As articulated below, courts will often consider the state's interests to be: the prevention of suicide; the preservation of the sanctity of life; the protection of innocent third parties; and the protection of the integrity of the medical profession. In this case, the court focuses on the protection of innocent third parties.

THE CASE

BARKETT, Chief Judge.

We review *In re Dubreuil*, [citation omitted], which held that a married but separated woman who chose not to receive a blood transfusion for religious reasons could be compelled to receive medical treatment because her death would cause the abandonment of four minor children. We quash the district court's decision because there was no abandonment proved in this case to override the patient's constitutional rights.

I. The Facts

The parties have agreed on the essential facts in this case. In the late evening of Thursday, April 5, 1990, Patricia Dubreuil was admitted to Memorial Hospital in Hollywood, Florida, through its emergency room. Patricia was in an "advanced stage" of pregnancy. At the time of her admission, she did not have a private attending physician, so Memorial Hospital assigned an obstetrician from its staff to

211

render necessary obstetrical services. Upon admission, Patricia signed a standard consent form agreeing to the infusion of blood if it were to become necessary.

By the early morning hours of April 6, physicians determined that Patricia was ready to deliver her child and that a Caesarean section delivery would be appropriate. She consented to the Caesarean section, but notwithstanding the routine consent form she had signed, she withheld consent to the transfusion of blood on the basis of her values and religious convictions as a Jehovah's Witness. Michael Dubreuil was subsequently delivered by Caesarean section at approximately 5:30 a.m. on April 6.

At the time of delivery Patricia experienced a significant loss of blood because of a severe blood condition that prevents her blood from clotting properly. Attending physicians determined that a blood transfusion was required to save her life, but Patricia still refused to consent. Because of the extreme medical emergency that existed on the morning of April 6, medical authorities, with police assistance, contacted Luc Dubreuil, Patricia's estranged husband. He had not accompanied Patricia when she went to the hospital hours earlier. When Luc arrived shortly thereafter, he consented to the blood transfusion. Physicians relied upon Luc's written consent and transfused a quantity of blood into Patricia during the morning of April 6.

Luc and Patricia were still married but were separated and living apart when this incident arose. They are the natural parents of the newborn infant, Michael, and three other minor children, Cary, Tina, and Tracy, who at the time, respectively, were twelve, six, and four years old and living with their mother. Luc was not a Jehovah's Witness. Luc's consent was supported by Patricia's two brothers, who were not Jehovah's Witnesses, while Patricia's mother, who is a Jehovah's Witness, backed her daughter's decision.

After the transfusion early on April 6, physicians apparently believed that transfusions would continue to be needed. Unsure of its legal obligations and responsibilities under these circumstances, the hospital petitioned the circuit court for an emergency declaratory judgment hearing to determine the hospital's authority or duty to administer blood transfusions to Patricia over her objections. A hearing was scheduled for 3 p.m. on April 6. The parties do not know whether the trial court was aware that a transfusion had already been given at the time of the hearing, but they believe the trial court was aware that transfusions would continue to be needed throughout the day.

The trial court conducted the hearing as scheduled, attended by counsel representing Patricia and the hospital. No testimony was taken, but during the hearing the hospital's counsel received a telephone call advising that Patricia, who had been unconscious, had just become conscious, appeared lucid, and was able to communicate. When asked at that time whether she would consent to a blood transfusion, Patricia again refused. At 3:30 p.m. on April 6, the trial court orally announced judgment in favor of the hospital, allowing it to administer blood as physicians deemed necessary. Subsequently, according to an affidavit later executed by Patricia, the hospital continued to administer blood, and Patricia survived.

The trial court issued a written order on April 11, concluding that "there has been no suggestion as to the means or methods of caring for the four minor children of Patricia Dubreuil, if she should die. In the absence of some suggestion or showing as to the availability of proper care and custody of the four minor children, in the event of the death of Patricia Dubreuil, this court believes that the demands of the state (and society) outweigh the wishes of Patricia Dubreuil and that every medical effort should be made to prolong her life so that she can care for her four minor children until their respective majorities." [Citation omitted.] Patricia moved for rehearing, indicating that she continued to object to blood transfusion and that she had an "extended family as well as friends who are willing to assist in the rearing of [her] minor children in the event of her demise." The Circuit Court denied rehearing on April 12. The Fourth District affirmed by a 2-1 vote. Patricia sought discretionary review here, arguing that the decision below violates her state and federal constitutional rights of privacy, bodily self-determination, and religious freedom. We recognize that the present case is moot given that Patricia received blood and was released from the hospital. However, we accept jurisdiction because the issue is one of great public importance, is capable of repetition, and otherwise might evade review. [Citations omitted.]

II. The Rights of Privacy and Free Exercise of Religion

We begin our analysis with the overarching principle that article I, section 23 of the Florida Constitution guarantees that "a competent person has the constitutional right to choose or refuse medical treatment, and that right extends to all relevant decisions concerning one's health." [Citations omitted.] In cases like this one, the privacy right overlaps with the right to freely exercise one's religion to protect the right of a person to refuse a blood transfusion because of religious convictions. [Citation omitted.]

In cases where these rights are litigated, a party generally seeks to invoke the power of the State, through the exercise of the court's judicial power, either to enforce the patient's rights or to prevent the patient from exercising those rights. We have set forth the following guiding principles: "The state has a duty to assure that a person's wishes regarding medical treatment are respected. That obligation serves to protect the rights of the individual from intrusion by the state unless the state has a compelling interest great enough to override this constitutional right. The means to carry out any such compelling state interest must be narrowly tailored in the least intrusive manner possible to safeguard the rights of the individual." [Citations omitted.] Among the factors we have identified that could be considered in determining whether to give force to a patient's right to refrain from medical treatment is the protection of innocent third parties, [citation omitted], often discussed in terms of "abandonment." [Citation omitted.]

The arguments made in this Court present two basic issues. First, we must determine whether it is appropriate for a hospital to assert the state interests in an attempt to defeat a patient's decision to forgo emergency medical treatment. Second, assuming the state interests were properly presented in this case, we must decide whether Patricia's rejection of a blood transfusion constituted, as the district court found, abandonment of the couple's minor children and amounted to a state interest that was compelling enough to override her constitutional rights of privacy and religious freedom, by the least intrusive means available.

III. Asserting the State Interests

Patricia argues that Memorial Hospital should not have intervened in her private decision to refuse a blood transfusion. She claims that the "State" has never been a party in this action, has not asserted any interest, and that the hospital has no authority to assume the State's responsibilities. The hospital argues in its brief that as a public health care facility owned and operated by a special taxing district established under Florida law, it acted as a unit of local government and stood in the shoes of the State for the purposes of asserting the state interests. However, at oral argument, the hospital expressed substantial discomfort in assuming the role of the State in such proceedings. Consequently, both parties agreed that a procedure should be established by which the State can properly intervene if there is reason to do so.

In most prior Florida decisions where state interests were asserted under analogous medical emergency situations, the State Attorney joined as a party at some point in the proceedings. [Citations omitted.]

[. . .]

We recognize that in situations like these, health care providers generally have sought judicial intervention to determine their rights and obligations to avoid liability. In *John F. Kennedy Memorial Hospital, Inc. v. Bludworth*, [citation omitted], we held that health care providers, when terminating life support in accordance with their patient's wishes, are relieved of potential civil and criminal liability as long as they act in good faith, and that no prior court approval of the health care provider's action is required. We believe the same principles apply here. When a health care provider, acting in good faith, follows the wishes of a competent and informed patient to refuse medical treatment, the health care provider is acting appropriately and cannot be subjected to civil or criminal liability.

Although this procedure absolves the health care facility of any obligation to go to court, we recognize the need for the State and interested parties to have the opportunity to seek judicial intervention if appropriate. Accordingly, a health care provider wishing to override a patient's decision to refuse medical treatment must immediately provide notice to the State Attorney presiding in the circuit where the controversy arises, and to interested third parties known to the health care provider. The extent to which the State Attorney chooses to engage in a legal action, if any, is discretionary based on the law and facts of each case. This procedure should eliminate needless litigation by health care providers while honoring the patient's wishes and giving other interested parties the right to intervene if there is a good faith reason to do so. [Citation omitted.]

Even though the State did not properly join this action, the hospital [. . .] stood in the State's shoes, assuming the heavy burden of proving that the prevention of abandonment outweighed Patricia Dubreuil's constitutional right to refuse medical treatment. The court below accepted the hospital's argument and adjudicated the case on the merits. Accordingly, we address the merits of the district court's decision.

IV. Protecting Innocent Third Parties

The state interest raised in this case is the protection of innocent third parties, which the parties and courts in other jurisdictions under similar circumstances have termed the prevention of abandonment of minor children. Until *Dubreuil*, no other reported Florida appellate decision had found abandonment in this context.

[. . .]

Norma Wons, a 38-year-old woman, had been suffering from dysfunctional uterine bleeding, and physicians said she could die without a blood transfusion. However, she refused based on her religious convictions as a Jehovah's Witness. Norma lived with her husband Henrich and their two minor children, who were twelve and fourteen years of age. Henrich was also a Jehovah's Witness and supported Norma's decision. Henrich worked to support the family, and during Norma's illness the children had been cared for in Henrich's absence by Norma's sixty-two-year-old mother, who was in good health. Testimony established that if Norma were to die, her mother and two brothers, who also were Jehovah's Witnesses, would assist in taking care of the children. The trial court ruled that Norma's refusal would deny the children the intangible right to be reared by two loving parents, and the state interest in protecting the two minor children overrode Norma's right to refuse lifesaving medical treatment. The Third District reversed, finding that there was no showing of an abandonment of the minor children to override Norma's constitutional rights. The district court said that "the societal interest in protecting Mrs. Wons' two minor children [cannot] override Mrs. Wons' constitutional right to refuse a blood transfusion under the circumstances of this case. This is so because, simply put, Mrs. Wons' probable, but not certain, demise by refusing the subject blood transfusions will not result in an abandonment of her two minor children. According to the undisputed testimony below, she has a tightly knit family unit, all practicing Jehovah's Witnesses, all of whom fully support her decision to refuse a blood transfusion, all of whom will care for and rear the two minor children in the event she dies. Her husband will, plainly, continue supporting the two children with the aid of her two brothers; her mother, a sixty-two-year-old woman in good health, will also care for the children while her husband is at work. Without dispute, these children will not become wards of the state and will be reared by a loving family." [Citation omitted.]

This Court generally approved the district court's rationale and held that the state interest in maintaining a home with two parents for the minor children does not override a patient's constitutional rights of privacy and religion to refuse a potentially lifesaving blood transfusion. [Citation omitted.]

[. . .]

The trial court in *Dubreuil* found abandonment and held it to be an overriding state interest. The court distinguished *Wons*, noting that Luc no longer lived with

Patricia and the children; Luc was not a Jehovah's Witness and consented to the transfusion; and Patricia presented no evidence of how the children would be cared for in the event of her death.

In a split decision, the district court affirmed by reasoning that *Wons* put the burden on the hospital to prove abandonment, and under the emergency circumstances and limited evidence presented, the hospital carried its burden. The district court focused on the fact that no evidence was presented about Luc, his ability to care for the couple's children, or the ability or willingness of any others to help care for the children in the event of Patricia's death. The court rejected the argument that a presumption against finding abandonment should exist in the absence of firsthand evidence to the contrary, suggesting that if any presumption were to apply, it would be a presumption in favor of finding abandonment given the ages of the children and the preexisting custody conditions. The district court concluded that because there was no showing that the children of tender years would be protected in the event of their parent's death, the trial court did not abuse its discretion by concluding that "there was an overriding interest in the state as parens patriae that out-balances the mother's free exercise and privacy right to reject the transfusion." [Citation omitted.]

In dissent, Judge Warner observed that Luc, as the natural father, is the children's legal guardian and is responsible for their care as a matter of Florida law. [. . .] Judge Warner relied on our decision in *Wons* to conclude that because the hospital failed to present compelling evidence that abandonment would result from the rejection of medical treatment, no compelling state interest was established to override Patricia's decision. [Citation omitted.]

In her argument to this Court, Patricia urges us to eliminate from this line of cases any consideration given to the state interest in protecting innocent third parties from abandonment, claiming that it is inherently unsound and dangerous and cannot be consistently applied. She argues, for example, that it will lead beyond blood transfusions to major medical procedures ranging from Caesarean sections to heart bypass surgery; or it will allow courts to compel a pregnant Catholic woman who is the single parent of a minor child to have an abortion against her religious beliefs if taking the pregnancy to term would endanger the mother's life. She also argues that the rule eventually will go well beyond the protection of minor children, compelling a single adult, who cares for her dependent elderly parent or grandparent, to receive unwanted medical treatment in order to advance the state interest in protecting the elderly dependent.

Patricia's argument has some merit. Parenthood, in and of itself, does not deprive one of living in accord with one's own beliefs. Society does not, for example, disparage or preclude one from performing an act of bravery resulting in the loss of that person's life simply because that person has parental responsibilities.

Nonetheless, we decline at this time to rule out the possibility that some case not yet before us may present a compelling interest to prevent abandonment. Therefore, we think the better course is the one we took in *Wons*, where we held that "these cases demand individual attention" and cannot be covered by a blanket rule." [Citation omitted.]

Next, Patricia argues that even if the prevention of abandonment may be a valid state interest, there was no proof in this record that an abandonment would have occurred had Patricia died after refusing medical treatment. We agree. Both the circuit and district courts failed to properly consider the father of the four children, Luc Dubreuil. Under Florida law, as Judge Warner's dissent correctly observed, a child with two living natural parents has two natural guardians who share equally the responsibilities of parenting. "If one parent dies, the natural guardianship shall pass to the surviving parent, and the right shall continue even though the surviving parent remarries. If the marriage between the parents is dissolved, the natural guardianship shall belong to the parent to whom the custody of the child is awarded." [Citation omitted.] Thus, Florida law unambiguously presumes that had Patricia died under these circumstances, Luc would have become the sole legal guardian of the couple's four minor children and would have been given full responsibility for their care in the absence of any contravening legal agreement or order.

The State could rebut this strong legal presumption only by presenting clear and convincing evidence that Luc would not properly assume responsibility for the children under the circumstances. [. . .]

Likewise, there was no evidence presented as to whether anyone else, including the families of Luc and Patricia, would take responsibility for the children. To the contrary, Patricia said in an affidavit on rehearing that extended family members and friends were willing to assist in raising the children in the event of Patricia's death. Moreover, we do not know if Luc or any other interested party was given the opportunity to address these issues. According to the parties' stipulation, neither Luc nor any other family members attended the emergency hearing, and the record contains no evidence that notice of the hearing was provided. [Citations omitted.]

We conclude that the district court erred in holding that sufficient evidence was presented to satisfy the heavy burden required to override the patient's constitutional right to refuse medical treatment. The State alone bore that burden, which the hospital, standing in the State's shoes, did not carry. Moreover, the district court erred by suggesting that absent firsthand proof, the law should presume abandonment under these circumstances. To the contrary, the law presumes that when one parent is no longer able to care for the couple's children, the other parent will do so. The district court's decision effectively presumed that Luc had abandoned his children when he separated from his wife. That presumption is unacceptable. The state cannot disparage a person's parental rights nor excuse a person's parental responsibilities based on martial status alone. [Citation omitted.] Likewise, although not intended by the district court, its rationale could be read by some to perpetuate the damaging stereotype that a mother's role is one of caregiver, and the father's role is that of an apathetic, irresponsible, or unfit parent. [Citations omitted.] We do not want the district court's rationale misinterpreted to reinforce these outdated ideas in a manner that effectively denies a woman her constitutional right to refuse medical treatment as guaranteed by article I, sections 3 and 23 of the Florida Constitution. Such an interpretation would also undermine the principle of shared parental responsibility, to which this state adheres. [Citations omitted.]

For the foregoing reasons, we quash the district court's decision. It is so ordered.

Dissenting Opinion

[Dissenting opinion of Justice Overton omitted.]

McDONALD, Justice, dissenting.

Admittedly, the courts travel in treacherous waters when they place any restrictions upon the free exercise of a person's religious beliefs. Such restriction should occur only when there is another compelling interest great enough to override this strong constitutional right. The trial judge found that the circumstances of this case meet this test. I agree with him.

There is no controversy or contest to the fact that unless Mrs. Dubreuil received blood transfusions she would die. The majority holds that this is a choice she can make if done in the exercise of her religious belief. The trial judge found, and I agree, that the children's right to have a mother outweighs the mother's right to observe her religious beliefs. Considering the age of these children, as opposed to the age of the children in *Wons v. Public Health Trust*, [citation omitted], this would be true whether Mr. Dubreuil faithfully performed all of his parental responsibilities or not.

Children of tender age desperately need the nurturing of a mother. Mrs. Dubreuil, according to all reports, is a fit and loving mother. It would be a legal mistake to let her expire because of the observance of her religious beliefs and leave these children motherless. [. . .] Children need, and are entitled to have, their mothers; this need is sufficiently great to outweigh one's free exercise of religious beliefs. The majority states: "Parenthood in and of itself does not deprive one of living in accord with one's own beliefs." [Citation omitted.] I suggest that parenthood, under some circumstances at least, can indeed deprive one of the right to live in accord with one's own beliefs. Parenthood requires many adjustments and often great sacrifice for the welfare of a person's children. Nearly every living creature of every species recognizes the duty to nurture its offspring. Their lives are changed in doing so. Humans should not allow religious beliefs, no matter how deeply seated or appropriately held, to neglect this fundamental duty. Mothers do not abandon the nest. Were this less than a life or death decision, or involved adolescents as opposed to young children, I would feel less fervent.

Under the facts here, a compelling interest great enough to override Mrs. Dubreuil's exercise of her religious beliefs or right of privacy clearly exists. I believe the majority makes a tragic mistake.

APPENDIX K

MODEL CRIMINAL CODE

Defining Murder

INTRODUCTORY NOTE

The state law of every state sets forth provisions defining different crimes involving the taking of a human life. Generally, different crimes, and various grades of each crime, are defined based upon the element of intent and the degree of malice involved in the taking of the life. The greater degree of malice involved, the greater the punishment for the crime. The following statute is a hypothetical criminal code provision that defines the crime of homicide.

THE STATUTE

Homicide Defined

(1) A person is guilty of homicide if he purposely, knowingly, recklessly or negligently causes the death of another human being.

(2) Homicide consists of the individual crimes of murder, manslaughter and negligent homicide.

Murder Defined

(1) Homicide is murder when:

(a) A human life is taken purposely or knowingly with malice aforethought; or

(b) A human life is taken as the result of acts which exhibit extreme indifference to the value of human life.

Manslaughter Defined

Homicide is manslaughter when a homicide which would otherwise be murder is committed under the influence of extreme mental duress or emotional disturbance for which there is a reasonable explanation or excuse. The reasonableness of the explanation or excuse is to be evaluated from the perspective of a person in the actor's situation under the circumstances as he believed them to be.

Negligent Homicide Defined

Homicide is negligent homicide when a human life is taken as the result of acts which are negligent.

APPENDIX L

IN RE T.A.C.P.

Supreme Court of Florida
609 So.2d 588 (1992)

INTRODUCTORY NOTE

A great deal of controversy has surrounded use of anencephalic infants as a source of transplantable organs. The controversy has arisen from the interception of legal definitions of death with, what many consider to be, a truly unique medical condition. The following case discusses the very difficult issues arising when the parents of an anencephalic infant seek to donate their child's organs to others.

THE CASE

KOGAN, Justice.

We have for review an order of the trial court certified by the Fourth District Court of Appeal as touching on a matter of great public importance requiring immediate resolution by this Court. We frame the issue as follows: Is an anencephalic newborn considered "dead" for purposes of organ donation solely by reason of its congenital deformity? [. . .]

I. Facts

At or about the eighth month of pregnancy, the parents of the child T.A.C.P. were informed that she would be born with anencephaly. This is a birth defect invariably fatal, in which the child typically is born with only a "brain stem" but otherwise lacks a human brain. In T.A.C.P.'s case, the back of the skull was entirely missing and the brain stem was exposed to the air, except for medical bandaging. The risk of infection to the brain stem was considered very high. Anencephalic infants sometimes can survive several days after birth because the brain stem has a limited capacity to maintain autonomic bodily functions such as breathing and heartbeat. This ability soon ceases, however, in the absence of regulation from the missing brain.

In this case, T.A.C.P. actually survived only a few days after birth. The medical evidence in the record shows that the child T.A.C.P. was incapable of developing any sort of cognitive process, may have been unable to feel pain or experience sensation due to the absence of the upper brain, and at least for part of the time was placed on a mechanical ventilator to assist her breathing. At the time of the hearing below, however, the child was breathing unaided, although she died soon thereafter.

On the advice of physicians, the parents continued the pregnancy to term and agreed that the mother would undergo caesarean section during birth. The parents agreed to the caesarean procedure with the express hope that the infant's organs would be less damaged and could be used for transplant in other sick children. Although T.A.C.P. had no hope of life herself, the parents both testified in court that they wanted to use this opportunity to give life to others. However, when the parents requested that T.A.C.P. be declared legally dead for this purpose, her health care providers refused out of concern that they thereby might incur civil or criminal liability.

The parents then filed a petition in the circuit court asking for, a judicial determination. After hearing testimony and argument, the trial court denied the request on grounds that section 382.009(1), Florida Statutes (1991), would not permit a determination of legal death so long as the child's brain stem continued to function. [. . .]

II. The Medical Nature of Anencephaly

Although appellate courts appear never to have confronted the issue, there already is an impressive body of published medical scholarship on anencephaly. From our review of this material, we find that anencephaly is a variable but fairly well defined medical condition. Experts in the field have written that anencephaly is the most common severe birth defect of the central nervous system seen in the United States, although it apparently has existed throughout human history.

A statement by the Medical Task Force on Anencephaly ("Task Force") printed in the New England Journal of Medicine generally described "anencephaly" as "a congenital absence of major portions of the brain, skull, and scalp, with its genesis in the first month of gestation." [Citation omitted.] The large opening in the skull accompanied by the absence or severe congenital disruption of the cerebral hemispheres is the characteristic feature of the condition. [Citation omitted.] The Task Force defined anencephaly as diagnosable only when all of the following four criteria are present: (1) A large portion of the skull is absent. (2) The scalp, which extends to the margin of the bone, is absent over the skull defect. (3) Hemorrhagic, fibrotic tissue is exposed because of defects in the skull and scalp. (4) Recognizable cerebral hemispheres are absent. [Citation omitted.] Anencephaly is often, though not always, accompanied by defects in various other body organs and systems, some of which may render the child unsuitable for organ transplantation. [Citation omitted.] Thus, it is clear that anencephaly is distinguishable from some other congenital conditions because its extremity renders it uniformly lethal. [. . .] We emphasize that the child T.A.C.P. clearly met the four criteria described above. [. . .]

The Task Force stated that most reported anencephalic children die within the first few days after birth, with survival any longer being rare. After reviewing all available medical literature, the Task Force found no study in which survival beyond a week exceeded nine percent of children meeting the four criteria. [Citation omitted.] Two months was the longest confirmed survival of an anencephalic, although there are unconfirmed reports of one surviving three months and another surviving fourteen months. The Task Force reported, however, that these survival rates are confounded somewhat by the variable degrees of medical care afforded to anencephalics. [Citation omitted.] Some such infants may be given considerable life support while others may be given much less care. [Citation omitted.]

The Task Force reported that the medical consequences of anencephaly can be established with some certainty. All anencephalics by definition are permanently unconscious because they lack the cerebral cortex necessary for conscious thought. Their condition thus is quite similar to that of persons in a persistent vegetative state. Where the brain stem is functioning, as it was here, spontaneous breathing and heartbeat can occur. In addition, such infants may show spontaneous movements of the extremities, "startle" reflexes, and pupils that respond to light. Some may show feeding reflexes, may cough, hiccup, or exhibit eye movements, and may produce facial expressions. [Citation omitted.] The question of whether such infants actually suffer from pain is somewhat more complex. It involves a distinction between "pain" and "suffering." The Task Force indicated that anencephaly in some ways is analogous to persons with cerebral brain lesions. Such lesions may not actually eliminate the reflexive response to a painful condition, but they can eliminate any capacity to "suffer" as a result of the condition. Likewise, anencephalic infants may reflexively avoid painful stimuli where the brain stem is functioning and thus is able to command an innate, unconscious withdrawal response; but the infants presumably lack the capacity to suffer. [Citation omitted.] It is clear, however, that this incapacity to suffer has not been established beyond all doubt. [Citation omitted.]

After the advent of new transplant methods in the past few decades, anencephalic infants have successfully been used as a source of organs for donation. However, the Task Force was able to identify only twelve successful transplants using anencephalic organs by 1990. Transplants were most successful when the anencephalic immediately was placed on life support and its organs used as soon as possible, without regard to the existence of brain-stem activity. However, this only accounted for a total of four reported transplants. [Citation omitted.]

There appears to be general agreement that anencephalics usually have ceased to be suitable organ donors by the time they meet all the criteria for "whole brain death," i.e., the complete absence of brain-stem function. [Citation omitted.] There also is no doubt that a need exists for infant organs for transplantation. Nationally, between thirty and fifty percent of children under two years of age who need transplants die while waiting for organs to become available. [Citation omitted.]

III. Legal Definitions of "Death" & "Life"

As the parties and amici have argued, the common law in some American jurisdictions recognized a cardiopulmonary definition of "death": A human being was not considered dead until breathing and heartbeat had stopped entirely, without possibility of resuscitation. [Citations omitted.] However, there is some doubt about the exact method by which this definition was imported into the law of some states. Apparently the definition was taken from earlier editions of Black's Law Dictionary, which itself did not cite to an original source. [Citation omitted.] The definition thus may only have been the opinion of Black's earlier editors. We have found no authority showing that Florida ever recognized the original Black's Law Dictionary definition or any other definition of "death" as a matter of our own common law. Even if we had adopted such a standard, however, it is equally clear that modern medical technology has rendered the earlier Black's definition of "death" seriously inadequate. With the invention of life-support devices and procedures, human bodies can be made to breathe and blood to circulate even in the utter absence of brain function. As a result, the ability to withhold or discontinue such life support created distinct legal problems in light of the "cardiopulmonary" definition of death originally used by Black's Dictionary. For example, health care providers might be civilly or criminally liable for removing transplantable organs from a person sustained by life support, or defendants charged with homicide might argue that their victim's death actually was caused when life support was discontinued. [Citation omitted.]

In light of the inadequacies of a cardiopulmonary definition of "death," a number of jurisdictions began altering their laws in an attempt to address the medical community's changing conceptions of the point in time at which life ceases. An effort was made to synthesize many of the new concerns into a Uniform Determination of Death Act issued by the National Conference of Commissioners on Uniform State Laws. The uniform statute states: "An individual who has sustained either (1) irreversible cessation of circulatory and respiratory functions, or (2) irreversible cessation of all functions of the entire brain, including the brain stem, is dead. A determination of death must be made in accordance with accepted medical standards." [Citation omitted.] Thus, the uniform act both codified the earlier common law standard and extended it to deal with the specific problem of "whole brain death." While some American jurisdictions appear to have adopted substantially the same language, Florida is not among these. [Citation omitted.] Indeed, Florida appears to have struck out on its own. The statute cited as controlling by the trial court does not actually address itself to the problem of anencephalic infants, nor indeed to any situation other than patients actually being sustained by artificial life support. The statute provides: "For legal and medical purposes, where respiratory and circulatory functions are maintained by artificial means of support so as to preclude a determination that these functions have ceased, the occurrence of death may be determined where there is the irreversible cessation of the functioning of the entire brain, including the brain stem, determined in accordance with this section." [Citation omitted.] A later subsection goes on to declare: "Except for a diagnosis of brain death, the standard set forth in this section is not the exclusive standard for determining death or for the withdrawal of life-support systems." [Citation omitted.] This language is highly significant for two reasons. First, the statute does not purport to codify the common law standard applied in some other jurisdictions, as does the uniform act. [. . .] Second, the statutory framers clearly did not intend to apply the statute's language to the anencephalic infant not being kept alive by life support. To the contrary, the framers expressly limited the statute to that situation in which "respiratory and circulatory functions are maintained by artificial means of support."

There are a few Florida authorities that have addressed the definitions of "life" and "death" in somewhat analogous though factually distinguishable contexts. Florida's Vital Statistics Act, for example, defines "live birth" as the complete expulsion or extraction of a product of human conception from its mother, irrespective of the duration of pregnancy, which, after such expulsion, breathes or shows any other evidence of life such as beating of the heart, pulsation of the umbilical cord, and definite movement of the voluntary muscles, whether or not the umbilical cord has been cut or the placenta is attached. [Citation omitted.] Conversely, "fetal death" is defined as death prior to the complete expulsion or extraction of a product of human conception from its mother if the 20th week of gestation has been reached and the death is indicated by the fact that after such expulsion or extraction the fetus does not breathe or show any other evidence of life such as beating of the heart, pulsation of the umbilical cord, or definite movement of voluntary muscles. [Citation omitted.] From these definitions, it is clear that T.A.C.P. was a "live birth" and not a "fetal death," at least for purposes of the collection of vital statistics in Florida. These definitions obviously are inapplicable to the issues at hand today, but they do shed some light on the Florida legislature's thoughts regarding a definition of "life" and "death."

Similarly, an analogous (if distinguishable) problem has arisen in Florida tort law. In cases alleging wrongful death, our courts have held that fetuses are not "persons" and are not "born alive" until they acquire an existence separate and independent from the mother. [Citation omitted.] We believe the weight of the evidence supports the conclusion that T.A.C.P. was "alive" in this sense because she was separated from the womb, and was capable of breathing and maintaining a heartbeat independently of her mother's body for some duration of time thereafter. Once again, however, this conclusion arises from law that is only analogous and is not dispositive of the issue at hand.

We also note that the 1988 Florida Legislature considered a bill that would have defined "death" to include anencephaly. [Citation omitted.] The bill died in committee. While the failure of legislation in committee does not establish legislative intent, it nevertheless supports the conclusion that as recently as 1988 no consensus existed among Florida's lawmakers regarding the issue we confront today. The parties have cited to no authorities directly dealing with the question of whether anencephalics are "alive" or "dead." Our own research has disclosed no other federal or Florida law or precedent arguably on point or applicable by analogy. We thus are led to the conclusion that no legal authority binding upon this Court has decided whether an anencephalic child is alive for purposes of organ donation. In the absence of applicable legal authority, this Court must weigh and consider the public policy considerations at stake here.

IV. Common Law & Policy

Initially, we must start by recognizing that [Florida statutory law] provides a method for determining death in those cases in which a person's respiratory and circulatory functions are maintained artificially. [Citation omitted.] Likewise, we agree that a cardiopulmonary definition of death must be accepted in Florida as a matter of our common law, applicable whenever [the statute] does not govern. Thus, if cardiopulmonary function is not being maintained artificially as stated in [the statute], a person is dead who has sustained irreversible cessation of circulatory and respiratory functions as determined in accordance with accepted medical standards. We have found no credible authority arguing that this definition is inconsistent with the existence of death, and we therefore need not labor the point further.

The question remaining is whether there is good reason in public policy for this Court to create an additional common law standard applicable to anencephalics. Alterations of the common law, while rarely entertained or allowed, are within this Court's prerogative. [Citation omitted.] However, the rule we follow is that the common law will not be altered or expanded unless demanded by public necessity, [citation omitted] or where required to vindicate fundamental rights. [Citation omitted.] We believe, for example, that our adoption of the cardiopulmonary definition of death today is required by public necessity and, in any event, merely formalizes what has been the common practice in this state for well over a century. Such is not the case with petitioners' request. Our review of the medical, ethical, and legal literature on anencephaly discloses absolutely no consensus that public necessity or fundamental rights will be better served by granting this request.

We are not persuaded that a public necessity exists to justify this action, in light of the other factors in this case--although we acknowledge much ambivalence about this particular question. We have been deeply touched by the altruism and unquestioned motives of the parents of T.A.C.P. The parents have shown great humanity, compassion, and concern for others. The problem we as a Court must face, however, is that the medical literature shows unresolved controversy over the extent to which anencephalic organs can or should be used in transplants.

There is an unquestioned need for transplantable infant organs. [Citations omitted.] Yet some medical commentators suggest that the organs of anencephalics are seldom usable, for a variety of reasons, and that so few organ transplants will be possible from anencephalics as to render the enterprise questionable in light of the ethical problems at stake--even if legal restrictions were lifted. [Citations omitted.]

Others note that prenatal screening now is substantially reducing the number of anencephalics born each year in the United States and that, consequently, anencephalics are unlikely to be a significant source of organs as time passes. [Citation omitted.] And still others have frankly acknowledged that there is no consensus and that redefinition of death in this context should await the emergence of a consensus. [Citations omitted.]

A presidential commission in 1981 urged strict adherence to the Uniform Determination of Death Act's definition, which would preclude equating anencephaly with death. [Citation omitted.] Several sections of the American Bar Association have reached much the same conclusion. [Citation omitted.] Some legal commentators have argued that treating anencephalics as dead equates them with "nonpersons," presenting a "slippery slope" problem with regard to all other persons who lack cognition for whatever reason. [Citation omitted.] [. . .]

We express no opinion today about who is right and who is wrong on these issues--if any "right" or "wrong" can be found here. The salient point is that no consensus exists as to: (a) the utility of organ transplants of the type at issue here; (b) the ethical issues involved; or (c) the legal and constitutional problems implicated.

V. Conclusions

Accordingly, we find no basis to expand the common law to equate anencephaly with death. We acknowledge the possibility that some infants' lives might be saved by using organs from anencephalics who do not meet the traditional definition of "death" we reaffirm today. But weighed against this is the utter lack of consensus, and the questions about the overall utility of such organ donations. The scales clearly tip in favor of not extending the common law in this instance.

To summarize: We hold that Florida common law recognizes the cardiopulmonary definition of death as stated above; and Florida statutes create a "whole-brain death" exception applicable whenever cardiopulmonary function is being maintained artificially. There are no other legal standards for determining death under present Florida law. Because no Florida statute applies to the present case, the determination of death in this instance must be judged against the common law cardiopulmonary standard. The evidence shows that T.A.C.P.'s heart was beating and she was breathing at the times in question. Accordingly, she was not dead under Florida law, and no donation of her organs would have been legal. [. . .] We answer the question posed by this case in the negative and approve the result reached below. It is so ordered.

APPENDIX M

STRUNK v. STRUNK

Court of Appeals of Kentucky
445 S.W.2d 145 (1969)

INTRODUCTORY NOTE

Strunk v. Strunk discusses the concept of substituted judgment. Substituted judgment is a legal construct whereby a medical decision is made on behalf of an incompetent person with the aim that the decision made will be the same decision that the incompetent person would have made for himself if he were capable of making the decision without assistance. As noted in the dissenting opinion, the use of the substituted judgment standard can have far-reaching social and ethical consequences.

THE CASE

OSBORNE, Judge.

The specific question involved upon this appeal is: Does a court of equity have the power to permit a kidney to be removed from an incompetent ward of the state upon petition of his committee, who is also his mother, for the purpose of being transplanted into the body of his brother, who is dying of a fatal kidney disease? We are of the opinion it does.

The facts of the case are as follows: Arthur L. Strunk, 54 years of age, and Ava Strunk, 52 years of age, of Williamstown, Kentucky, are the parents of two sons. Tommy Strunk is 28 years of age, married, an employee of the Penn State Railroad and a part-time student at the University of Cincinnati. Tommy is now suffering from chronic glomerulus nephritis, a fatal kidney disease. He is now being kept alive by frequent treatment on an artificial kidney, a procedure which cannot be continued much longer.

Jerry Strunk is 27 years of age, incompetent, and through proper legal proceedings has been committed to the Frankfort State Hospital and School, which is a state institution maintained for the feebleminded. He has an I.Q. of approximately 35, which corresponds with the mental age of approximately six years. He is further handicapped by a speech defect, which makes it difficult for him to communicate with persons who are not well acquainted with him. When it was determined that Tommy, in order to survive, would have to have a kidney the doctors considered the possibility of using a kidney from a cadaver if and when one became available or one from a live donor if this could be made available. The entire family, his mother, father and a number of collateral relatives were tested. Because of incompatibility of blood type or tissue none were medically acceptable as live donors. As a last resort, Jerry was tested and found to be highly acceptable. This immediately presented the legal problem as to what, if anything, could be done by the family, especially the mother and the father to procure a transplant from Jerry to Tommy.

The mother as a committee petitioned the county court for authority to proceed with the operation. The court found that the operation was necessary, that under the peculiar circumstances of this case it would not only be beneficial to Tommy but also beneficial to Jerry because Jerry was greatly dependent upon Tommy, emotionally and psychologically, and that his well-being would be jeopardized more severely by the loss of his brother than by the removal of a kidney.

Appeal was taken to the Franklin Circuit Court where the chancellor reviewed the record, examined the testimony of the witnesses and adopted the findings of the county court.

A psychiatrist, in attendance to Jerry, who testified in the case, stated in his opinion the death of Tommy under these circumstances would have "an extremely traumatic effect upon him"(Jerry).

The Department of Mental Health of this Commonwealth has entered the case as amicus curiae and on the basis of its evaluation of the seriousness of the operation as opposed to the traumatic effect upon Jerry as a result of the loss of Tommy, recommended to the court that Jerry be permitted to undergo the surgery. Its recommendations are as follows: "Jerry Strunk, a mental defective, has emotions and reactions on a scale comparable to that of normal person. He identifies with his brother Tom; Tom is his model, his tie with his family. Tom's life is vital to the continuity of Jerry's improvement at Frankfort State Hospital and School. The testimony of the hospital representative reflected the importance to Jerry of his visits with his family and the constant inquiries Jerry made about Tom's coming to see him. Jerry is aware he plays a role in the relief of this tension. We the Department of Mental Health must take all possible steps to prevent the occurrence of any guilt feelings Jerry would have if Tom were to die. The necessity of Tom's life to Jerry's treatment and eventual rehabilitation is clearer in view of the fact that Tom is his only living sibling and at the death of their parents, now in their fifties, Jerry will have no concerned, intimate communication so necessary to his stability and optimal functioning. The evidence shows that at the present level of medical knowledge, it is quite remote that Tom would be able to survive several cadaver transplants. Tom has a much better chance of survival if the kidney transplant from Jerry takes place."

Upon this appeal we are faced with the fact that all members of the immediate family have recommended the transplant. The Department of Mental Health has likewise made its recommendation. The county court has given its approval. The circuit court has found that it would be to the best interest of the ward of the state that the procedure be carried out. Throughout the legal proceedings, Jerry has been represented by a guardian ad litem, who has continually questioned the power of the state to authorize the removal of an organ from the body of an incompetent who is a ward of the state. We are fully cognizant of the fact that the question before us is unique. Insofar as we have been able to learn, no similar set of facts has come before the highest court of any of the states of this nation or the federal courts. [. . .] The right to act for the incompetent in all cases has become recognized in this country as the doctrine of substituted judgment and is broad enough not only to cover property but also to cover all matters touching on the well-being of the ward. [. . .]

The medical practice of transferring tissue from one part of the human body to another (autografting) and from one human being to another (homografting) is rapidly becoming a common clinical practice. In many cases the transplants take as well where the tissue is dead as when it is alive. This has made practicable the establishment of tissue banks where such material can be stored for future use. Vascularized grafts of lungs, kidneys and hearts are becoming increasingly common. These grafts must be of functioning, living cells with blood vessels remaining anatomically intact. The chance of success in the transfer of these organs is greatly increased when the donor and the donee are genetically related. It is recognized by all legal and medical authorities that several legal problems can arise as a result of the operative techniques of the transplant procedure. [Citation omitted.]

The renal transplant is becoming the most common of the organ transplants. This is because the normal body has two functioning kidneys, one of which it can reasonably do without, thereby making it possible for one person to donate a kidney to another. Testimony in this record shows that there have been over 2500 kidney transplants performed in the United States up to this date. The process can be effected under present techniques with minimal danger to both the donor and the donee. [. . .]

Review of our case law leads us to believe that the power given to a committee under [state law] would not extend so far as to allow a committee to subject his ward to the serious surgical techniques here under consideration unless the life of his ward be in jeopardy. Nor do we believe the powers delegated to the county court by virtue of the above statutes would reach so far as to permit the procedure which we are dealing with here.

We are of the opinion that a chancery court does have sufficient inherent power to authorize the operation. The circuit court having found that the operative procedures in this instance are to the best interest of Jerry Strunk and this finding having been based upon substantial evidence, we are of the opinion the judgment should be affirmed. We do not deem it significant that this case reached the circuit court by way of appeal as opposed to a direct proceeding in that court.

Judgment affirmed.

Dissenting Opinion

STEINFELD, Judge (dissenting).

Apparently because of my indelible recollection of a government which, to the everlasting shame of its citizens, embarked on a program a genocide and experimentation with human bodies I have been more troubled in reaching a decision in this case than in any

other. My sympathies and emotions are torn between a compassion to aid an ailing young man and a duty to fully protect unfortunate members of society.

The opinion of the majority is predicated upon the authority of an equity court to speak for one who cannot speak for himself. However, it is my opinion that in considering such right in this instance we must first look to the power and authority vested in the committee, the appellee herein. [State statutes] do nothing more than give the committee the power to take custody of the incompetent and the possession, care and management of his property. Courts have restricted the activities of the committee to that which is for the best interest of the incompetent. [Citations omitted.] The authority and duty have been to protect and maintain the ward, to secure that to which he is entitled and preserve that which he has. [Citations omitted.] The wishes of the members of the family or the desires of the guardian to be helpful to the apparent objects of the ward's bounty have not been a criterion.

[. . .]

The majority opinion is predicated upon the finding of the circuit court that there will be psychological benefits to the ward but points out that the incompetent has the mentality of a six-year-old child. It is common knowledge beyond dispute that the loss of a close relative or a friend to a six-year-old child is not of major impact. Opinions concerning psychological trauma are at best most nebulous. Furthermore, there are no guarantees that the transplant will become a surgical success, it being well known that body rejection of transplanted organs is frequent. The life of the incompetent is not in danger, but the surgical procedure

advocated creates some peril. [. . .]

Unquestionably the attitudes and attempts of the committee and members of the family of the two young men whose critical problems now confront us are commendable, natural and beyond reproach. However, they refer us to nothing indicating that they are privileged to authorize the removal of one of the kidneys of the incompetent for the purpose of donation, and they cite no statutory or other authority vesting such right in the courts. The proof shows that less compatible donors are available and that the kidney of a cadaver could be used, although the odds of operational success are not as great in such case as they would be with the fully compatible donor brother.

I am unwilling to hold that the gates should be open to permit the removal of an organ from an incompetent for transplant, at least until such time as it is conclusively demonstrated that it will be of significant benefit to the incompetent. The evidence here does not rise to that pinnacle. To hold that committees, guardians or courts have such awesome power even in the persuasive case before us, could establish legal precedent, the dire result of which we cannot fathom. Regretfully I must say no.

NEIKIRK and PALMORE, JJ., join with me in this dissent.

APPENDIX N

MOORE v. THE REGENTS OF THE UNIVERSITY OF CALIFORNIA

Supreme Court of California, en banc
271 Cal.Rptr. 146, 51 Cal.3d 120, 793 P.2d 479 (1990)

INTRODUCTORY NOTE

Moore v. The Regents of the University of California is a much cited and often discussed case that established that a physician has a duty to inform a patient when the physician has a research or pecuniary interest in a patient's treatment. As a result of the *Moore* decision, physicians in California who conduct research on human subjects must disclose their research and financial interests to the research subjects when the physician stands to gain from the patient taking part in a research protocol, from treatment provided to the patient, or from research conducted on a body part or product removed from the patient. That disclosure is generally made to the patient in the informed consent form. An excerpt from the *Moore* case follows.

THE CASE

I. INTRODUCTION

We granted review in this case to determine whether plaintiff has stated a cause of action against his physician and other defendants for using his cells in potentially lucrative medical research without his permission. Plaintiff alleges that his physician failed to disclose preexisting research and economic interests in the cells before obtaining consent to the medical procedures by which they were extracted. [. . .] We hold that the complaint states a cause of action for breach of the physician's disclosure obligations, but not for conversion.

II. FACTS

[. . .]

The plaintiff is John Moore (Moore), who underwent treatment for hairy-cell leukemia at the Medical Center of the University of California at Los Angeles (UCLA Medical Center). The five defendants are: (1) Dr. David W. Golde (Golde), a physician who attended Moore at UCLA Medical Center; (2) the Regents of the University of California (Regents), who own and operate the university; (3) Shirley G. Quan, a researcher employed by the Regents; (4) Genetics Institute, Inc. (Genetics Institute); and (5) Sandoz Pharmaceuticals Corporation and related entities (collectively Sandoz).

Moore first visited UCLA Medical Center on October 5, 1976, shortly after he learned that he had hairy-cell leukemia. After hospitalizing Moore and "withdr[awing] extensive amounts of blood, bone marrow aspirate, and other bodily substances," Golde confirmed that diagnosis. At this time all defendants, including Golde, were aware that "certain blood products and blood components were of great value in a number of commercial and scientific efforts" and that access to a patient whose blood contained these substances would provide "competitive, commercial, and scientific advantages."

On October 8, 1976, Golde recommended that Moore's spleen be removed. Golde informed Moore "that he had reason to fear for his life, and that the proposed splenectomy operation . . . was necessary to slow down the progress of his disease." Based upon Golde's representations, Moore signed a written consent form authorizing the splenectomy.

Before the operation, Golde and Quan "formed the intent and made arrangements to obtain portions of [Moore's] spleen following its removal" and to take them to a separate research unit. Golde gave written instructions to this effect on October 18 and 19, 1976. These research activities "were not intended to have . . . any relation to [Moore's] medical . . . care." However, neither Golde nor Quan informed Moore of their plans to conduct this research or requested his permission. Surgeons at UCLA Medical Center, whom the complaint does not name as defendants, removed Moore's spleen on October 20, 1976.

Moore returned to the UCLA Medical Center several times between November 1976 and September 1983. He did so at Golde's direction and based upon representations "that such visits were necessary and required for his health and well-being, and based upon the trust inherent in and by virtue of the physician-patient relationship . . . ." On each of these visits Golde withdrew additional samples of "blood, blood serum, skin, bone marrow aspirate, and sperm." On each occasion Moore traveled to the UCLA Medical Center from his home in Seattle because he had been told that the procedures were to be performed only there and only under Golde's direction.

"In fact, [however,] throughout the period of time that [Moore] was under [Golde's] care and treatment, . . . the defendants were actively involved in a number of activities which they concealed from [Moore] . . . .." Specifically, defendants were conducting research on Moore's cells and planned to "benefit financially and competitively . . . [by exploiting the cells] and [their] exclusive access to [the cells] by virtue of [Golde's] on-going physician-patient relationship . . .."

Sometime before August 1979, Golde established a cell line from Moore's T-lymphocytes. On January 30, 1981, the Regents applied for a patent on the cell line, listing Golde and Quan as inventors. "[B]y virtue of an established policy . . ., [the] Regents, Golde, and Quan would share in any royalties or profits . . . arising out of [the] patent." The patent issued on March 20, 1984, naming Golde and Quan as the inventors of the cell line and the Regents as the assignee of the patent.

The Regent's patent also covers various methods for using the cell line to produce lymphokines. Moore admits in his complaint that "the true clinical potential of each of the lymphokines . . . [is] difficult to predict, [but] . . . competing commercial firms in these relevant fields have published reports in biotechnology industry periodicals predicting a potential market of approximately $3.01 Billion Dollars by the year 1990 for a whole range of [such lymphokines] . . .."

With the Regents' assistance, Golde negotiated agreements for commercial development of the cell line and products to be derived from it. Under an agreement with Genetics Institute, Golde "became a paid consultant" and "acquired the rights to 75,000 shares of common stock." Genetics Institute also agreed to pay Golde and the Regents "at least $330,000 over three years, including a pro-rata share of [Golde's] salary and fringe benefits, in exchange for . . . exclusive access to the materials and research performed" on the cell line and products derived from it. On June 4, 1982, Sandoz "was added to the agreement," and compensation payable to Golde and the Regents was increased by $110,000. "[T]hroughout this period, . . . Quan spent as much as 70 [percent] of her time working for [the] Regents on research" related to the cell line.

III. DISCUSSION

A. Breach of Fiduciary Duty and Lack of Informed Consent

Moore repeatedly alleges that Golde failed to disclose the extent of his research and economic interests in Moore's cells before obtaining consent to the medical procedures by which the cells were extracted. These allegations, in our view, state a cause of action against Golde for invading a legally protected interest of his patient. This cause of action can properly be characterized either as the breach of a fiduciary duty to disclose facts material to the patient's consent or, alternatively, as the performance of medical procedures without first having obtained the patient's informed consent.

Our analysis begins with three well-established principles. First, "a person of adult years and in sound mind has the right, in the exercise of control over his own body, to determine whether or not to submit to lawful medical treatment." [Citations omitted.] Second, "the patient's consent to treatment, to be effective, must be an informed consent." [Citations omitted.] Third, in soliciting the patient's consent, a physician has a fiduciary duty to disclose all information material to the patient's decision. [Citations omitted.]

These principles lead to the following conclusions: (1) a physician must disclose personal interests unrelated to the patient's health, whether research or economic, that may affect the physician's professional judgment; and (2) a physician's failure to disclose such interests may give rise to a cause of action for performing medical procedures without informed consent or breach of fiduciary duty.

To be sure, questions about the validity of a patient's consent to a procedure typically arise when the patient alleges that the physician failed to disclose medical risks, as in malpractice cases, and not when the patient alleges that the physician had a personal interest, as in this case. The concept of informed consent, however, is broad enough to encompass the latter. "The scope of the physician's communication to the patient . . . must be measured by the patient's need, and that need is whatever information is material to the decision." [Citation omitted.]

Indeed, the law already recognizes that a reasonable patient would want to know whether a physician has an economic interest that might affect the physician's professional judgment. As the Court of Appeal has said, "[c]ertainly a sick patient deserves to be free of any reasonable suspicion that his doctor's judgment is influenced by a profit motive." [Citation omitted.] The desire to protect patients from possible conflicts of interest has also motivated legislative enactments. Among these is Business and Professions Code section 654.2. Under that section, a physician may not charge a patient on behalf of, or refer a patient to, any organization in which the physician has a "significant beneficial interest, unless [the physician] first discloses in writing to the patient, that there is such an interest and advises the patient that the patient may choose any organization for the purposes of obtaining the services ordered or requested by [the physician]." [Citations omitted.] Similarly, under Health and Safety Code section 24173, a physician who plans to conduct a medical experiment on a patient must, among other things, inform the patient of "[t]he name of the sponsor or funding source, if any, . . . and the organization, if any, under whose general aegis the experiment is being conducted." [Citation omitted.]

It is important to note that no law prohibits a physician from conducting research in the same area in which he practices. Progress in medicine often depends upon physicians, such as those practicing at the university hospital where Moore received treatment, who conduct research while caring for their patients.

Yet a physician who treats a patient in whom he also has a research interest has potentially conflicting loyalties. This is because medical treatment decisions are made on the basis of proportionality--weighing the benefits *to the patient* against the risks *to the patient.* As another court has said, "the determination as to whether the burdens of treatment are worth enduring for any individual patient depends upon the facts unique in each case," and "the patient's interests and desires are the key ingredients of the decision-making process." [Citation omitted.] A physician who adds his own research interests to this balance may be tempted to order a scientifically useful procedure or test that offers marginal, or no, benefits to the patient. The possibility that an interest extraneous to the patient's health has affected the physician's judgment is something that a reasonable patient would want to know in deciding whether to consent to a proposed course of treatment. It is material to the patient's decision and, thus, a prerequisite to informed consent. [Citation omitted.]

Golde argues that the scientific use of cells that have already been removed cannot possibly affect the patient's medical interests. The argument is correct in one instance but not in another. If a physician has no plans to conduct research on a patient's cells at the time he recommends the medical procedure by which they are taken, then the patient's medical interests have not been impaired. In that instance the argument is correct. On the other hand, a physician who does have a preexisting research interest might, consciously or unconsciously, take that into consideration in recommending the procedure. In that instance the argument is incorrect: the physician's extraneous motivation may affect his judgment and is, thus, material to the patient's consent.

We acknowledge that there is a competing consideration. To require disclosure of research and economic interests may corrupt the patient's own judgment by distracting him from the requirements of his health. But California law does not grant physicians unlimited discretion to decide what to disclose. Instead, "it is the prerogative of the patient, not the physician, to determine for himself the direction in which he believes his interests lie." [Citation omitted.] "Unlimited discretion in the physician is irreconcilable with the basic right of the patient to make the ultimate informed decision . . .." [Citation omitted.]

Accordingly, we hold that a physician who is seeking a patient's consent for a medical procedure must, in order to satisfy his fiduciary duty and to obtain the patient's informed consent, disclose personal interests unrelated to the patient's health, whether research or economic, that may affect his medical judgment.

1. Dr. Golde

[. . .]

Moore alleges that, prior to the surgical removal of his spleen, Golde "formed the intent and made arrangements to obtain portions of his spleen following its removal from [Moore] in connection with [his] desire to have regular and continuous access to, and possession of, [Moore's] unique and rare Blood and Bodily Substances." Moore was never informed prior to the splenectomy of Golde's "prior formed intent" to obtain a portion of his spleen. In our view, these allegations adequately show that Golde had an undisclosed research interest in Moore's cells at the time he sought Moore's consent to the splenectomy. Accordingly, Moore has stated a cause of action for breach of fiduciary duty, or lack of informed consent, based upon the disclosures accompanying that medical procedure.

We next discuss the adequacy of Golde's alleged disclosures regarding the postoperative takings of blood and other samples. In this context, Moore alleges that Golde "expressly, affirmatively and impliedly represented . . . that these withdrawals of his Blood and Bodily Substances were necessary and required for his health and well-being." However, Moore also alleges that Golde actively concealed his economic interest in Moore's cells during this time period. "[D]uring each of these visits . . ., and even when [Moore] inquired as to whether there was any possible or potential commercial or financial value or significance of his Blood and Bodily Substances, or whether the defendants had discovered anything . . . which was or might be . . . related to any scientific activity resulting in commercial or financial benefits . . ., the defendants repeatedly and affirmatively represented to [Moore] that there was no commercial or financial value to his Blood and Bodily Substances . . . and in fact actively discouraged such inquiries."

Moore admits in his complaint that defendants disclosed they "were engaged in strictly academic and purely scientific medical research . . .." However, Golde's representation that he had no financial interest in this research became false, based upon the allegations, at least by May 1979, when he "began to investigate and initiate the procedures . . . for [obtaining] a patent" on the cell line developed from Moore's cells.

In these allegations, Moore plainly asserts that Golde concealed an economic interest in the postoperative procedures. Therefore, applying the principles already discussed, the allegations state a cause of action for breach of fiduciary duty or lack of informed consent.

We thus disagree with the superior court's ruling that Moore had not stated a cause of action because essential allegations were lacking. We discuss each such allegation. First, in the superior court's view, Moore needed but failed to allege that defendants knew his cells had potential commercial value *on October 5, 1976* (the time blood tests were first performed at UCLA Medical Center) and had *at that time* already formed the intent to exploit the cells. We agree with the superior court that the absence of such allegations precludes Moore from stating a cause of action based upon the procedures undertaken on October 5, 1976. But, as already discussed, Moore clearly alleges that Golde had developed a research interest in his cells by October 20, 1976, when the splenectomy was performed. Thus, Moore can state a cause of action based upon Golde's alleged failure to disclose that interest before the splenectomy.

The superior court also held that the lack of essential allegations prevented Moore from stating a cause of action based on the splenectomy. According to the superior court, Moore failed to allege that the operation lacked a therapeutic purpose or that the procedure was totally unrelated to therapeutic purposes. In our view, however, neither allegation is essential. Even if the splenectomy had a therapeutic purpose, it does not follow that Golde had no duty to disclose his additional research and economic interests. As we have already discussed, the existence of a motivation for a medical procedure unrelated to the patient's health is a potential conflict of interest and a fact material to the patient's decision.

APPENDIX O

QUARANTINE STATUTES

Wyoming and New Mexico State Codes

INTRODUCTORY NOTE

Most states have statutes that provide for quarantine measures to be taken in the event of an outbreak of a contagious disease. Many such statutes were enacted many years ago to combat tuberculosis and are not often enforced. The Wyoming and New Mexico statutes included in this Appendix are examples of such enactments.

THE STATUTES

Wyoming Statutes, Title 35, Sections 4-103 and 4-105

Section 35-4-103. Investigation of diseases; quarantine; regulation of travel; employment of police officers to enforce quarantine; report of county health officer; supplies and expenses. It shall be the duty of the department of health, immediately after the receipt of the information that there is any smallpox, cholera, scarlet fever, diphtheria or other infectious or contagious disease, which is a menace to the public health, in any portion of this state, to order the county health officer by telegram or telephone, if he is not at hand to proceed immediately to said case and there to investigate said case or cases, and to report to the state health officer, by telephone or telegram, the results of said investigation, and it shall be the duty of the state health officer, if in his judgment the occasion requires, to direct the county health officer to declare said infected place to be in quarantine and to place any and all restrictions upon the ingress and egress thereat as in his judgment, or in the judgment of the state health officer shall be necessary to prevent the spread of the disease from the infected locality; and it shall be the duty of the said county health officer when he shall have declared any city or town or other place to be in quarantine, so to control the population of said city, town or other place, and make such disposition of the same, as shall in his judgment best protect the people and at the same time prevent the spread of the disease among the same. And when deemed necessary for the

protection of the public health the state health officer shall establish and maintain a state quarantine, and shall enforce such practical regulations regarding railroads, stage lines, or other lines of travel into and out of the state of Wyoming as they so deem proper and necessary for the protection of the public health, and the expenses incurred in maintaining said state quarantine shall be paid out of the funds of the state treasury appropriated for this purpose and in the manner in which other expenses of the department are audited and paid. The county health officer, or the department, are hereby authorized to employ a sufficient number of police officers who shall be under the control of the county health officer, to enforce and carry out any and all quarantine regulations the department may prescribe, which said regulations shall be made public in the most practicable manner, in the several counties, cities, towns or other places where the quarantine may be established. And where quarantine is established by the county health officer, he shall make immediate report of his actions and doings in the premises to the state health officer and from time to time so long as quarantine shall continue.
[. . .]

Section 35-4-105. Escape from quarantine deemed crime; punishment. Any person or persons confined in any quarantine established in this state under the provisions of this act who shall escape therefrom or attempt to escape therefrom, without having been dismissed upon the certificate or authority of the county health officer may be charged with a crime and shall be quarantined for tuberculosis or other emergent disease or condition that might pose comparable risk for transmission in the absence of strict quarantine, and confined to a site designated by the state health officer and the director of the department of health until such disease is cured or becomes inactive or noninfectious. Upon conviction of a violation of this section, a person may be punished by a fine of not more than five hundred dollars ($500.00) or imprisonment for not more than one (1) year.

New Mexico Statutes Annotated, Section 24-1-3

The Department of Health has authority to:
    a. [omitted]
    b. supervise the health and hygiene of the state;
    c. investigate, control and abate the causes of disease, especially epidemics, sources of mortality and other conditions of public health;
    d. [omitted]
    e. close any public place and forbid gatherings of people when necessary for the protection of the public health;
    [subsections f. through i. omitted]
    j. bring action in court for the enforcement of health laws and regulations and orders issued by the department;
    [subsections k. through m. omitted]

n. maintain and enforce regulations for the control of communicable diseases deemed to be dangerous to public health;

[subsections o. through t. omitted]

u. do all other things necessary to carry out its duties.

APPENDIX P

VACCO, ET AL. v. QUILL, ET AL.

United States Supreme Court
(June 26, 1997)

INTRODUCTORY NOTE

In this case, the U.S. Supreme Court rejected the arguments of New York physicians that the Equal Protection Clause of the U.S. Constitution protects the interest of terminally ill, mentally competent patients to be assisted by a physician in ending their lives. The Court held that a New York statute prohibiting physician assisted suicide was not invalid. The decision sets forth a good discussion of the rights of terminally ill persons and how those rights are, and should be, balanced the state's interest in preserving life. The Court also discusses the legal distinction between allowing a person to die and assisting a person to commit suicide.

THE CASE

Chief Justice Rhenquist delivered the opinion of the Court.

In New York, as in most States, it is a crime to aid another to commit or attempt suicide, [footnote omitted] but patients may refuse even lifesaving medical treatment. [Footnote omitted.] The question presented by this case is whether New York's prohibition on assisting suicide therefore violates the Equal Protection Clause of the Fourteenth Amendment. We hold that it does not.

Petitioners are various New York public officials. Respondents Timothy E. Quill, Samuel C. Klagsbrun, and Howard A. Grossman are physicians who practice in New York. They assert that although it would be "consistent with the standards of [their] medical practice[s]" to prescribe lethal medication for "mentally competent, terminally ill patients" who are suffering great pain and desire a doctor's help in taking their own lives, they are deterred from doing so by New York's ban on assisting suicide. [Citations omitted.] Respondents, and three gravely ill patients who have since died, [footnote omitted] sued the State's Attorney General in the United States District Court. They urged that because New York permits a competent person to refuse life sustaining medical treatment, and because the refusal of such treatment is "essentially the same thing" as physician assisted suicide, New York's assisted suicide ban violates the Equal Protection Clause. [Citation omitted.]

The District Court disagreed: "[I]t is hardly unreasonable or irrational for the State to recognize a difference between allowing nature to take its course, even in the most severe situations, and intentionally using an artificial death producing device." [Citation omitted.] The court noted New York's "obvious legitimate interests in preserving life, and in protecting vulnerable persons," and concluded that "[u]nder the United States Constitution and the federal system it establishes, the resolution of this issue is left to the normal democratic processes within the State." [Citation omitted.]

The Court of Appeals for the Second Circuit reversed. [Citation omitted.] The court determined that, despite the assisted suicide ban's apparent general applicability, "New York law does not treat equally all competent persons who are in the final stages of fatal illness and wish to hasten their deaths," because "those in the final stages of terminal illness who are on life support systems are allowed to hasten their deaths by directing the removal of such systems; but those who are similarly situated, except for the previous attachment of life sustaining equipment, are not allowed to hasten death by self administering prescribed drugs." [Citation omitted.]. In the court's view, "[t]he ending of life by [the withdrawal of life support systems] is nothing more nor less than assisted suicide." [Citations omitted.] The Court of Appeals then examined whether this supposed unequal treatment was rationally related to any legitimate state interests, [footnote omitted] and concluded that "to the extent that [New York's statutes] prohibit a physician from prescribing medications to be self administered by a mentally competent, terminally ill person in the final stages of his terminal illness, they are not rationally related to any legitimate state interest." [Citations omitted.] [We granted certiorari and now reverse.]

The Equal Protection Clause commands that no State shall "deny to any person within its jurisdiction the equal protection of the laws." This provision creates nosubstantive rights. [Citation omitted.] Instead, it embodies a general rule that States must treat like cases alike but may treat unlike cases accordingly. [Citations omitted.]

New York's statutes outlawing assisting suicide affect and address matters of profound significance to all New Yorkers alike. They neither infringe fundamental rights nor involve suspect classifications. [Citations omitted.] [. . .]

On their faces, neither New York's ban on assisting suicide nor its statutes permitting patients to refuse medical treatment treat anyone differently than anyone else or draw any distinctions between persons. Everyone, regardless of physical condition, is entitled, if competent, to refuse unwanted lifesaving medical treatment; no one is permitted to assist a suicide. Generally speaking, laws that apply evenhandedly to all "unquestionably comply" with the Equal Protection Clause. [Citations omitted.]

The Court of Appeals, however, concluded that some terminally ill people--those who are on life support systems--are treated differently than those who are not, in that the former may "hasten death" by ending treatment, but the latter may not "hasten death" through physician assisted suicide. [Citation omitted.] This conclusion depends on the submission that ending or refusing lifesaving medical treatment "is nothing more nor less than assisted suicide." [Citation omitted.] Unlike the Court of Appeals, we think the distinction between assisting suicide and withdrawing life sustaining treatment, a distinction widely recognized and endorsed in the medical profession [footnote omitted] and in our legal traditions, is both important and logical; it is certainly rational. [Citation omitted.]

The distinction comports with fundamental legal principles of causation and intent. First, when a patient refuses life sustaining medical treatment, he dies from an underlying fatal disease or pathology; but if a patient ingests lethal medication prescribed by a physician, he is killed by that medication. [Citations omitted.]

Furthermore, a physician who withdraws, or honors a patient's refusal to begin, life sustaining medical treatment purposefully intends, or may so intend, only to respect his patient's wishes and "to cease doing useless and futile or degrading things to the patient when [the patient] no longer stands to benefit from them." [Citation omitted.] The same is true when a doctor provides aggressive palliative care; in some cases, painkilling drugs may hasten a patient's death, but the physician's purpose and intent is, or maybe, only to ease his patient's pain. A doctor who assists a suicide, however, "must, necessarily and indubitably, intend primarily that the patient be made dead." [Citation omitted.] Similarly, a patient who commits suicide with a doctor's aid necessarily has the specific intent to end his or her own life, while a patient who refuses or discontinues treatment might not. [Citations omitted.]

The law has long used actors' intent or purpose to distinguish between two acts that may have the same result. [Citations omitted.]

Given these general principles, it is not surprising that many courts, including New York courts, have carefully distinguished refusing life sustaining treatment from suicide. [Citations omitted.] In fact, the first state court decision explicitly to authorize withdrawing lifesaving treatment noted the "real distinction between the self infliction of deadly harm and a self determination against artificial life support." [Citation omitted.] And recently, the Michigan Supreme Court also rejected the argument that the distinction "between acts that artificially sustain life and acts that artificially curtail life" is merely a "distinction without constitutional significance--a meaningless exercise in semantic gymnastics [. . .]. [Citation omitted.]

Similarly, the overwhelming majority of state legislatures have drawn a clear line between assisting suicide and withdrawing or permitting the refusal of unwanted lifesaving medical treatment by prohibiting the former and permitting the latter. [Citation omitted.] And "nearly all states expressly disapprove of suicide and assisted suicide either in statutes dealing with durable powers of attorney in health care situations, or in 'living will' statutes." [Citations omitted.] Thus, even as the States move to protect and promote patients' dignity at the end of life, they remain opposed to physician assisted suicide.

New York is a case in point. The State enacted its current assisted suicide statutes in 1965. [Footnote omitted.] Since then, New York has acted several times to protect patients' common law right to refuse treatment. [Citations omitted.] In so doing, however, the State has neither endorsed a general right to "hasten death" nor approved physician assisted suicide. Quite the opposite: The State has reaffirmed the line between "killing" and "letting die." [Citations omitted.]

This Court has also recognized, at least implicitly, the distinction between letting a patient die and making that patient die. In Cruzan v. Director, Mo. Dept. of Health [citation omitted], we concluded that "[t]he principle that a competent person has a constitutionally protected liberty interest in refusing unwanted medical treatment may be inferred from our prior decisions," and we assumed the existence of such a right for purposes of that case. [Citation omitted.] But our assumption of a right to refuse treatment was grounded not, as the Court of Appeals supposed, on the proposition that patients have a general and abstract "right to hasten death," [citation omitted], but on well established, traditional rights to bodily integrity and freedom from unwanted touching. [Citations omitted.] In fact, we observed that "the majority of States in this country have laws imposing criminal penalties on one who assists another to commit suicide." [Citation omitted.] Cruzan therefore provides no support for the notion that refusing life sustaining medical treatment is "nothing more nor less than suicide."

For all these reasons, we disagree with respondents' claim that the distinction between refusing lifesaving medical treatment and assisted suicide is "arbitrary" and "irrational." [Citation omitted.] Granted, in some cases, the line between the two may not be clear, but certainty is not required, even were it possible. [Citation omitted.] Logic and contemporary practice support New York's judgment that the two acts are different, and New York may therefore, consistent with the Constitution, treat them differently. By permitting everyone to refuse unwanted medical treatment while prohibiting anyone from assisting a suicide, New York law follows a longstanding and rational distinction.

The judgment of the Court of Appeals is reversed.

Justice O'Connor, concurring.

Death will be different for each of us. For many, the last days will be spent in physical pain and perhaps the despair that accompanies physical deterioration and a loss of control of basic bodily and mental functions. Some will seek medication to alleviate that pain and other symptoms.

The Court frames the issue in this case as whether the Due Process Clause of the Constitution protects a "right to commit suicide which itself includes a right to assistance in doing so," [citation omitted] and concludes that our Nation's history, legal traditions, and practices do not support the existence of such a right. I join the Court's opinions because I agree that there is no generalized right to "commit suicide." But respondents urge us to address the narrower question whether a mentally competent person who is experiencing great suffering has a constitutionally cognizable interest in controlling the circumstances of his or her imminent death. I see no need to reach that question in the context of the facial challenges to the New York and Washington laws at issue here. [Citations omitted.] The parties and amici

agree that in these States a patient who is suffering from a terminal illness and who is experiencing great pain has no legal barriers to obtaining medication, from qualified physicians, to alleviate that suffering, even to the point of causing unconsciousness and hastening death. [Citations omitted.] In this light, even assuming that we would recognize such an interest, I agree that the State's interests in protecting those who are not truly competent or facing imminent death, or those whose decisions to hasten death would not truly be voluntary, are sufficiently weighty to justify a prohibition against physician assisted suicide. [Citations omitted.]
[. . .]

Justice Stevens, concurring in the judgments.

The Court ends its opinion with the important observation that our holding today is fully consistent with a continuation of the vigorous debate about the "morality, legality, and practicality of physician assisted suicide" in a democratic society. [Citation omitted.] I write separately to make it clear that there is also room for further debate about the limits that the Constitution places on the power of the States to punish the practice.

[. . .]

History and tradition provide ample support for refusing to recognize an open ended constitutional right to commit suicide. Much more than the State's paternalistic interest in protecting the individual from the irrevocable consequences of an ill advised decision motivated by temporary concerns is at stake. There is truth in John Donne's observation that "No man is an island." [Footnote omitted.] The State has an interest in preserving and fostering the benefits that every human being may provide to the community--a community that thrives on the exchange of ideas, expressions of affection, shared memories and humorous incidents as well as on the material contributions that its members create and support. The value to others of a person's life is far too precious to allow the individual to claim a constitutional entitlement to complete autonomy in making a decision to end that life. Thus, I fully agree with the Court that the "liberty" protected by the Due Process Clause does not include a categorical "right to commit suicide which itself includes a right to assistance in doing so." [Citation omitted.]

[. . .]

In Cruzan v. Director, Mo. Dept. of Health, [citation omitted], the Court assumed that the interest in liberty protected by the Fourteenth Amendment encompassed the right of a terminally ill patient to direct the withdrawal of life sustaining treatment. As the Court correctly observes today, that assumption "was not simply deduced from abstract concepts of personal autonomy." [Citation omitted.] Instead, it was supported by the common law tradition protecting the individual's general right to refuse unwanted medical treatment. [Citation omitted.] We have recognized, however, that this common law right to refuse treatment is neither absolute nor always sufficiently weighty to overcome valid countervailing state interests. [. . .] In most cases, the individual's constitutionally protected interest in his or her own physical autonomy, including the right to refuse unwanted medical treatment, will give way to the State's interest in preserving human life.

Cruzan, however, was not the normal case. Given the irreversible nature of her illness and the progressive character of her suffering, [footnote omitted] Nancy Cruzan's interest in refusing medical care was incidental to her more basic interest in controlling the manner and timing of her death. In finding that her best interests would be served by cutting off the nourishment that kept her alive, the trial court did more than simply vindicate Cruzan's interest in refusing medical treatment; the court, in essence, authorized affirmative conduct that would hasten her death. When this Court reviewed the case and upheld Missouri's requirement that there be clear and convincing evidence establishing Nancy Cruzan's intent to have life sustaining nourishment withdrawn, it made two important assumptions: (1) that there was a "liberty interest" in refusing unwanted treatment protected by the Due Process Clause; and (2) that this liberty interest did not "end the inquiry" because it might be outweighed by relevant state interests. [Citation omitted.] I agree with both of those assumptions, but I insist that the source of Nancy Cruzan's right to refuse treatment was not just a common law rule. Rather, this right is an aspect of a far broader and more basic concept of freedom that is even older than the common law. [Footnote omitted.] This freedom embraces, not merely a person's right to refuse a particular kind of unwanted treatment, but also her interest in dignity, and in determining the character of the memories that will survive long after her death. [Footnote omitted.] In recognizing that the State's interests did not outweigh Nancy Cruzan's liberty interest in refusing medical treatment, Cruzan rested not simply on the common law right to refuse medical treatment, but--at least implicitly--on the even more fundamental right to make this "deeply personal decision." [Citation omitted.]

Thus, the common law right to protection from battery, which included the right to refuse medical treatment in most circumstances, did not mark "the outer limits of the substantive sphere of liberty" that supported the Cruzan family's decision to hasten Nancy's death. [Citation omitted.] Those limits have never been precisely defined. [. . .]Whatever the outer limits of the concept may be, it definitely includes protection for matters "central to personal dignity and autonomy."

[. . .]

The Cruzan case demonstrated that some state intrusions on the right to decide how death will be encountered are also intolerable. The now deceased plaintiffs in this action may in fact have had a liberty interest even stronger than Nancy Cruzan's because, not only were they terminally ill, they were suffering constant and severe pain. Avoiding intolerable pain and the indignity of living one's final days incapacitated and in agony is certainly "[a]t the heart of [the] liberty . . . to define one's own concept of existence, of meaning, of the universe, and of the mystery of human life." [Citation omitted.]

While I agree with the Court that Cruzan does not decide the issue presented by these cases, Cruzan did give recognition, not just to vague, unbridled notions of autonomy, but to the more specific interest in making decisions about how to confront an imminent death. Although there is no absolute right to physician assisted suicide, Cruzan makes it clear that some individuals who no longer have the option of deciding whether to live or to die because they are already on the threshold of death have a constitutionally protected interest that may outweigh the State's interest in preserving life at all costs. The liberty interest at stake in a case like this differs from, and is stronger than, both the common law right to refuse medical treatment and the unbridled interest in deciding whether to live or die. It is an interest in deciding how, rather than whether, a critical threshold shall be crossed.

The state interests supporting a general rule banning the practice of physician assisted suicide do not have the same force in all cases. First and foremost of these interests is the "'unqualified interest in the preservation of human life,'" [citation omitted], which is equated with "'the sanctity of life.'" [Citation omitted.] That interest not only justifies--it commands--maximum protection of every individual's interest in remaining alive, which in turn commands the same protection for decisions about whether to commence or to terminate life support systems or to administer pain medication that may hasten death. Properly viewed, however, this interest is not a collective interest that should always outweigh the interests of a person who because of pain, incapacity, or sedation finds her life intolerable, but rather, an aspect of individual freedom.

Many terminally ill people find their lives meaningful even if filled with pain or dependence on others. Some find value in living through suffering; some have an abiding desire to witness particular events in their families' lives; many believe it a sin to hasten death. Individuals of different religious faiths make different judgments and choices about whether to live on under such circumstances. There are those who will want to continue aggressive treatment; those who would prefer terminal sedation; and those who will seek withdrawal from life support systems and death by gradual starvation and dehydration. Although as a general matter the State's interest in the contributions each person may make to society outweighs the person's interest in ending her life, this interest does not have the same force for a terminally ill patient faced not with the choice of whether to live, only of how to die. Allowing the individual, rather than the State, to make judgments "'about the "quality" of life that a particular individual may enjoy.'" [citation omitted], does not mean that the lives of terminally ill, disabled people have less value than the lives of those who are healthy. [Citation omitted.] Rather, it gives proper recognition to the individual's interest in choosing a final chapter that accords with her life story, rather than one that demeans her values and poisons memories of her. [. . .]

Similarly, the State's legitimate interests in preventing suicide, protecting the vulnerable from coercion and abuse, and preventing euthanasia are less significant in this context. I agree that the State has a compelling interest in preventing persons from committing suicide because of depression, or coercion by third parties. But the State's legitimate interest in preventing abuse does not apply to an individual who is not victimized by abuse, who is not suffering from depression, and who makes a rational and voluntary decision to seek assistance in dying. Although, as the New York Task Force report discusses, diagnosing depression and other mental illness is not always easy, mental health workers and other professionals expert in working with dying patients can help patients cope with depression and pain, and help patients assess their options. [Citation omitted.]

Relatedly, the State and amici express the concern that patients whose physical pain is inadequately treated will be more likely to request assisted suicide. Encouraging the development and ensuring the availability of adequate pain treatment is of utmost importance; palliative care, however, cannot alleviate all pain and suffering. [. . .]An individual adequately informed of the care alternatives thus might make a rational choice for assisted suicide. For such an individual, the State's interest in preventing potential abuse and mistake is only minimally implicated.

The final major interest asserted by the State is its interest in preserving the traditional integrity of the medical profession. The fear is that a rule permitting physicians to assist in suicide is inconsistent with the perception that they serve their patients solely as healers. But for some patients, it would be a physician's refusal to dispense medication to ease their suffering and make their death tolerable and dignified that would be inconsistent with the healing role. [. . .] Furthermore, because physicians are already involved in making decisions that hasten the death of terminally ill patients--through termination of life support, withholding of medical treatment, and terminal sedation--there is in fact significant tension between the traditional view of the physician's role and the actual practice in a growing number of cases. [Footnote omitted.]

[. . .]

In New York, a doctor must respect a competent person's decision to refuse or to discontinue medical treatment even though death will thereby ensue, but the same doctor would be guilty of a felony if she provided her patient assistance in committing suicide. [Footnote omitted.] Today we hold that the Equal Protection Clause is not violated by the resulting disparate treatment of two classes of terminally ill people who may have the same interest in hastening death. I agree that the distinction between permitting death to ensue from an underlying fatal disease and causing it to occur by the administration of medication or other means provides a constitutionally sufficient basis for the State's classification. [Footnote omitted.[Unlike the Court, however, [citation omitted], I am not persuaded that in all cases there will in fact be a significant difference between the intent of the physicians, the patients or the families in the two situations.

There may be little distinction between the intent of a terminally ill patient who decides to remove her life support and one who seeks the assistance of a doctor in ending her life; in both situations, the patient is seeking to hasten a certain, impending death. The doctor's intent might also be the same in prescribing lethal medication as it is in terminating life support. A doctor who fails to administer medical treatment to one who is dying from a disease could be doing so with an intent to harm or kill that patient. Conversely, a doctor who prescribes lethal medication does not necessarily intend the patient's death--rather that doctor may seek simply to ease the patient's suffering and to comply with her wishes. The illusory character of any differences in intent or causation is confirmed by the fact that the American Medical Association unequivocally endorses the practice of terminal sedation--the administration of sufficient dosages of pain killing medication to terminally ill patients to protect them from excruciating pain even when it is clear that the time of death will be advanced. The purpose of terminal sedation is to ease the suffering of the patient and comply with her wishes, and the actual cause of death is the administration of heavy doses of lethal sedatives. This same intent and causation may exist when a doctor complies with a patient's request for lethal medication to hasten her death. [Footnote omitted.]

[. . .]

There remains room for vigorous debate about the outcome of particular cases that are not necessarily resolved by the opinions announced today. How such cases may be decided will depend on their specific facts. In my judgment, however, it is clear that the so called "unqualified interest in the preservation of human life," [citation omitted], is not itself sufficient to outweigh the interest in liberty that may justify the only possible means of preserving a dying patient's dignity and alleviating her intolerable suffering.

[Concurring opinion of Justice Souter omitted.]

GLOSSARY

THE PRINCIPLES OF BIOETHICS DECISION-MAKING

The Philosophical Foundation of Bioethics

INTRODUCTORY NOTE

Bioethics scholars have formulated and rely upon several key concepts in discussing bioethical issues. Ideally, those concepts should be relied upon and applied by practitioners in making, and assisting others to make, bioethical decisions. Set forth below is a brief summary of the four principles of bioethics that have been formulated by Tom L. Beauchamp and James F. Childress in their book, *Principles of Biomedical Ethics*.

KEY TERMS AND CONCEPTS

Autonomy. The principle of autonomy stems from the notion that, in general, we believe as a society that individuals should be able to make their own decisions and act freely, without interference from others. Autonomy may be applied to specific situations to support an individual's right to control his or her own body. Many times this principle is discussed in the context of respecting the right of an individual to refuse medical care. Naturally, there are situations in which respect for autonomy must give way to other concerns, but autonomy should be one of the principles that we look to in our decision-making process.

Beneficence. Another one of the principles formulated by Beauchamp and Childress, beneficence represents the notion that we should act in ways that will result in "good" things happening. This principle may be viewed as related to a utilitarian stance that we should act, both as individuals and a society, to produce good. Beneficence is clearly related to nonmaleficence and the two principles may be viewed as two sides of the same coin.

253

Justice. Perhaps the most difficult of Beauchamp and Childress' four principles to define, justice implicates fairness. It suggests that similar situations should be treated in similar ways, not unlike the concept of legal precedent. Justice implies that inequality may be bad. The related concept of "distributive justice" can be viewed as requiring that those who incur a burden should reap the benefits. This concept is often discussed with regard to clinical trials, such that populations who participate in clinical trials should be afforded the benefits resulting from those trials. Justice implies fairness, both on a societal and individual level.

Nonmaleficence. The principle of nonmaleficence demands that we should not inflict harm on others. Of course, there will be situations in which it is unavoidable that we cause harm, but the principle of nonmaleficence requires that in determining which path to take, we should make every effort not to hurt others in any way. Again, nonmaleficence can be viewed as integrally related to beneficence.

INDEX

International Library of Ethics, Law, and the New Medicine

1. L. Nordenfelt: *Action, Ability and Health.* Essays in the Philosophy of Action and Welfare. 2000
ISBN 0-7923-6206-3

2. J. Bergsma and D.C. Thomasma: *Autonomy and Clinical Medicine.* Renewing the Health Professional Relation with the Patient. 2000
ISBN 0-7923-6207-1

3. S. Rinken: *The AIDS Crisis and the Modern Self.* Biographical Self-Construction in the Awareness of Finitude. 2000
ISBN 0-7923-6371-X

4. M. Verweij: *Preventive Medicine Between Obligation and Aspiration.* 2000
ISBN 0-7923-6691-3

5. F. Svenaeus: *The Hermeneutics of Medicine and the Phenomenology of Health.* Steps Towards a Philosophy of Medical Practice. 2001
ISBN 0-7923-6757-X

6. D.M. Vukadinovich and S.L. Krinsky: *Ethics and Law in Modern Medicine.* Hypothetical Case Studies. 2001
ISBN 1-4020-0088-X

KLUWER ACADEMIC PUBLISHERS – DORDRECHT / BOSTON / LONDON